THE LONDON STAGE
1729-1747

A Critical Introduction

THE
LONDON STAGE
1729-1747

A Critical Introduction

BY

Arthur H. Scouten

SOUTHERN ILLINOIS UNIVERSITY PRESS
CARBONDALE AND EDWARDSVILLE

FEFFER & SIMONS, INC.
LONDON AND AMSTERDAM

FOREWORD

THE LONDON STAGE, 1660–1800, now completed in eleven volumes, has resulted from a co-operative scholarly venture lasting for thirty-three years. The five authors have called upon aid from dozens of specialists in the field, and from the staffs of many a library to compile the day-by-day account of what went on upon the London stage, including the booths at fairs and the opera houses, for a hundred-and-forty-year period. Each has acknowledged his debt in the Preface to his own part.

The basic compilation provides the reader with factual and revisitable evidence in strict chronological order as to dates, plays, casts, facilities, scenes, costumes, theatrical management, specialty acts, music, dance, box receipts, and hundreds of illuminating items from contemporary comments in letters, journals, diaries, pamphlets, periodicals, and newspapers. The headnotes to each year tell of the composition of the acting companies, summarize forthcoming theatrical events, and suggest trends and novelties as well as the proportions of tragedy, comedy, history, and musicals to be presented.

Since the eleven-volume reference work may be too massive for individuals to possess, the authors now make available, in this series of five paperbacks, their Critical Introductions to each part. These are both factual and interpretive. Interpretations of identical basic material will, of course, vary as the years go on and as each up-coming stage historian brings to bear upon it his own predilections and interests. The authors, however, planned from the beginning to give the results of their own insights gained from searching out the details, organizing the facts, and living with the fragments of evidence for over a quarter of a century apiece.

Dr. Van Lennep, who undertook the difficult period embraced in Part 1, died before it was completed. The Critical Introduction for that period was prepared by professors Avery and Scouten, who were helping him with the calendar of events for the Restoration era.

The authors hope that these introductions will serve all readers interested in stage history. Each volume deals fully with theatrical events recorded in the blocks of time indicated. Together they tell the cumulative story of a flow of activities dominated by the manager-actor-dramatists who characterized each period—Davenant and Betterton, Cibber, Fielding and Rich, Garrick, and Sheridan and Kemble. All readers are referred for details to the full documentation presented in the complete calendar.

G. W. S., Jr.

New York University
21 April 1968

CONTENTS

INTRODUCTION

THE LONDON STAGE
1729-1747

The Playhouses: Location and Description

THEATRE ROYAL, DRURY LANE (1674-1791)

NO CHANGES are known to have been made in the structure of the Drury Lane theatre. Its continuance as a Theatre Royal was ratified on 25 April 1732: "at a hearing before the L[ord] Chancellor, L[ord] Chief Justice Raymond, and Baron Comyns, the Court unanimously agreed, that the Patent granted by his Majesty to R. Wilks, C. Cibber, and Barton Booth, Esq; for the Play-House in Drury-Lane, was a lawful Grant; and it passed the Broad Seal accordingly."[1] "The Patent is for 21 years."[2]

THE KING'S OPERA HOUSE IN THE HAYMARKET (1705-1789)

The opera house also continued without change, but some notices appear concerning its size and capacity. At a production in 1732, the author of *The German Spy* noted that "The Stage was now above 100 Foot long, 40 Foot broad, and 32 Foot high."[3] The reporter may have been the victim

---

[1] *Daily Post*, 27 April 1732; John Genest, *Some Account of the English Stage from the Restoration in 1660 to 1830.* III (Bath, 1832), 336.

[2] *St. James's Evening Post*, 27 April, as quoted by the *Grub St. Journal* of 4 May 1732.

[3] As quoted by Richard Southern in "Lediard and Early 18th Century Scene Design," *Theatre Notebook*, II (April 1948), 54.

of an optical illusion, though the figures for width and height seem reasonable. At a performance on 27 January 1736, the *Daily Advertiser* reports the house was so full that "there were above 440 Ladies and Gentlemen in the Pit and Boxes, besides the Subscribers"; unfortunately, the number of subscribers for this season is not known. It generally ranged from 50 to 200. In advance notices for Farinelli's benefit night in 1735, the *Daily Advertiser* states that "a Contrivance will be made to accommodate 2,000 People." Whatever the contrivance was, the normal capacity was probably not much over 1,400. For a performance on 28 March 1738, two witnesses attempt estimates. "In the evening I went to Handel's Oratorio," the Earl of Egmont entered in his diary, "where I counted nearly 1,300 persons besides the gallery and upper gallery. I suppose he got this night £1,000."4 The young musician Charles Burney, later to be the great Dr. Burney, states that at least 500 people were seated on the stage.5

THEATRE ROYAL, LINCOLN'S INN FIELDS (1714–1744)

Use of the new theatre in Lincoln's Inn Fields ended during this period, as John Rich moved his company to his new house in Covent Garden, the last production taking place on 11 December 1744.6

THE NEW THEATRE IN THE HAYMARKET (1720–1820)

Situated almost directly across from the King's Opera House, the New Haymarket (frequently called the little theatre or the French theatre) was used by several different companies, particularly Fielding's in the 1730's and Foote's in the 1740's. The only change in its structure before mid-century was an alteration enlarging its single gallery during the brief occupancy in 1744 by Theophilus Cibber.7

---

4 Earl of Egmont, *The Diary of the Earl of Egmont*, II (London, 1920), 474.

5 As quoted by Otto Erich Deutsch, *Handel: A Documentary Biography* (New York, n.d.), p. 455.

6 Sources and fuller information concerning dated productions can be found in the Theatrical Seasons, under date.

7 *Daily Advertiser*, 20 Sept. 1744.

ODELL'S THEATRE IN AYLIFFE STREET, GOODMAN'S FIELDS
(1729–1732)

The great interest in the drama engendered by the success of *The Beggar's Opera* and *The Provoked Husband* during the spring of 1728 soon led to physical expansion. The first new house was located at the other end of town, in Ayliffe Street, in Goodman's Fields. The entrepreneur was Thomas Odell, who "obtained Letters Patent" to erect a theatre by subscription.[8] Information about it comes from opponents, for the *London Evening Post* of 25–27 September 1729 noted that the justices of the peace near Whitechapel were working to prevent "the Erecting of a Playhouse in Ayliffe Street, which is now about." By 30 September "seven or eight Persons" had applied to the justices "to prohibit the theatre" (*Daily Post*). On 7 October was published a lengthy statement by Samuel Cowper and Samuel Sadleir, clerks to the justices "acting for the Division of the Tower" (*Daily Post*). These clerks report that "a Gentleman" had undertaken to secure letters patent, and they state that "great Numbers of Gentlemen and substantial Merchants and Tradesmen" residing in and near the Tower had applied to the justices, who had, in turn, "order'd Caveats to be entered . . . to prevent the Gentleman obtaining Letters Patent for erecting the said Theatre" (*Daily Post*).

A news item in the *Weekly Journal* predicts that the theatre would open on Monday 27 October.[9] Actually, the opening came on the last day of October, in an old workshop which had been converted into a theatre, for no new structure had been erected.[10] The first play was Farquhar's *The Recruiting Officer*, the same play which John Rich had used to open the Lincoln's Inn Fields theatre in 1714. The significance of the performance, however, lay in the fact that for the first time since Charles II had issued patents at the beginning of the Restoration three regular companies were playing legitimate drama in London.

According to the opening announcement, the new playhouse had pit, boxes, and a single gallery; and the manager had "Constables attending Nightly," at his own expense, "to prevent Disorders." The "Prologue to the Town" spoken that night appeared in the *British Journal* on 8 November.

8 From Watson Nicholson, *The Struggle for a Free Stage in London* (Boston, 1906), p. 25, who cited *The Coffee-House Morning Post* of 24 Sept. 1729.

9 *Weekly Journal*, 25 Oct.

10 *Daily Journal*, 31 Oct.; *Biographia Dramatica; or, A Companion to the Playhouse* (1782), I, xxxviii; Sir John Hawkins, *The Life of Samuel Johnson* (London, 1787), p. 73.

It provides a conventional statement of desire to please, instruct, and be virtuous. From a very late source, the *Biographia Dramatica* of 1782, we learn that Odell "got no less than one hundred pounds a week by this undertaking." In *A Letter to the Right Hon. Sir Richard Brocas* (1730), it was reported that the fixed overhead did not exceed £16 nightly (as contrasted against a nightly charge of forty pounds at the patent houses), and that the performers had not acted a single night under fifty pounds, with the receipts usually amounting to about sixty pounds. Prices here were three shillings for the boxes, two for the pit, and one for the gallery, more modest charges than at the larger theatres.

Opposition to Odell's new theatre continued. On 30 November 1729 Arthur Bedford, indefatigable foe of the stage, preached in the Parish Church of St. Butolph's, Aldgate, a sermon "Occasioned by the erecting of a Play-House in the Neighborhood," soon published by "Request of several of the Auditors." Bedford cited the new theatre and included the statement of the justices opposing it, but his main attack was upon the danger of attending any playhouse. The pamphlet *A Letter to . . . Sir Richard Brocas* warned of the danger to industry which occurs when a playhouse is situated in a working-class district and made the accurate prediction that success of this new house would mean "*many more*" theatres there. On 28 April 1730 matters came to a climax with a petition to the King from the Lord Mayor and Alderman of London asking that the players at Goodman's Fields, who "pretend to act by authority," be silenced. According to Watson Nicholson, who cites the *Post Boy* of 30 April 1730, the King withdrew his approval, and the company ceased acting with the performance of 28 April, even though Odell had appeared before the king and asked royal leave to continue.[11] Under circumstances which are not clear, Odell commenced production again on 11 May and continued playing until the end of the regular season.

In spite of a notice in the *St. James's Evening Post*, 30 July 1730, that Odell had taken a fourteen-year lease on a piece of ground near Tottenham Court to build a playhouse there, he re-opened Goodman's Fields on 16 September 1730 and operated with much less visible opposition throughout a second season. By the beginning of 1731–32, however, Odell had relinquished the management to Henry Giffard, an actor possessing considerable managerial ability. Production continued throughout the season, and the final performance at this house took place on 23 May 1732.

[11] Nicholson, *Struggle for a Free Stage*, p. 28; *Grub St. Journal*, 7 May 1730.

THE NEW THEATRE IN AYLIFFE STREET, GOODMAN'S FIELDS
(1732–1742)

Immediately upon becoming manager of Odell's playhouse, Giffard began negotiations to build a new theatre in the same area. His published proposals indicated that he would obtain a forty-one-year lease and endeavor to raise £1,500 by subscription, 25 shares at £60 each.[12] From a later source, we learn that he leased the ground from Sir William Leman for a term of sixty-one years, and that he found twenty-three subscribers at £100 each, providing a working capital of £2,300.[13] He hoped to receive all the subscription money by 1 May 1732, and he intended to engage an architect whose plan must be approved by a majority of the subscribers. No money would be withdrawn from the bank without the consent of at least seven subscribers, and whatever was left after erecting the building would go towards the purchase of scenes and costumes. In return for his subscription, each sharer would receive one shilling for each acting night (a later document specifies 1s. 6d. instead[14]) as well as a pass for pit, box, or gallery, and Giffard hoped to offer 160 performances during a season. Some of the subscribers were substantial merchants,[15] whose influence would protect the new venture. Three years later, Giffard testified that he put "all his Fortune" into the playhouse and expended "many thousand Pounds" for costumes, scenery, and decorations.[16]

The new playhouse was under construction by early summer, with Edward Shepherd as the architect; on 14 July 1732 the *Daily Advertiser* reported that the structure was being roofed and would be ready for occupancy in September. It opened on 2 October 1732 with *1 Henry IV*. Its decor, according to the *Daily Advertiser* of 4 October, included a large oval over the pit in which was represented His Majesty, who was attended by Peace, Liberty, and Justice, "trampling Tyranny and Oppression under his Feet"; around the oval were the heads of Shakespeare, Dryden, Congreve,

---

12 *Proposals by Henry Giffard for erecting a Theatre by Subscription in or near Goodman's Fields* (1731), a broadside copy in the Guildhall Library, London.

13 *Journal of the House of Commons*, XXII, 452; *The Case of the Several Persons upon whose Subscription the Theatre in Goodman's Fields hath been built* (London, 1735). British Museum copy.

14 *The Case of the Several Persons.*

15 *Journal of the House of Commons*, XXII, 453.

16 From broadsides (now in the British Museum) issued by Giffard during 1735 when Parliament was considering a bill to regulate the theatres. One is entitled "The Case of Henry Giffard, Proprietor of the Theatre in Goodman's Fields, in relation to a Bill now depending in Parliament."

and Betterton. To the left, the spectators could see a painting of the scene in which Cato points to the dead body of his son Marcus; in the middle, the stabbing of Julius Caesar in the Senate; and on the right, Marc Antony and Octavia (*All for Love*) with their children. On the sounding board over the stage was a painting of Apollo and the nine Muses done by Oram and Hayman (*Daily Advertiser*, 12 September). Like Odell's house, this theatre had a single gallery, pit, and boxes, including stage boxes and "balconies" on the stage.

From the curiosity and diligence of the late eighteenth-century and early nineteenth-century scene designer William Capon, a considerable amount of information survives concerning the designs and physical dimensions of this theatre. Capon examined the structure in 1786, when he was preparing scenes for the Royalty Theatre, and again in 1802, making sketches and measurements on both visits. A print was made from his final sketch and published by Robert Wilkinson in *Londina Illustrata* (1820), together with detailed notes written by Capon. The sketch itself, as well as separate annotations by Capon, also survives and is in the possession of R. L. Eddison.[17] James (Bowes) Winston, manager of the Haymarket theatre at that time and engaged in compiling a history of the London theatres, made a copy of Capon's sketch and notations, and added further data based on separate manuscript notes of Capon's.[18] Winston's copy is now at the Folger Library. Capon found the outside length to be 88 feet and the inside width 47 feet (though he earlier gave 90 by 52). Space for the side boxes reduced the width of the pit to 30 feet, where Capon found only seven rows, to his evident surprise. In a "puff" which Giffard himself may have written for the *Daily Advertiser* of 29 December 1733, advertising a new entertainment, the statement is made that the "Stage is made more than 50 Foot long." This contemporary entry yields some corroboration to Capon's measurement of the depth of the stage, 47 feet, 6 inches. The width he gives as 20 feet, 6 inches, surely too narrow for building on the stage, a favorite practice of Giffard's. Capon specifically says "from wall

[17] Mr. Eddison has very kindly supplied me with a copy of Capon's own annotations and provided me with an account of the slight differences between the sketch in his possession, a reproduction of which, together with the annotations, appeared in *Theatre Notebook* in 1960. I am further indebted to Miss Sybil Rosenfeld, editor of *Theatre Notebook*, for her good offices in notifying me of the discovery of Capon's original sketch and making the material available to me in advance of its publication in *Theatre Notebook*.

[18] As Capon was designing scenes for different London theatres when Winston was manager at the New Haymarket, it seems most likely that the two were acquainted and that Winston had full access to Capon's notes. For Capon's activities, see Sybil Rosenfeld, "Scene Designs of William Capon," *Theatre Notebook*, X (July 1956), 118–22.

to wall"; yet the measurement from the inside of the exterior walls was 47 feet. He may also have been guided by the horizontal grooves in the floor for the sliding flats (see his note No. 3). If his measurement of the stage is correct, two very important observations can be made. First, by way of interest, what an intimate stage for a Garrick performance! No wonder the contemporary audiences could see his facial expressions so clearly. (See the letter of Thomas Newton in the Calendar of Performances under date of 15 December 1741.) Secondly, even if the stage were slightly wider than the distance given by Capon, the sketch shows that the auditorium flared or fanned out from the stage, and this theatre becomes the first to have such an architectural design.

From the sketch we can see that the orchestra was located in the usual position, that there were side and front boxes, and that there was only one gallery. The indication of a single gallery is also supported by contemporary notices of admission prices. As Capon states that the steps to the gallery remained in 1786, and it is unlikely that they would have been redesigned and rebuilt, we may get a clue to the height of the building. There are forty-two steps. With the high risers of eight and nine inches that can be seen today in older buildings, the height was from twenty-eight feet to possibly thirty-one feet.

The dressing rooms were on either side of the Green Room, on the northeast side of the building. The gallery entrance was at the southwest corner. Since new doorways had been cut, it is difficult to ascertain the position of entrances to the pit. The stage entrance was at the southeast end of the structure, with the box office just around the corner from it. Inside the theatre, the pit was fifteen feet deep and the boxes seventeen feet, six inches, marked for seven rows in the pit and nine rows of boxes.

What does this sketch yield concerning the seating capacity of this theatre? Starting with the most certain dimension, we can see that seven rows in a pit 30 feet wide would seat 120 people, allowing 21 inches a person, as Garrick calculated later at Drury Lane. Nine rows of front boxes at an average width of 40 feet would permit 207 spectators. The length of the space taken up by the two tiers of side boxes is not sure; from the sketch it may have been 19 or 20 feet. Allowing 2 feet per person, we may estimate a total of 80 people here. Even Capon is making conjectures about the gallery, but if we accept his marking of ten rows, at probably 42 feet with the curve, there might be space for 250 in the gallery. Boxes and raised balconies on the stage, for which our source is the contemporary advertisements, should yield capacity for 50 people. Capacity seating and receipts would be as follows:

	At advanced prices			At common prices, with no building on the stage	
	CAPACITY	RATE	TOTAL	RATE	TOTAL
Boxes on Stage	50	5s.	£12 10s.		
Side Boxes	80	4s.	16	3s.	£12
Front Boxes	207	4s.	41 8s.	3s.	31 1s.
Pit	120	2s.	12	2s.	12
Gallery	250	1s.	12 10s.	1s.	12 10s.
Total	707		£94 8s.		£67 11s.

If my estimates for the boxes and stage building are too low, the total attendance would be increased to about 750, or what some modern stage historians have conjectured. This total would be considerably short of the Drury Lane capacity, and so much smaller than the capacity of the theatre in Lincoln's Inn Fields that we can understand Giffard's decision to move there in 1736. On this point, the *Daily Advertiser* of 18 September 1736 argued (again Giffard may have composed the entry) that Giffard's company would have "so great an Advantage of room above that they have at the other Theatre."

On the other hand, even if my estimate is high, the Goodman's Fields theatre was no £30 house, a figure so frequently noted by older stage historians, including Capon and Winston. I have never understood how Giffard could support a company of sixty to seventy players, singers, and high-paid dancers in a £30 house and keep building new scenery and get up new entertainments. If as few as twenty people sat in each of the nine rows of front boxes, at four shillings apiece, they would pay £36, without a spectator in the pit, gallery, or side boxes.

After Giffard removed to Lincoln's Inn Fields in 1736, Goodman's Fields was dark for four years. After the passage of the Licensing Act, it fell under the restrictions which confined plays to the patent houses, and in 1737 Giffard was apparently ready to abandon the whole enterprise, for he advertised: "To be Sold, The Interest of the Theatre and Materials in Goodman's Fields, Inquire of Mr Giffard at his House in Grange Court, in Cary Street."[19] On 26 July 1736 an auction was announced for 1 August of a "Large Quantity of Theatrical Goods" lately the property of Henry

[19] *London Daily Post and General Advertiser*, 5 May 1737.

Giffard: "Mens and Womens Cloaths, or Cloath, Velvet, and Silk embroider'd, laced and plain, properly adapted to all the Entertainments of the Stage; as also various Sets of Scenes, with Machines and other Decorations, belonging to several Pantomime Interludes; large Glass Lustres, rich Screens, and Velvet Chairs with Gilt Frames, a large Harpsichord, with a Quantity of Musick in Score" (*London Daily Post and General Advertiser*). On 16 September the notice appeared that the lease "having upwards of 50 Years to come" for the "late Theatre in Goodman's Fields" was for sale (*London Daily Post and General Advertiser*). Those interested were to apply to Edward Shepherd, the architect who had designed the structure, at his home in Audley Street, Grosvenor Square. Shepherd also had for sale "the Dwelling-House adjoining the Theatre."

Nothing further is known about these proposed sales, but apparently they did not materialize, for on 15 October 1740 Giffard reopened the theatre. In 1741–42 he introduced Garrick there to a London audience. On 27 May 1742, Thomas Walker sang his original role of Macheath in *The Beggar's Opera*, for the final performance in this theater. The building itself was converted into a chapel and then a warehouse.[20]

THE THEATRE ROYAL IN COVENT GARDEN (1732–1808)

The tremendous and unprecedented financial successes of his pantomimes as well as of *The Beggar's Opera* undoubtedly led John Rich to make plans in 1730 for the erection of a new theatre. Towards this end, he evidently issued proposals to invite subscriptions from interested financial backers. According to H. Saxe Windham, "the prospectus was issued in December 1730 and . . . by January 1731, £6000 was subscribed."[21] Early in January 1731, three London newspapers report that the project had been underwritten. Issue No. 9131 of the *Daily Courant* for Tuesday 12 January 1730/1 has the following statement: "We hear the subscription for building a new Theatre in Bow-Street, Covent Garden, for Mr Rich, amounts to upward of 6000 *l*. and that the same will be very speedily begun by that ingenious Architect James Sheppard, Esq." This notice was quoted by the *Grub St. Journal*, issue No. 54, Thursday 14 January 1730/1, and the

20 C. B. Hogan, *Shakespeare in the Theatre, 1701–1800*, I (Oxford, 1952), 463.

21 Henry Saxe Wyndham, *Annals of Covent Garden from 1732 to 1897*, I (London, 1906), 24; however, on I, 23, Wyndham gives the date of 11 Dec. 1731. Basil Francis, "John Rich's 'Proposals,'" *Theatre Notebook*, XII (Autumn 1957), 17, and in a personal letter, also gives the date of the prospectus as 11 Dec. 1731.

substance repeated in the *Universal Spectator*, issue No. 119, Saturday 16 January 1730/1. Actually, no money had yet been deposited, but these reports show that news of a subscription was being circulated. Various rumors continued to appear, the *Daily Courant* of 9 February 1730/1 announcing, incorrectly, that a Mr Gibbs was the architect, and the *Daily Advertiser* of 2 March 1730/1 stating that the new theatre would be designed upon the model of the Opera House.

On 28 February 1730/1, the *British Journal* reported that buildings on the intended site of the new theatre were being torn down. However, Rich did not secure the location until 16 March 1730/1 or 25 of March 1731,[22] when he leased from the Duke of Bedford a "parcel of Ground contiguous to Bow Street and Covent Garden," the property being 120 feet in length from east to west and 100 feet in width from north to south.[23] The lease was to run sixty-one years from Lady Day 1731 (i.e., 25 March), at a rental of £100 yearly.

Immediately after securing the lease, Rich came to an oral agreement with the architect Edward Shepherd, so that Shepherd might begin construction pending the legal signing of the articles of agreement.[24] Work did begin at once, as the *Daily Advertiser* of 29 April 1731 reports that the foundations were being dug. On 3 June 1731 the formal building contract was validated. Recently discovered by Basil Francis, in the archives of the bank of C. Hoare and Co., the document contains a signal example of John Rich's financial trickery.[25] In the proposals for subscription, Rich was seeking a capital sum of £15,000 with which to erect and furnish the theatre, but in this secret building agreement Shepherd had contracted to do the work for £5,600. The wily manager evidently expected to derive a large profit from the entire transaction. However, as sometimes happens in such cases, he was cheated on one hand by the architect, through improper building materials and failure to follow specifications, so much so that extended litigation in Chancery followed, and on the other, the subscribers barely paid in enough to satisfy the amount of the building contract.

To finance the construction Rich proposed to issue fifty shares, each subscriber paying £100 on signing the contract, another £100 on Lady

[22] 16 March is the date given by Howard P. Vincent, in "John Rich and the First Covent Garden Theatre," *Journal of English Literary History*, XVII (Dec. 1950), 296–306, quoting John Rich's Bill in Chancery, C11 2662/1, sworn 15 March 1733. The latter date comes from the text of Rich's prospectus, British Museum Add. MSS 32,428.

[23] British Museum Add. MSS 32,428.

[24] Vincent, "John Rich and the First Covent Garden Theatre," pp. 296–306.

[25] Francis, "John Rich's 'Proposal,'" p. 17.

Day 1732, and a final £100 when the theatre was completed. Upon full payment, a subscriber would receive an assignment of one-fiftieth part of the premises for as much of the term of sixty-one years, less one month, as yet remained. For this lease a subscriber would have reserved for him the rental of two shillings on each acting night at Covent Garden or at any other theatre where Rich or his assigns might act plays by virtue of the present or subsequent grant of authority from the Crown. The two-shilling rental was to have first claim upon the nightly receipts of the playhouse; in addition, each subscriber might see plays without charge in any part of the theatre except behind the scenes.

It appears that Rich must have issued his proposals for subscriptions at different times. One prospectus, now in the British Museum, is dated 11 December 1731.[26] Nevertheless, in the unsigned copy of the building contract of 3 June 1731, mention is made of the fact that Rich had already offered fifty shares to subscribers, and the statement is further made that "severall persons have accordingly Subscribed & paid the first payment of 100l into Mr Hoare's hands."[27] Such information, on this date, would certainly indicate a prospectus antedating that of 11 December 1731, unless this unsigned document is really a memorandum written at a much later date than 3 June 1731.

Records of the subscribers' names survive in the British Museum copy of Rich's prospectus. Forty-six persons signed, including their Graces of Norfolk, Bedford, Chandos, and Richmond, with four signers taking an extra share to subscribe the total of fifty.[28] Records of their payments have recently been found in the ancient ledgers kept by the banking firm of C. Hoare and Co., together with the disbursements to the builder, Edward Shepherd, and the other persons concerned. From the kind permission granted to us to have these ledgers examined and reproduced, we have been able to review the entire situation. Even with the discovery of these documents, the exact circumstances of financing are not yet clear. As quoted above, the agreement of 3 June 1731 shows that some money had already been paid by that date. On the other hand, the first payments

26 My colleague Emmett L. Avery suggests that this prospectus is misdated 1731 and should be 1730. Basil Francis, as cited above, writes that the date is correct. An argument against dating it in 1730 is that Rich includes in the document a statement that he has leased land from the Duke of Bedford, a lease that was not drawn up before March 1730/1. My solution, based on the builder's contract of 3 June 1731, is that more than one solicitation for subscriptions was made.

27 From a copy of the building contract in the possession of C. Hoare and Co., made available to me by the kindness of Mr. H. P. R. Hoare, and secured for me by Professor Fred L. Bergmann.

28 Francis, "John Rich's 'Proposal,'" p. 17.

received by the bank were on 10 January 1731/2, that is, 1732.[29] The ledger for disbursements shows that payments were made to Shepherd immediately, and the debits are for the same months as the payments, so that no further enlightenment can be derived from them. In fact, the entries suggest that Shepherd was waiting in the bank to draw out each subscription payment as it was made.[30]

Of the forty-six persons who earlier underwrote the cost, only twenty-eight names appear in the ledger for receipts of payments, and only seventeen paid the full amount of a share, £300. Five people are listed who paid £200 and five who paid but £100. As it is highly unlikely that a person would deposit £100 and neither withdraw the money nor pay the rest, it may be that the clerk entered the name of the actual person who delivered the money (knowing him to be the servant of one of the noblemen who subscribed). If this explanation is accepted, the total number of sponsors increases to twenty-two (one person being credited with an extra payment). The money came in slowly. Up to 4 April 1733 only £5,650 had been deposited, four months after the theatre opened. The final entry in the ledgers is dated 4 October 1733, when James Brydges, Duke of Chandos, paid £300 to bring the total to £6,700.

Completion of the theatre was almost as slow. Though the *Daily Advertiser* as of 6 August 1731 had expected that the building would be ready for use by the winter season, several delays were encountered. On 6 November the *Weekly Journal* reported that a section of the roof had fallen in, and throughout the fall John Rich was bitterly complaining about Shepherd's absence from supervising the work.[31] Shepherd, by this time, was of course busy with the construction of the Goodman's Fields theatre, which he was to complete first. Even on 18 September 1732, nearly three months before the opening, the *Daily Advertiser* stated that Lambert and Harvey were still engaged in painting scenery and that Signor Ameconi was executing on the ceiling his design exhibiting Apollo in an assembly of the Muses with Shakespeare dignified by the laurel. To

[29] I am indebted to Professor Fred L. Bergmann for studying and copying these ledgers for me and to Mr. H. P. R. Hoare for re-examining the entries and confirming the date as 10 Jan. 1731/2.

[30] The question may arise as to how Shepherd was able to continue the construction when the payments were so greatly delayed. Fortunately, it turns out that Edward Shepherd was also a client of C. Hoare and Co. From the ledger for his transactions, Mr. H. P. R. Hoare assures me that Shepherd had considerable means and had a balance of £3,300 when he started work on the Covent Garden theatre. As the work went on, Shepherd sold South Sea Bonds to pay the construction bills.

[31] Vincent, "John Rich and the First Covent Garden Theatre," pp. 296–306.

the last minute, delays plagued Rich, for he postponed one opening date, 27 November, moved the wardrobe on 1 December, and finally on 7 December 1732 presented *The Way of the World* as the first play in the new house. In spite of all the delays and the charges of poor workmanship and shoddy materials, Edward Shephard had designed and built a superb auditorium, not only in elegance of appearance but also with acoustics far superior to those of the first theatre in Lincoln's Inn Fields or the Opera House in the Haymarket. Reverberation was short because of the drapery in the front and side boxes. Echoes were avoided by flat ceilings, and orchestral tone was good because the building was made out of wood. A contemporary writer stated that Covent Garden seemed "best calculated . . . for splendor and admiration" and that "the figure of a satire over the pit . . . has an admirable propriety in it, and deserves more praise than all the painting beside."[32]

From the depositions in the litigation between Rich and Shepherd it appears that Covent Garden had a pit, boxes (with "the King's front box" as at Lincoln's Inn Fields, side boxes, and balconies and boxes over the stage boxes), and first and second galleries; scene room, coffee room, wardrobe, and privies, concerning whose number, disposition, and convenience there was lively controversy. Rich had Lincoln's Inn Fields in mind in setting specifications for his new house; in his diary and depositions he frequently referred to the fact that one detail or another should correspond with the like element in the older theatre.

Unfortunately, there is little exact information on the seating capacity of Covent Garden at this time. The receipts on the opening night (£115) were much below the £160 or £180 ordinarily realized from a large audience at Lincoln's Inn Fields, but the run of *Achilles* in February 1733 brought income comparable to that for Gay's earlier ballad opera. With receipts of £207 11s. 6d. for *Achilles* on its first night (10 February 1733) and income in the range between £160 and £180 during its run, Covent Garden would seem to have had a capacity similar to that at Lincoln's Inn Fields. Another body of data in a copy made by Frederick Latreille of a Covent Garden account book for 1735–36 which J. H. Haslewood saw in the mid-nineteenth century but which now is lost sheds some information. For a performance of *The Funeral* on 31 May 1736 the servants were issued tickets (240 box, 497 pit, and 500 gallery) to sell for their collective benefit. On 31 July 1736 when they settled their accounts they had sold 120 box, 310 pit,

---

[32] *A Critical Review of the Public Buildings* (1734), pp. 29–30; See also Richard Southern, *Oxford Companion to the Theatre*, s.v. "Scenery."

and 351 gallery tickets. From a Covent Garden account book for 1740–41[33] the list of benefits adds more detail on tickets sold for some locations:

	BOX	PIT	GALLERY
12 November 1740	29	75	56
19 November 1740	48	160	107
12 December 1740	17	113	134
1 April 1741	35	268	222
8 April 1741	218	498	199

(All figures represent tickets sold by the benefitting players and not total attendance in each category.)

The data for 1735–36 and 1740–41 suggest that Covent Garden could accommodate 240 spectators in the boxes, 498 in the pit, and at least 351 in the first gallery. If the number of tickets issued for the gallery on 31 May 1736 accurately represents its capacity, then 500 auditors could be accommodated there, but, as a compromise, let us assume that the first gallery was no larger than that at Lincoln's Inn Fields, which held 450. Furthermore, if the second gallery at Covent Garden, like its counterpart at Rich's old theatre, held half as many spectators as the first gallery, it had room for 225 persons. These assumptions would set the capacity at around 240 in the boxes, 498 in the pit, 450 in the first gallery, and 225 in the second gallery, a total of 1,413, although the figure of 498 individuals in the pit seems somewhat large in proportion to the other areas of the theatre.

Using some of these same figures but a somewhat different statistical method, H. W. Pedicord has estimated the capacity of Covent Garden in 1732 as about 1,335 persons.[34] This figure is similar to an estimate reported in the *London Daily Post and General Advertiser*, 20 February 1736, concerning the crowd the preceding evening, where there were "at least 1300 Persons present," with pit and boxes at half a guinea, first gallery at four shillings, and upper gallery at 2s. 6d. bringing an estimated revenue of £450. These various data make it clear that Covent Garden could certainly hold more than 1,300 and possibly as many as 1,400, but they do not totally clarify the number which could be accommodated in each portion of the house.

33 British Museum Add. MSS 32,251.
34 *The Theatrical Public in the Time of Garrick* (New York, 1954), pp. 6–9.

THE GREAT ROOM OR THEATRE IN YORK BUILDINGS, VILLARS (VILLIERS) STREET (1703-1737)

The Music Room or "Consort-Room" in York Buildings was remodelled and used as a theatre in the summer of 1703, "with a Stage built for Performances," according to the *Daily Courant* of 24 July 1703, and decorated with "a beautiful Ceiling . . . painted by Verrio."[35] William Pinkethman was the promoter: "Tickets given out by Pinkeman" reads the announcement. About 1731 it was remodelled again, and boxes may have been constructed at this time, for the theatre had stage boxes, front boxes, pit, and a gallery (*Daily Advertiser*, 28 August 1734). The first production came on 5 April 1731, when *Sophonisba* was played by "Lilliputians." Clusters of performances were announced during the summer, and again in 1734. Aaron Hill's *Zara* received its premiere here on 29 May 1735. In 1737 a production of *The Fair Penitent* was offered, according to the *Daily Advertiser*, on Monday, 31 January, the first performance that I have noticed on 31 January when the preceding day (the anniversary of the martyrdom of Charles I) fell on a Sunday. A final production was announced for 2 May 1737, and no further performances were given after the passage of the Licensing Act. The structure was demolished about 1758.[36]

THE THEATRES IN RICHMOND

Performances at the Richmond theatres were listed in Part 2 of this Work, and are included in the Calendar of Performances in the present volume up to the end of the 1737 summer season because of the close connection between the companies there and those in the London theatres. The two principal managers were the elder Pinkethman and Thomas Chapman, both of whom were primarily members of London companies. After 1737 the connections are no longer so close, and the Richmond houses are more properly classified as provincial houses. Performances were given in the summer season from 1730 to 1736.

35 *Public Advertiser*, 8 April 1758 (kindly supplied me by C. B. Hogan).
36 *Ibid.*

THE TENNIS COURT IN JAMES STREET (1713–1756)

Plays, concerts, and puppet shows were conducted at a number of places in the Haymarket, so that the identity and location of each place of entertainment were not clear to all contemporary Londoners, much less to us. The position of the opera house and of Potter's little theatre is certain, but some confusion exists concerning the theatre or theatres at or by the tennis court in James Street.

Around 1634 one Simon Osbaldeston had built a tennis court on the south side of James (now Orange) Street.[37] The first notice of a performance there comes on 26 November 1713, the location specified by the *Daily Courant* as "at the Tennis-Court in James Street . . . near the Haymarket." On 4 May 1714, the *Daily Courant* announced that "the Little Tennis Court is in James Street, near the Haymarket," where a concert for the benefit of Glash would be given; and on 12 March 1718 the same paper listed an entertainment at "The Tennis-Court, near the Haymarket." In 1726, Powell and Fawkes offer a puppet show at the "Old Tennis Court in James Street,"[38] and Pinchbeck showed a "Musical Clock" there on 22 April 1732 (*Daily Advertiser*). But the first announcement of regular plays does not appear until 1734, when a group of "Lilliputians" offer *The London Merchant* with *The Devil to Pay* for Easter Monday, 22 April 1734 (*Daily Advertiser*). The location is designated as "at the Tennis-Court in James Street." A month later, casts appear in the *Daily Advertiser*, the players are from other London theatres. *Cato* was scheduled for 23 May, and the location was "the Old Tennis Court in James Street." After a few more performances nothing is heard until 1738, when on 13 March Mrs Charlotte Charke offered a puppet show, "At the Old Tennis-Court in James Street, near the Haymarket."[39] Notices in 1734 had listed boxes, pit, gallery, and second gallery, with Mrs Charke using the terms "rail'd gallery" and upper gallery. She adds that it is called Punch's Theatre, but this designation is to inform the readers of the puppet show; otherwise, the bill reads like that for a regular theater.

[37] *London County Council Survey of London* XX (1940), 109. Miss Elizabeth G. Scanlon, in "Tennis Court Theatres in England and Scotland," *Theatre Notebook*, X (October 1955), 10–15, states that the tennis court was built in 1673 by Col. Thomas Panton. It is true that Col. Panton began paying taxes on this tennis court in 1673, but it is more likely that he had recently acquired ownership of the property than that he had built a new court on the same location.

[38] From a newspaper clipping in the Osborne Collection at the Guildhall Library, according to George Speaight, *The History of the English Puppet Theatre* (London, 1955), p. 102.

[39] *Daily Advertiser*, 13 March 1734; Charlotte Charke, *A Narrative of the Life of Mrs. Charlotte Charke* (London, 1755), pp. 75, 112.

On 29 March 1739, there appears the first indication of a different site. Edward Pinchbeck announced on that date a puppet show at "Punch's Theatre, adjoining the tennis-court in James Street, near the Haymarket,"[40] tickets to be secured "at the Lancashire Witch opposite the Theatre." Unfortunately, the whole matter is further complicated by an advertisement on 2 January 1740 of *The Lover His Own Rival* with *Cupid's Triumph*, performed by actors, to be given "at Punch's Theatre, at the Old Tennis-Court."[41] That the tennis court was being used is supported by an announcement in the *Daily Advertiser* of 28 November 1740 for a production of *Henry IV* by moving waxworks "at the Old Tennis Court near the Hay-market." On 11 May 1741, however, a company of actors began a summer season "At the Old Tennis-Court in James-Street, near the Haymarket" with *Cato* and *The Cobler of Preston*,[42] and their announcements for 16 and 19 May gave the same location. But at this point a change in nomenclature appears: on 16 June the advertisement by the same troupe in the *Daily Advertiser* designated the location as "the Theatre near the Tennis-Court," as did their notice of 29 September. Yet only a week later, 6 October, the location is called "the New Theatre in James-street, near the Haymarket," and the place is so designated for the remaining performances of plays (*Daily Advertiser*). The troupe continued at this theatre for several years, in fact on 23 March 1743 ambitiously offering Dryden's *Aurengzebe*, "acted but once these 20 Years" (*London Daily Post and General Advertiser*). They still consider it necessary to warn gentlemen sending their servants for tickets "(for fear of a Mistake) to take Notice, that the Playhouse adjoins to the Tennis-Court" (*Daily Advertiser*, 15 April 1743). Pinchbeck was still the manager. On Wednesday, 12 March 1746, they risk an illegal Lenten performance. A curious notice appears on 20 April 1747 announcing a forthcoming benefit production for Miss Cymber at the New Theatre in the Haymarket: "Several of Miss Cymber's Friends mistaking the House for The Theatre in James St., are desir'd to observe this is facing the Opera House in the Haymarket" (*Daily Advertiser*). At this time Foote with his "Diversions of the Morning" and his "cup of Tea" was supposedly the talk of the town; and it is difficult to believe that Londoners were unacquainted with the location of the New Theatre in the Haymarket

---

40 *Daily Advertiser. The London Daily Post and General Advertiser* of 19 Dec. is even more specific: "at his Theatre adjoining to the Tennis Court in James Street."

41 *London Daily Post and General Advertiser*. See also Allardyce Nicoll, *A History of Early Eighteenth Century Drama, 1700–1750* (Cambridge, 1929), p. 369.

42 Elizabeth G. Scanlan, giving the Latreille MS as her source, states that during the "Season of May 19 to October 12, 1741" the performances were given on a different or *second* tennis court in James St.—"Tennis Court Theatres in England and Scotland," p. 11.

or that they were more familiar with the James Street theatre than with Foote's theatre.

As time passed, the chief entertainment was puppet shows, but the theatre usually opened on Easter Monday for legitimate drama. Pinchbeck finally gave up the place in January 1750, advertising the property for sale, with or without "Properties and Scenes."[43] From a notice in the following month, we learn that the "New Theatre" was "60 Feet long" and "nearly 40 wide" (*Daily Advertiser*, 2 February).[44] A regular play was scheduled there on 16 December 1751, however (*Daily Advertiser*). On 24 December 1754, George Alexander Stevens, in advertising a lecture on *Pilgrim's Progress*, identified the location as "the Lecture Room, formerly the Theatre in James Street, near the Tennis Court" (*Public Advertiser*). However, on 18 March 1756, the *Daily Advertiser* reported an accident to one Simpson, an acrobatic and slack-rope walker, who ran a sword into his leg in a performance "at the Theatre, James Street, near the Haymarket." By 11 May 1757 the tennis court building was again being used for tennis.[45] For the rest of the century it was the center of the game in England.

HICKFORD'S GREAT ROOMS OR CONCERT ROOMS

The first location given for Hickford's Room was the north side of James Street, "Opposite the Royal Tennis Court."[46] The first concert given there was on 25 March 1713 (*Daily Courant*). The announcement in the *Daily Courant* for 21 March 1715 is quite clear, "At the Great Room in James Street, near the Hay-market." No mention of any other approach to this concert room is made before 1715; then advertisements begin to

43 *Daily Advertiser*, 2 Feb. 1750.

44 From these dimensions, we may infer that the structure was probably separate from the tennis court itself. The problem still remains of deciding how many different theatrical establishments were located here. The outside total may be four: (1) a theatre at the tennis court, (2) a second theatre on a separate tennis court in James St. (Mrs Scanlan's view), (3) an "adjacent" room for puppet shows, and (4) a "New Theatre" near the tennis court. But if the different promotors, over a period of years, were simply using varying terminology, then there was only one theatrical house. In support of this conclusion, George Speaight writes me that he has never found advertisements for any two productions in James St. on the same day, throughout this fifty-year period. This is negative evidence, but our own records support it.

45 "This Day, at one o'clock, will be play'd a Match at Tennis, between four of the best Players in England. . . . It is Played at the Tennis Court in James Street, in the Haymarket."— *Daily Advertiser*, 11 May 1757.

46 Mrs Robert Harrison and William H. G. Flood, *Grove's Dictionary of Music and Musicians*, s.v. "Hickford's Rooms."

speak of another passage way on Panton Street. By 1719 the notices stated that "Coaches and Chairs may come into James Street or into Panton Street, there being a passage into the room both ways."[47] Beginning in 1724 the place was called Hickford's Great Room in Panton Street, and thereafter was always so designated. In 1738 Hickford gave up the place and moved away: "In 1738 there are no concerts recorded in connection with Hickford at the Panton Street room, his name does not appear at all, nor are the entertainments such as he was generally associated with."[48] The entertainments that were being presented were puppet shows, and these continued until mid-century. However, the younger Yates occasionally got together a troupe and offered plays there, as on 26 December 1745 (Daily Advertiser).

On 9 February 1739 Hickford opened a new concert room in Brewer Street, Golden Square. This place was large, carefully designed, and had excellent accoustics. "It is a room of good proportions, 50 feet by 30 feet broad, lofty and with a coved ceiling lighted by one large window at the Southern end, in front of which is the Platform, small and rather low, and there is a gallery opposite, over the door."[49] John Lockman's *Rosalinda* had its premier here on 4 January 1740, and J. C. Smith's oratorio *David's Lamentation over Saul and Jonathan* was also first produced here (Daily Advertiser, 22 February 1740). The once celebrated Signora Cuzzoni gave her final London performance at this house, on 23 May 1751 (General Advertiser).

HAMPTON COURT

There was much agitation about performances at Hampton Court in the autumn of 1731. Three different papers of 3 September carried notices that the Drury Lane company had received orders to play at Hampton Court the next week.[50] On 7 September the report is that six plays were to be produced, and on 11 September Wilks and Cibber had gone to Hampton Court to get the theatre in order (Daily Post). On 23 September the whole project was apparently laid aside as the King's physicians decided that the lighting in the theatre would "greatly incommode the King's eyesight" (St. James's Evening Post). Their decision was not final, as a messenger was sent to Wilks on 29 September to notify him that the theatre in Hampton Court was ready and to notify Cibber to attend at Court with "a list of such plays as the players have in readiness to perform" so that a selection

47 *Ibid.*   48 *Ibid.*   49 *Ibid.*
50 *Daily Post, Universal Spectator, Craftsman.*

could be made (*Universal Spectator*). The first piece actually staged was *The Recruiting Officer* on 18 October for the special entertainment of the Duke of Lorrain.[51]

BOOTHS AND THEATRES, BOWLING GREEN, SOUTHWARK

Apart from the temporary booths erected for performances during the time of Southwark Fair, in September, at least three permanent structures on the Bowling Green were used for winter productions. The first winter production came on 26 December 1732, at a theatre on the Bowling Green. It contained boxes, pit, and two galleries, and the house was made "commodious and warm, and the Passages new laid and rang'd with Lamps." The three permanent houses which can be distinguished are the "Til'd Booth," the "Old Theatre," and the "New Theatre." C. B. Hogan identifies yet another as Phillip's Booth,[52] but when casts are given for the "New Theatre" Phillips and his wife appear in them. The different places which operated during 1729-47, whether in the time of the Fair or in the winter season, are listed below. Several of the entries are undoubtedly identical, but the list is given for convenience. The dates in parentheses are given to aid in finding the performances in the Calendar.

Booth in Blue Maid Alley (1729)
New Playhouse in Birdcage Alley (1730)
Booth behind the Marshalsea Gate (1731)
Booth in the Half Moon Inn Yard (1731)
Booth by Queen's Arms Tavern, near Marshalsea Gate (1731)
Old Tiled Booth (8 September 1734)
Booth, Bowling Green (7 April 1735)
Old Playhouse, bottom of Mermaid Court, by Queen's Arms, near the Marshalsea (1736)
Lee's Old Theatrical Playhouse, turning from Axe and Battle Yard, behind Marshalsea Prison (1735)
New built Booth opposite the Old Tiled Booth (1743)
Booth at Great Fives Court (1746)
Old Theatre (1746)
New Theatre (1746)

[51] *Daily Courant*; *Daily Advertiser*; *Lord Hervey and His Friends, 1726-1738*, ed. the Earl of Ilchester (London, 1950) p. 103.
[52] Hogan, *Shakespeare in the Theatre*, 1, 464-65.

SADLER'S WELLS (1733-1765)

A music room had been constructed at Sadler's Wells in 1683, which fifty years later was converted into a theatre, opening on 12 March 1733 as a pantomime house with *The Harlot's Progress*.53 From a notice in the *Daily Advertiser* of 29 March 1737, it was improved and redecorated. Unlike the legitimate theatres of the time, its progress was characterized by long runs, e.g., the new pantomine *Harlequin in Turkey* having 82 consecutive performances in the summer season of 1748, and *The Adventures of Harlequin in China* 121 in 1737. It was closed for three years after the Licensing Act (though the terms of the Act did not proscribe it), and opened again in 1740. An attendance of 600 was thought worth a news item in the *Daily Advertiser* of 28 August 1744. It was a summer house, running from Easter Monday to sometime in early October. Its performances are not included in the calendar of performances, as it showed nothing but pantomime; however, for certain inquiries in this period, it is important to know of the existence of Sadler's Wells.

NEW WELLS, LONDON SPA, CLERKENWELL (1734-1750)

Located in lower Rosoman Street, the New Wells in Clerkenwell, opened in the spring of 1734.54 Like Sadler's Wells, it was a pantomime house, and had long runs. One piece, *A Hint to the Theatres*, was advertised on 1 June 1737 as having been performed "over 200 successive nights." This show had opened on Easter Monday 1736 and closed on 7 November 1737 after many more than 200 performances. This house provided a novelty— the two o'clock matinee, with the main performance at five. However, the company from time to time showed legitimate drama, and all such performances are entered in our Calendar. In 1741 the matinee was at five and the night performance at seven. The last performance of a play was on 29 December 1748. C. B. Hogan states that it was closed about 1750 and demolished in 1756.55

---

53 *Daily Advertiser*. See also *Theatre Notebook*, I (Oct. 1945), 2.
54 Hogan, *Shakespeare in the Theatre*, I, 464.
55 *Ibid.*

NEW WELLS, LEMON (LEMAN) STREET, HOOPER'S SQUARE, GOODMAN'S FIELDS (1739–1752)

There was still a third structure used for theatrical performances in Goodman's Fields, though its identity was not clear to older stage historians. C. B. Hogan has recently called attention to this house, and some account of it should be given.[56] It was sometimes called "The Theatre in Lemon Street" and sometimes the New Wells. It really was a wells, as Hogan points out; it had a pump room and a taphouse.[57] Our first notice of it comes in the *Daily Post* of 20 April 1739: "Mr W. Hallam, of the Theatre Royal, Covent Garden, having taken the Dwelling-house and Bowling-Green in Hooper's Square, the lower End of Lemon-street, Goodman's Fields, has repaired and beautified them both in a very handsome manner, and will open the House on Monday next, and the Bowling-Green on Thursday."

The opening was delayed slightly, but on 18 June William Hallam began a summer season of pantomime. He continued for six summer seasons; then in November 1744 got a company together and began offering legitimate drama. The theatre then stayed open the year round, reverting to a pantomime house on Easter Monday, and playing a winter season of spoken drama until legal proceedings were brought against the proprietor in the spring of 1747, probably by James Lacy on behalf of Drury Lane.[58] He disbanded his company, whence Lewis Hallam took some of the players to the Eastern seaboard colonies in America. However, he continued with surreptitious performances while the litigation against him was going on. From Miss Rosenfeld's account, we get an excellent sidelight: In October 1750, she writes, "Sir Samuel Gower, one of the J. P.'s, was implicated in the matter, and in February 1751, a complaint was made to the Lord Chancellor that Gower had not only refused to stop the performances but had blatantly taken his family to see them and given every encouragement to the actors."[59]

Hallam made some improvements in the theatre. On 27 October 1746 he announced that "The House is alter'd in a more Theatrical Manner,

[56] "The New Wells, Goodman's Fields, 1739–1752," *Theatre Notebook*, III (July 1949), 67–72.

[57] *Ibid.*, p. 69.

[58] From Proceedings recorded in the Middlesex Sessions Books, as quoted by Sybil Rosenfeld, "Theatres in Goodman's Fields," *Theatre Notebook*, I (Oct. 1945), 50.

[59] *Ibid.*

is made warm, and Front Boxes made at the upper end of the Pit" (*Daily Advertiser*). The size and design of the theatre are not known. That it had some capacity is attested by the fact that it had two galleries and that the pit was deep enough so that ten rows could be "rail'd in" with the boxes.

THE NEW WELLS AND THE NEW THEATRE, SHEPHERD'S MARKET, MAYFAIR

It is very difficult, if not impossible, to distinguish between what was advertised as the "New Wells, Mayfair" and the "New Wells, Shepherd's Market, Mayfair, near Piccadilly." Advertisements appear first for the former, Miss Sybil Rosenfeld points out, citing a benefit performance for Miss Lincoln on 13 March 1742.[60] These notices continue in the *Daily Advertiser* through 1743 and the spring of 1744. Then, on 1 May 1744 appeared a notice for Hallam's "New Theatre adjoining to the Market House (*Daily Advertiser*). The bill continues, "As this is a regular Theatre, Ladies and Gentlemen will be entertained in a more decent and commodious manner than they can possibly be in a Booth." Miss Rosenfeld believes the new theatre to be located on the second floor of Shepherd's Market, and that it was built by the architect Edward Shepherd, yet she notices the difficulty created by Hallam's statement that his new theatre is "adjoining" the Market house. Several explanations are possible. Hallam may have been indulging in exaggeration; probably he had a booth just like the other three that were performing there. Again, the structure called the New Wells in 1742 and 1743 may have been abandoned or demolished and replaced by new accommodations on the second floor of Shepherd's Market. If so, the name, New Wells, would remain, but its location would have changed.

Immediate remonstrance came from the authorities, whereupon Shepherd replied that he was operating under a patent granted by Charles I for "Great and Little Brookfield in the Parish of St George, Hanover Square" (*Daily Advertiser*, 2 May 1745).

Whatever the explanation, performances of regular plays were given at the New Wells, Shepherd's Market, intermittently until 16 May 1749. All of them are entered in the Calendar, though records of pantomimes are omitted.

---

[60] "Shepherd's Market Theatre and May Fair Wells," *Theatre Notebook*, V (July 1951), 89–92. Shepherd's Market was near Curzon St., and east of Hyde Park.

THE FAIRS

BARTHOLOMEW FAIR. In the time of Bartholomew Fair, the last Wednesday to Saturday in August, the leading players from the London theatres set up booths in Smithfield or West Smithfield, sometimes as many as five or six, and put on continuous performances from two in the afternoon until ten at night. The repertory was completely different, with old favorites like the story of *Dick Whittington and His Cat*, the *Blind Beggar of Bethnal Green*, and even Biblical stories. Large crowds attended, and on occasion the Prince of Wales or the Duke of Cumberland could be found at a booth. Performances ceased for a time after the Licensing Act, except for pantomimes, rope-dancing, juggling, and slack-rope walking, but in 1741 the players were back, putting six booths into operation and favoring the crowd with the representation of "Kouli Kan," or of *Darius King of Persia, with the Humours of Sir Andrew Ague-cheek*. Such programs, in four to six booths, continued through 1747.

At times the productions were carefully got up. The context as well as the content of the following advance notice suggest an entirely proper and competent presentation:

A booth is building in Smithfield for the use of Mr Cibber, Mr Griffin, Mr Bullock, and Mr H. Hallam, where they are to perform the tragedy of *Tamerlane*, with the fall of *Bajazet*; intermix'd with the comedy of the *Miser*; the entertainment is to conclude with the *Ridotto al Fresco*. The scenes, habits, and all the decorations, are very magnificent, and entirely new; the boxes are to be gilt, and adorn'd in the handsomest manner, for the reception of the quality, and the whole will be illuminated with a number of glass lusters.—*Daily Post*, 11 August; *Grub St. Journal*, 16 August 1733.

SOUTHWARK FAIR. As soon as Bartholomew Fair ended, the operators of booths moved south of the Thames and advertised the same program for the duration of Southwark Fair, which usually lasted a week. A list of the booths has been given above, under Southwark.

TOTTENHAM COURT FAIR. On 4 August the Tottenham Court Fair opened and extended for about two weeks. In addition to some booths, a "New Theatre" in Tottenham Road is announced from 4 to 11 August 1731. The manager was J. Petty. Performances were continuous from 10 A.M. to 9 P.M. By 1736 the "New Theatre" was being called Petty's "Old Theatre," as opposed to a new theatre "in the Pound." Plays were offered through August 1743, after which the magistrates stopped performances permanently.

WELSH FAIR. The Welsh Fair evidently coincided with the time of Bartholomew Fair, and booths were erected for it in the London Spa Fields only infrequently. Plays were acted before 1737, to be replaced by pantomimes after that date.

MAYFAIR. Mayfair extended for the first two weeks of May. In the 1740's a number of troupes set up booths there, and a good many plays were acted. Such activity met with considerable opposition. Legal steps were taken to restrict not only plays and pantomimes, as was achieved by 1749, but also the assembling of people during the Fair, and abolishing the Fair itself, which was done in 1764.[61]

In addition, plays were sometimes acted at Stationer's Hall, Ludgate Street, at such taverns as the Crown and Anchor and the Castle Tavern, Paternoster Row, at Hampstead, where there was a summer company in 1734, according to the *Daily Journal*, and even at Broughton's Amphitheatre, where fashionable young men usually attended to see the prizefights.

THE THEATRICAL SEASON

Performances at eighteenth-century theatres are best studied in terms of the theatrical season, and our calendar of day by day performances is organized on this basis. Hence, some explanation may be given concerning the nature and patterns of the theatrical season. Many of the older practices remained, but important and far-reaching changes were evolving between 1729 and 1747. Both Drury Lane and John Rich's company (whether at Lincoln's Inn Fields or the new house in Covent Garden) began production in mid-September, acting on alternate days until early or mid-October, when London society had returned to the city. The theatres were dark on 23 and 24 December, in anticipation of Christmas, and again on 30 January, the fast day in memory of Charles I. In January and February came the premieres. During the Lenten season no performances were given on Wednesdays and Fridays, or throughout the whole of Passion Week. In the middle of March the benefit programs began. And about the last week in May the season ended. If there were summer acting, it was by the younger members of the company, to whom the house was given over.

[61] *Ibid.*

However, as soon as two additional companies began performances in the fall of 1729 many of these customs and traditions were altered. Actors earned no money when the house was dark; consequently, the managers of the new houses began to act whenever they could draw an audience. The Haymarket company led the way by acting on 23 December in 1729, 1730, and 1732; it was joined by the Goodman's Fields troupe and in 1736 by the Drury Lane players. By the 1740's the patent houses regularly acted on 23 December, and the date had been added to the acting season. Other changes took place around the Christmas period. Boxing Day (26 December) was a holiday, and a lower middle class group were seeking entertainment. To meet this demand, plays, pantomimes, and puppet shows were given at the smaller theatres and concert rooms, and variety of afterpieces at the principal theatres yielded to the production of pantomimes during the Christmas holidays.

The Haymarket company also took the lead in performing on Wednesdays and Fridays in Lent, giving seven performances in the Lenten season of 1730. In 1731, after Ash Wednesday, the Haymarket theatre was open on ten Wednesdays and Fridays, the premiere of Fielding's *Tragedy of Tragedies* coming on Wednesday 24 March. It was followed on Friday, 26 March, by Lincoln's Inn Fields, where *Acis and Galatea* was given. Offering a musical piece was not considered improper; concerts had been given on Lenten Wednesdays and Fridays earlier in the century. Handel proceeded to test this convention by bringing out his oratorio *Esther* for its first night on Ash Wednesday of 1732. Some musicologists have tried to explain this innovation away by labelling it a rehearsal, but Otto Deutsch has assembled incontrovertible evidence from primary sources to disprove this designation.[62] Meanwhile, the New Haymarket was open on nine Lenten Wednesdays and Fridays.

The first known production of a play on Ash Wednesday took place on 14 February 1733, when *The Beggar's Opera* was offered at the New Haymarket. Handel followed on the next Friday with the oratorio *Judith*, and the opera *Rosamund* was played at Lincoln's Inn Fields on Wednesday 7 March, with the New Haymarket still performing on Wednesdays and Fridays. The New Haymarket company now made a sharp break with tradition by staying open and offering regular plays during Passion Week. On Monday came the *Beaux Stratagem*, on Tuesday the *Mock Doctor*, with *Love Runs all Dangers* on Wednesday and Thursday. On the latter night Walpole himself joined the audience. Remonstrances against such an out-

[62] *Handel*, p. 285.

right violation of tradition came from the church, and the calendar shows no performances on Lenten Wednesdays and Fridays in 1734 (save for a performance at York Buildings on Wednesday, 27 March), until nearly the end of Lent, when Henry Fielding came upon the scene. Using the New Haymarket troupe, he brought out *Don Quixote in England* for its premiere on Friday, 5 April, and continued its production through the first four days of Passion Week. He was joined by the King's Opera House, where an opera was given, and on Monday and Wednesday by Lincoln's Inn Fields, with oratorios on both nights. Two of these musical productions received sanction, the opera being selected by royal command, and the Prince of Wales was in attendance at the second oratorio.

In 1735 a company of French players took over the New Haymarket and performed on several Lenten Wednesdays and Fridays, but the practices of a foreign troupe would not affect contemporary attitudes. Meanwhile, the Drury Lane management arranged a gala benefit night for Owen Swiney on Wednesday, 26 February, before a crowded audience, and players at York Buildings acted on Wednesday, 12 and 19 March, and Friday, 22 March. Handel was now producing oratorios at Covent Garden, with that house open on seven Wednesdays and Fridays; the real straining of tradition came when he continued on throughout the first four days of Passion Week. He was followed on two of these days by the opera house's production of *David*.

The older taboos seem to have been pretty well upset in the spring of 1736, when every company played on some of the forbidden days. *Pasquin* was in its long run at the New Haymarket, and beginning with Friday, 12 March, Fielding kept the play on the boards each Wednesday and Friday. Covent Garden announced several benefit performances, giving six of these on various Wednesdays or Fridays. They were not charitable benefits, for which practice there was some precedent, but for well-known actors and dancers. On Friday, 16 April, as many theatres were open as on any day in the regular season. Drury Lane offered *Julius Caesar* as a charitable benefit for the executors of the late Mrs Heron's estate. At Goodman's Fields *The Conscious Lovers* was showing for the benefit of Norris and Havard. *Hamlet* was the attraction at Lincoln's Inn Fields for the benefit of Tony Aston, with a cast from the Covent Garden company; and *Pasquin* continued at the New Haymarket. Passion Week came on, but *Pasquin* continued two nights, when Fielding was ordered to desist. Lincoln's Inn Fields was also open on Monday and Tuesday, the first night with Rich's players and the next with Drury Lane personnel who played for the benefit of Moore, boxkeeper at Drury Lane, hardly a charitable benefit. On Thursday there was a concert for the benefit of Arne at Drury Lane.

Since the production of legitimate drama under the auspices of a special benefit performance seemed to be accepted, all the major companies proceeded to keep open daily in the Lenten season of 1737. Wednesday, 2 March, found a play for the benefit of a "decay'd Merchant" at Drury Lane, another play at the New Haymarket, and an opera at Covent Garden. All three were open again on the following Friday, though the Drury Lane performances was only for the benefit of an actor. On Wednesday, 9 March, three houses were still open; though the New Haymarket was dark, the *Busy Body* was offered at Goodman's Fields for the benefit of Mrs Lowe, a charitable performance.

Nevertheless, the theatrical productions on Lenten Wednesdays and Fridays were not acceptable to the authorities; on 10 March the storm broke. All productions on these days were forbidden, including operas.[63] In this crisis Handel proved more resourceful than Fielding. With all the companies interdicted, Handel turned to the ambiguities of semantics and offered an "Ode," *Alexander's Feast*, at Covent Garden on Wednesday 16 March. The Prince and Princess of Wales were in attendance and the production "was performed with great Applause, and to the satisfaction of a numerous Audience" (*Daily Journal*, 17 March). Handel promptly advertised another performance for Friday 18 March. Everyone in the theatrical world was watching for the outcome, and Giffard evidently thought another test might be made, for he announced a forthcoming performance, benefit the actor Haughton, on a forbidden day. The result of this effort appears in the following advertisement from the *Daily Advertiser* of 24 March: "An Order having been sent to Mr. Giffard, forbidding all Performances on Wednesdays and Fridays in Lent, Mr Haughton was oblig'd to defer his Benefit to this Day, when Tickets deliver'd out for Yesterday will be taken." Handel was the only one with the right answer. He shifted from the ode to oratorios and serenely continued into Passion Week, keeping Covent Garden open on Tuesday, Wednesday, and Thursday.

After the Licensing Act, the consequence was that both Drury Lane and Covent Garden were permitted to perform, and did perform, oratorios on Lenten Wednesdays and Fridays, that regular plays were prohibited on these days, and that all houses were to be shut during Passion Week.

[63] *Daily Post*, 11 March 1737; Charles Burney, *A General History of Music*, IV (London, 1789) 404.

The next development that need be remembered in studying the Calendar of performances is the evolution of a new theatrical season in the summer. Down through the first three decades of the century, the summer season meant the producing of repertory at the regular theatres by the younger members of the resident companies. But during the 1730's a new trend began. It arose through managerial recognition of the audience potential for the holiday time of Easter Week. Thus on Easter Monday 1733 we see John Rich dividing his company in order to offer productions at both Covent Garden and Lincoln's Inn Fields. On Easter Monday of the following year a company at James Street began its acting, and the New Wells, Clerkenwell, opened for pantomimes. When we turn to the next decade, a discernible though not a fixed pattern governs the productions. A pantomime house will sometimes open in the late winter, or even play the year round, but others will open on Easter Monday and close in late October. The most systematic procedure was established by William Hallam at the New Wells in Goodman's Fields. He regularly opened on Easter Monday and offered pantomimes until the end of October; but for three years, beginning in 1744, he assembled a group of actors and played straight legitimate drama up to Passion Week. When the house opened again on Easter Monday, the dancers were gathered, and nothing but pantomimes were offered. Finally, Samuel Foote began to give noonday performances in the New Haymarket, and, as time went on, to offer regular plays. Thus at mid-century, there remained the conventional theatrical season at the patent houses much as it had been at the beginning, but with the addition of a summer season consisting of two kinds of entertainment: pantomime houses and summer repertory at the New Haymarket. Summer stock at the patent houses was now discontinued for a considerable number of years.

The Licensing Act

THE REMARKABLE expansion of theatrical activity characterizing this period was checked in 1737 and completely halted in 1747 by the passage of a law designed to limit production of legitimate drama to the two patent houses and place the licensing of plays under the Lord Chamberlain. Consequently, a brief account may be given of governmental intervention immediately prior to 1737 and the final incorporation of a licensing act into statute law.

The story begins with Thomas Odell's actions after George II had approved a petition on 28 April 1730 to close Odell's new theatre in Ayliffe Street, Goodman's Fields.[64] According to the *Post Boy* of 30 April, Odell appealed in person to the King on 29 April, only to be denied.[65] From a notice that Watson Nicholson quotes from the *Coffee-House Morning Post* of 24 September 1729, the King had given "Letters-Patent" to Odell; now he was withdrawing Royal approval.[66] Odell proceeded to re-open his theatre on 11 May (*Daily Journal*). The peculiar feature about these happenings is that neither the Lord Chamberlain nor the Master of the Revels is mentioned in any of the reports; the Lord Mayor's objections and Odell's petition went directly to the Throne. Now it may be that Odell was later given permission to operate, but the general opinion in London was that he was performing without any permission, and it is even more certain that his successor Henry Giffard was producing plays without any Royal sanction.[67] In fact, Watson Nicholson states that in London the doubt was frequently expressed whether the Crown prerogative itself extended so far as to silence playhouse managers who were not holding privileges under the Crown.[68]

[64] *Grub St. Journal*, 7 May, where the reports from different newspapers are quoted.

[65] Nicholson, *The Struggle for a Free Stage*, p. 28.

[66] *Ibid.*, pp. 25, 28.

[67] P. J. Crean, "The Stage Licensing Act of 1737," *Modern Philology*, XXXV (1937–38), 240; and see *An Apology for the Life of Mr. T. C., Comedian* (1740).

[68] In 1735, when Parliament considered a proposal to regulate and restrain the playhouses, Giffard issued several broadsides opposing the pending legislation. One argued that in 1730, when petitioners attempted to close the first Goodman's Fields house, Odell received an opinion from "several of the most eminent lawyers" that he had "a Right by the Law of the Land" to give plays. See Nicholson, *Struggle for a Free Stage*, p. 33.

The next intervention of authority came in the summer of 1731, when the *Daily Advertiser* reports that the players acting *The Fall of Mortimer* at the New Theatre in the Haymarket were arrested and the play banned.[69] This time the individual players rather than management were dealt with.

A similar fate befell the production of *Hurlothrumbo* on 20 August 1731, the *Daily Post* reporting that the Constables dispersed the actors and stopped the performance, and *Fog's* explaining that the "constables . . . came to seize them by virtue of a Warrant from the Justices of Westminster."[70]

The first report of an attempt at parliamentary action appears in a letter from Charles Howard to Lord Carlisle, dated 24 May 1733: "and a Bill to regulate the Playhouses read the first time, a debate of about two hours upon it, but no Division."[71] Of this, nothing more is heard. In the fall of 1733 an attempt was made to test the scope of the existing statute concerning vagrancy, by arresting one of the seceding Drury Lane players (Harper) who left for the New Haymarket that season. The upshot of this court test was a fiasco, in that it proved nothing, and a severe defeat for the plaintiff, John Highmore, in his attempt to repress the revolters by legal means.

Meanwhile, Sir John Barnard, according to Sir John Hawkins' *Life of Dr. Johnson*, "had for some time been watching for such information as would bring the actors of Goodman's Fields Playhouse within reach of the vagrant laws: but none was laid before him that he could, with prudence, act upon." Accordingly, he asked leave to bring a new bill before parliament. The new bill was read the first time on 3 April 1735 and ordered to be printed.[72] "Petitions now poured in on the House of Commons,"[73] the only one of which holding any significance in the history of theatre regulations was that of Charles Lee, Master of the Revels, who alleged that the bill would infringe upon his rights.[74] The second reading came on 14 April, and apparently the members were ready to enact it into law, but Sir Robert Walpole misread Sir John Barnard's motivation in the whole matter. Barnard wanted theatres repressed for moral reasons; Walpole wanted only to get rid of the satirists who were leading whole audiences to laugh at him. Furthermore, Walpole wished to add a clause strengthening the power

69 *Daily Advertiser*, 23 Aug. 1731. See also the *Grub St. Journal*, 24 June 1731.

70 *Daily Post*, 23 Aug.; *Fog's Weekly Journal*, 28 Aug.

71 Carlisle MS. Historical Manuscript Commission, 15th Report, Part VI, Appendix (London, 1897), p. 115.

72 *Journal of the House of Commons*, XXII, 444.

73 Crean, "The Stage Licensing Act of 1737," pp. 224–26.

74 *Journal of the House of Commons*, XXII, 459.

of the Lord Chamberlain, but Barnard was interested in the authority of the House of Commons.[75] The consequence was that on 30 April the House voted 90 to 74 against considering the bill, a sharp setback for Walpole.

Defeated, Walpole waited two more years, during which time Fielding's satirical attacks continued on the stage of the New Haymarket, culminating in *The Historical Register for the Year 1736*. That Walpole resented such attacks is not a matter of modern historical inference. Attending a performance at the New Haymarket during Passion Week, Walpole heard one of the actors speak some lines containing a direct reflection upon himself and the Excise bill, and "immediately corrected the Comedian with his own Hands very severely." In May 1737, occurred the strange episode of *The Golden Rump*. The standard version of the story is that a play by this title, containing obscene allusions to, and scurrilous attacks upon, Walpole, was offered to Giffard.[76] Instead of producing it, he carried it to Walpole, who, with great indignation, read passages of it on the floor of the House of Commons, "and the feeling was unanimous that some effective check must be exercised over the theatrical productions."[77] Henry Fielding, however, entered some searching questions three years later concerning the validity of this simple explanation. (To follow Fielding's line of argument, the reader must remember that in the 1730's the phrase "Great Man" would be understood in London as meaning Walpole.) "Suppose, Sir," asks Fielding, "some *Golden Rump* Farce was wrote by a certain Great Man's own Direction, and as much Scurrility and Treason larded in it as possible. . . . Suppose Giffard had a private Hint how to act in this affair, and was promised great Things. . . . Suppose he was promised a *separate License*."[78]

Walpole now reverted to the earlier concern with the vagrancy acts and brought in not a new bill, but an amendment to a vagrancy statute of 12 Anne, on 20 May.[79] The *Daily Post* had picked it up by 23 May, abstracting the bill very accurately the day before it had its first reading. Within a week it had been passed by the House of Lords, where it had its first reading on 2 June and passed its third reading by June 6 (*Daily Advertiser*, 7 June). Royal assent came on 21 June.

75 Crean, "The Stage Licensing Act of 1737," p. 247.

76 *Ibid.*, p. 252.

77 *Ibid.*

78 *An Apology for the Life of Mr. T. C., Comedian.* Against this may be argued Giffard's offered sale of the costumes and properties of Goodman's Fields, and later his attempt to sell his shares; for Fielding (who states that he was writing on 2 May 1740) is the fact that he could hardly have known that Giffard was going to re-open his theatre in the fall.

79 Crean, "The Stage Licensing Act of 1737," p. 252.

The significant items in the Act were the restriction of the King's power to grant letters patent to Westminster (and his various residences, of course) only; the limiting of theatres to those having patents; authorization of the Lord Chamberlain to prohibit an individual theatrical performance; and the requirement that all new plays, additions to old plays, prologues and epilogues had to be licensed by the Lord Chamberlain.[80]

The terms of the Licensing Act of 21 June 1737 prohibited the acting of legitimate drama at any place not sanctioned by a Royal patent, as was Covent Garden, or licensed by the Lord Chamberlain, as was Drury Lane, creating a situation in the light of which all productions of the minor theatres must be considered. For a time all was quiet. Fielding withdrew from the theatre entirely, James Ralph made no attempt to continue at the New Haymarket, and Giffard disbanded his company. Yet before the next winter ended, a violation had already occurred.

"There is a common saying," wrote a pamphleteer in discussing the restriction of theatres, "that all Acts of Parliament have a Hole to creep out of."[81] Undoubtedly the new law would be tested to find a loophole. The first individual to pit himself against authority was a former member of Fielding's company, an unreconstructed actor named James Lacy. His later career as co-manager with Garrick at Drury Lane is well known, but I have seen no mention of his defiance of the Licensing Act in the winter of 1737–38. Nor do surviving newspapers carry any notices of his first performance. However, The London Daily Post and General Advertiser of 15 February 1738 contains a news article stating that on 13 February "Mr Lacey, who set up the Oratory in York Buildings, and was committed to Bridewell some time since by two of his Majesty's Justices of the Peace on the late Act of Parliament, was brought by Habeas Corpus to the King's Bench, in order to be bail'd." The court's decision was to return him to jail, whence he was discharged on 2 March. The article also relates that Lacy had applied for and received a licence to perform his "shew," and that it had been revoked. The account raises a number of questions. Why was the new statute being extended so far beyond its intentions to be applied to a soap-box orator giving a one-man show? Was any influential person backing Lacy's actions by having legal talent secure a writ of habeas corpus?

Soon upon his release from prison, Lacy started his performances anew, but meanwhile, another person issued a curious advertisement. It announced, "By Permission, according to Act of Parliament. At Punch's Theatre, at

80 Ibid., p. 254.
81 The Usefulness of the Stage to Religion and to Government, 2nd ed. (London, 1738), p. 22.

the Old Tennis-Court in James Street, near the Haymarket. *Henry VIII* written by Shakespeare; *Damon and Phillida*, written by Colley Cibber, Esq, Poet-Laureate" (*London Daily Post and General Advertiser*, 13 March). In addition, would be spoken "a new Ode, written by Mrs Charke, the Musick compos'd by an Eminent Hand." This production, scheduled for 13 March 1738, was to be a puppet show, presentation of which did not constitute an evasion of the Licensing Act. On the other hand, the notice was a close imitation of playbills for the regular theatres, with the customary naming of a famous author. Furthermore, singing an "Ode" was just on the border-line of infraction of the law. Finally, the promoter was the well known troublemaker, Charlotte Charke.

Lacy's advertisement announces his appearance for Sunday, 26 March 1738: "At the new Oratory in Villars-Street, York Buildings, an Oration on the following words of St. Matthew . . . by Mr Lacy. The Doors will be open'd at Six, and the Oration begin at Seven o'clock. In regard to the Expenses of the late Prosecution the Seats will be 2*s*." (*London Daily Post and General Advertiser*, 25 March). These notices, with some variations, were repeated on the 28, 29, and 30 March and on 2 and 9 April, by which time he had reduced his price to one shilling.

A third member of this cast of rebels makes his entrance on 1 May, when Tony Aston announced that he would exhibit "his most learned, Serious, Comic, and Whimsical Entire Rhapsodical Declamation" at the George Tavern at Charing Cross (*London Daily Post and General Advertiser*). This notice was not repeated; whether he was prevented by the magistrates or whether an audience failed to appear, there is no telling. Two seasons later, Tony Aston tried again, announcing for 12 and 14 March 1740, at the Crown and Cushion, his "Serious and Comic Oratory," including the specialty act of "The Drunken Man" (*London Daily Post and General Advertiser*).

A number of players advertised performances at different booths during the time of Bartholomew Fair in late August 1740. Strangely enough, the only booth offering a pantomime announced that it was performing by authority; Hallam, Hippisley and Chapman, and Yeates made no reference to obtaining a license in their advertisements.[82] More advertisements followed, so that we may assume that the plays were allowed to be performed.

Three seasons had passed without any organized attempt by a regular company to produce legitimate drama. However, in the fall of 1740 Henry Giffard brought his players together again and began to act plays at Good-

---

[82] *London Daily Post and General Advertiser*, 19, 21, 22 Aug. 1740; *Daily Advertiser*, 21 22 Aug.

man's Fields in an intended evasion of the law by means of a semantic device which brought him (and a number of later imitators) a temporary success. He announced, "At the late Theatre in Goodman's Fields a Concert of Vocal and Instrumental Musick, Divided into Two Parts. Prices 3s., 2s., 1s. N.B. Between the two parts of the Concert will be presented a Comedy, gratis, by Persons for their Diversion" (*Daily Advertiser*, 15 October). This phrasing came to be known as the "concert" formula, variations of which soon appeared as other theatrical promoters observed that Giffard was allowed to act. Possibly the first imitator was Middleton, in announcing performances at a booth set up on 4 August 1741 for the Tottenham Court Fair. At Fawkes and Pinchbeck's booth during Bartholomew Fair in August 1741 some kind of machine was used to present the siege of Cartagena; then followed a puppet show. Neither production constituted an infraction of the Licensing Act. However, the only "live" performance was announced as follows: "Before the Siege begins, will be spoke, given gratis, the Authentic Speech of the Admiral, which he made to the Officers the Morning before he begun the Attack" (*Daily Advertiser*).

The Goodman's Fields company went through the 1740–41 season without interference; in fact, the Lord Chamberlain's office seemed much more interested in exercising its rights of censorship than in its authority to prohibit unlicensed performances. In 1739 Henry Brooke's *Gustavus Vasa* and James Thomson's *Edward and Eleonora* were both prohibited, and in the following year a license was refused for William Paterson's *Arminius*. Paterson's innocuous tragedy did not contain any political or satirical matter for contemporary application and was probably condemned because of the author's handwriting.[83] John Kelly's *The Levee* was banned in 1741 on what were, at least, more logical grounds, as it was a ballad opera packed with immediate political satire.

After the financial success of Garrick's first season at the Goodman's Fields theatre, cognizance was finally taken of Giffard's violation of statute law and he was forced to desist. Giffard's next move was to take his company in the fall of 1742 to the theatre in Lincoln's Inn Fields which Rich had evacuated but for which he still paid rent. Here the concert formula was dropped, and Giffard boldly advertised "At the Theatre-Royal in Lincoln's Inn Fields, This Day will be presented a Comedy . . . at Common Prices" and acted intermittently throughout that season (*London Daily Post*

---

83 The *Daily Post* of 11 Jan. 1740 printed the order from the Lord Chamberlain forbidding the acting of *Arminius*. See Allardyce Nicoll, *A History of English Drama*, 1660–1900, II (Cambridge, 1949), 23, for an interesting account of the reasons for banning these plays.

and General Advertiser, 24 November 1742). The billing was accurate, inasmuch as that house was a "Theatre Royal" by virtue of the two patents granted by Charles II and inherited by John Rich, as an aftermath of the union of the two London companies in 1682.

Meanwhile, occasional applications for performances were being approved by the Lord Chamberlain. A ballad opera produced on 16 June 1742 at the New Haymarket was announced in the bills as acted "By Authority." On 18 February 1743 a group of actors from both Drury Lane and Covent Garden performed a play at the Great Theatrical Booth on the Bowling Green, Southwark, billing it as acted "By Permission"; then they proceeded to include the concert formula in the same advertisement. This odd combination was repeated in the bills for 25 February and 30 March at the same place.

After Macklin had been isolated as a result of the abortive actors' revolt of 1743, he collected some young performers and opened the New Haymarket on 6 February 1744 with a slightly different method of evading the law. In the advance notice in the *Daily Advertiser* of 21 January he wrote that *Othello* "will be perform'd by a set of Gentlemen for their own Diversion, no money will be taken at the Doors nor any person admitted but by printed Tickets; which will be deliver'd gratis by Mr Macklin at his House in Bow Street, Covent Garden." However, the advertisement on the actual day of performance included the usual concert formula. He was soon forced to stop. It so happened that unlicensed productions were being given at a number of different houses during this season. There had been two booths at the Tottenham Court Fair, five at Bartholomew Fair, two at the Southwark Fair, with one troupe acting sporadically on into the winter season, and four in Mayfair. Furthermore, the ubiquitous Charlotte Charke was occasionally offering plays at the James Street house. Most of the advertising for these various productions carried the concert formula, but there were some exceptions, those of the promoters in Mayfair, for example. It is not surprising then to learn of the presentment of the Middlesex Grand Jury in which, among other stipulations, the justices were called upon to apprehend all "Players of Interludes, Plays, and Drolls" (*Daily Advertiser*, 11 May 1744). What is surprising, and not easily explainable, is the list of theatres under scrutiny: the New Wells in Clerkenwell, the New Wells, Lemon Street, Goodman's Fields, and Hallam's booth in Mayfair were the only ones cited. Three other troupes performing in Mayfair had their current advertisements in the same issue of the *Daily Advertiser* that carried the grand jury presentment. Nor was the theatre in James Street mentioned

On the other hand, the Wells in Clerkenwell and the one in Goodman's Fields did not present "Interludes, Plays, and Drolls"; they featured tumbling, slack-wire equilibrists, and pantomimes. Both had opened on Easter Monday and continued with their regular programs, nor did the justices of the peace interfere with their productions. On 17 May the *Daily Advertiser* printed another presentment of the Middlesex Grand Jury, wherein the booths at Tottenham Court Fair were singled out for mention and the constables told to apprehend the players. Three weeks later Mrs Charke shifted from the James Street theatre to a house in Mayfair, couching her announcements in the usual concert formula, but quoting very low prices, 2s. 6d. and 1s. 6d. In her advertisement of 8 June 1744, she initiated another device for evading the law: "Each Person to be admitted for Sixpence at the door, which entitles them to a Pint of Ale, upon delivering the Ticket to the Waiter." This tactic may be considered the unfortunate Charlotte Charke's most permanent contribution to the English stage, as the device has been used, in one place or another, by houses of public entertainment ever since.

The Wells in Clerkenwell paid no attention to the legal action started against them, and in that summer drew the largest crowds to their pantomimes and tumbling shows that had ever been noted by the press. On the 25 August 1744, a writer in the *Daily Advertiser* estimated the attendance on the previous night at upwards of six hundred. But when some actors attempted to perform on the afternoon of 18 September 1744 at the Mile End Fair, the justice of the peace stopped the performance.

The next member of the Cibber clan to run afoul of the law was Theophilus, who announced in late August a production of *Romeo and Juliet*, to be held on 11 September 1744, "By Permission, by Act of Parliament," and when performances began his daily bills omitted the concert formula. Young Cibber did not really have permission however, as Justice de Veil soon informed him. Whereupon, Cibber initiated a still different device, also one that would be used by other promoters. It may be termed the "rehearsal." Its formula went as follows: "At Cibber's Academy in the Haymarket . . . will be presented a Concert . . . After the Concert will be exhibited Gratis a Rehearsal, in form, of the Play (often acted with great Applause) called Romeo and Juliet . . . The Characters personated by the Master of the Academy, his Assistants, Pupils and Servants" (*Daily Advertiser*).

Thomas de Veil read this bill and notified Cibber that such a production would constitute an infraction of the Licensing Act and if presented would be stopped.[84] The unbelieving Theophilus issued this rehearsal formula again in announcing a performance on 10 November, whereupon de Veil stopped the production. The Lord Chamberlain now allowed Cibber's daughter, Miss Jenny Cibber, to schedule a benefit for herself on 17 December, and this authority was duly proclaimed in the bills. Thinking she could succeed where her brother had failed, Charlotte Charke immediately announced an intended performance on 26 December. Knowing that her niece had acted under a license, Mrs Charke attempted to link the announced production of 26 December with her niece's performance on 17 December in the minds of the public, and she stated that tickets for the earlier performance would be taken on 26 December. De Veil, of course, thwarted her plans by interdicting the performance.[85]

All this while, when the law was so strictly enforced against actors at the New Haymarket, the New Wells in Goodman's Fields, which had been cited by the grand jury when the programs were not illegal, had changed on 24 November 1744 from entertainments of rope dancing and tumbling to the production of legitimate drama that was forbidden and put on plays for over a hundred nights during that season. Their bills carried the usual concert formula, sometimes saying the New Wells, sometimes "the late Wells." Late in the spring, however, their advertisements contained an amusing variation of the concert formula that has not been noticed by historians of the drama. In explanation of this advertisement, it must be remembered that the custom of this house for some years had been to open on Easter Monday with a program of rope dancing, tumbling, and pantomime, and play through the summer until into the fall season before closing. On Easter Monday of this season the decision had been made to continue a little later with regular plays. Accordingly, for that date, the house issued the following ironical alteration of the concert formula: "will be perform'd several new exercises of Rope Dancing and Tumbling, by M. Duge, Vangable and others, divided into two Parts. Box 2s. 6d., Pit and first Gallery 1s. 6d., Upper Gallery 1s. Between the two Parts of the Exercises will be given gratis The Tempest as alter'd by Mr Dryden and Sir William Davenant from Shakespear" (*Daily Advertiser*).

Hallam's troupe continued acting in the winter seasons of 1745–46 and 1746–47, regularly using the concert formula. For their opening performance in the fall of 1746, their advertisement located the house as the "Late Wells." On 13 November 1746, however, the bill fails to include the

[84] As quoted by T. Cibber, *A Serio-Comic Apology* (Dublin, 1748), p. 18.
[85] For the full details, see the theatrical seasons under the dates cited.

concert formula. Instead, their production is scheduled to take place at "the Theatre, at the Bottom of Lemon Street, Goodman's Fields," just as if no Licensing Act existed and no constables stood ready to enforce it. This was the last season for plays at this house, for the new management at Drury Lane in 1747 seeing advantage in monopoly called for the enforcement of the statute, and Hallam's troupe was dissolved.

In the years 1740–47, then, considerable activity continued at the minor houses in London. Apart from Giffard's and Hallam's companies, frequent though irregular productions occurred at the New Haymarket, at Shepherd's Market, in Southwark, and the James Street Theatre, together with a great increase of booths at the fairs, as may be seen by examining the Calendar for late August and early September. Yet only infrequent notices appear of actual intervention by the constables. An example that will serve for the period takes place in November, 1746: "Whereas a Pack of Strolling Players, who by the Laws now in Force are liable to be punish'd . . . as Vagrants and Vagabonds; have given printed Hand Bills and Tickets, particularly the Recruiting Officer and Flora to be presented at Yeates' Old Theatre in the Bowling Green, Southwark." (*Daily Advertiser*, 8 November). From the rest of this notice, we learn that the performance was scheduled for 3 November 1746, the players failed to appear, and the audience got no refunds, even though "several Gentlemen and Ladies paid for Tickets." Meanwhile some promoter had announced *The Beaux Stratagem* as a benefit performance at the same location, but after the fiasco of November 3 and the notice quoted above, the promoter got out a new advertisement in which the location for Farquhar's play was announced as the New Haymarket. On 4 November the town and borough of Southwark directed the constables "to suppress the Acting of Plays. By the Statute, no Plays to be acted out in Westminster . . . on forfeit of £50" (*London Courant*). The day was saved for the old theatre on the Bowling Green by one of technology's gifts to civilization: "By Desire of the United Body of Gentlemen Salesmen," a performance was announced on 6 November for that theatre, where *George Barnwell* would be the main play (*Daily Advertiser*). And in January the dancer Phillips, now lodging at 5, Faulcon Court, instead of one of the London prisons as usual, triumphantly announced a performance at this theatre every Wednesday (*Daily Advertiser*).

The most famous evasion of the Licensing Act was that achieved by Foote. When Foote had assembled a small company at the New Haymarket in the spring of 1747, he first scheduled his performance at night, using the concert formula. Furthermore, no money was to be taken in at the door, as all tickets were to be purchased in advance from the bookseller Waller. De Veil interdicted the production, and Foote realized that the concert formula had served its term of usefulness. He decided to draw upon a practice quite popular in the period, the public breakfastings, and use the jargon of their announcements in his attempt to evade the law. Furthermore, he decided to try for a noonday audience. Accordingly, for 25 April he announced: "On Saturday Noon, exactly at Twelve o'Clock, at the New Theatre in the Haymarket, Mr Foote begs the Favour of his Friends to come and drink a Dish of Chocolate with him; and 'tis hoped there will be a great deal of good Company, and some Joyous Spirits" (*Daily Advertiser*). He still retained the technique learned from Macklin, the advance sale of the tickets, with no money taken at the doors, saying "Tickets for the Entertainments to be had at George's Coffee House, Temple Bar." This procedure, while Macklin and Foote may have thought it a legal safeguard, is a risky device in the entertainment world; for the audience is automatically limited to those people who plan in advance to attend. Foote recognized this financial danger, and changed his advertisement the next day to read "Any Gentlemen, or Lady, with or without Tickets, will be admitted."

This phrasing represented a great improvement. If Foote would admit a person without a ticket, then he was not representing plays "For gain"; conversely, to the public, the notice meant that a person could pay at the door if he had not secured any tickets previously. Furthermore, the device of charging the customer for the dish of chocolate or tea (as Foote was also to do) instead of making him pay for the dramatic entertainment enabled Foote to evade the Act of 1737 and continue performances. Since it had been noticed that Mrs Charke's use of the same device had been unsuccessful, other factors must have been involved. The noonday time of performance was a main factor, for Foote was not at that hour competing against the major theatres for customers. Intangibles may also be considered; no one wanted to be "taken off" or mocked by Foote on the Haymarket stage. Garrick's biographers comment on his own timidity in his relations with Foote. Instead of insisting that de Veil or Fielding stop Foote's performance, Garrick temporized. A bold adventurer like Foote, having observed that Garrick did not push for his rights under the monopoly, would take advantage of the situation.

In the following season Foote contributed another variation. He resumed his matinees, but patterned his notices on the customary advertisements of auctions of pictures, as can be seen from his notice of 15 April 1748.

On Monday next at his Auction-Room, late New Theatre in the Hay-Market, Mr Foote will exhibit for the Satisfaction of the Curious, a choice Collection of *Pictures*, all warranted *Originals*, and entirely new. The auction to begin exactly at Twelve. Catalogues will be deliver'd at the Place of Sale, which Ladies and Gentlemen are desir'd to pay for at going in, and 'twill be allowed them in any Purchase they may make. The Sale will continue everyday till all the Catalogues are sold.—*Daily Advertiser.*

By such means, including the careful avoidance of naming the play to be performed, Foote was able to continue his productions.[86]

On 18 April 1748, a court order was promulgated to prohibit acting at the fairs. This time the Tottenham Court Fair, the Shepherd's Bush Fair, the Welsh Fair, the Mile-End Fair, Bow Fair and Mayfair were all cited. This order was more closely enforced than was previous edicts, and the gradually increasing number of performances was again cut back, if not stopped entirely. On 31 October 1748 Yeates announced a play for the old tiled booth at Southwark without including the concert formula, but calls it the last performance of the season, which of course it was not. But on 2 January 1749 he had resumed using the concert tag.

Hallam, who had taken some of his players to the American colonies, had clearly signified that he no longer intended to compete in London, and accordingly was able to obtain special concessions. On 4 April 1748, 27 February 1749, and on six nights between 13 and 30 November 1752, he was given to understand that he could perform a limited number of nights. He did not include the concert phrasing in advertising each of these performances as a special benefit for himself, but neither did he assert that he had obtained permission. He did say that there would be no further performing but on each particular occasion.

The legislation passed by parliament in 1752 and again in 1755 for the regulation of such places as Sadler's Wells required these places of entertainment to be licensed by magistrates for afternoon productions. This legislation gave the small houses more legal status than they previously had, but only if the proprietor secured a license, and a magistrate was not likely to give a promoter a license to act plays in violation of the Act of 1737. Consequently, we may regard the fifteen years between 1737 and 1752 as being a transition period when the Licensing Act might or might

---

[86] One could argue that since Foote and his troupe were engaged chiefly in imitations and "take-offs" no regular play was being produced. On the other hand, years later the production of this season was revived and known as *Taste*. Furthermore, in one bill Foote promises a new "Dessert"; the context clearly implies a changed afterpiece.

not be enforced, or, if enforced to interdict performances at such theatres as the New Haymarket or the two theatres in Goodman's Fields, productions might be relatively safe at smaller theatres, great rooms, or tennis courts. But the statute of 1752 was primarily concerned with these latter places, and the acting of plays would no longer be overlooked. After 1752, then, we read no more about the eight theatrical booths at Bartholomew Fair or four booths at Southwark Fair; instead, we see notices that the sets and furniture of the theatre in James Street are for sale.

The pattern of evasion for testing licensing law enforcement moved then from the "concert" formula to that of the "pint of wine," to "tumbling," to the "rehearsal," to the "dish of tea," to the "auction," to the "final benefit performance"—through a gamut of neat vocabulary shifts and finally because of economic pressure into desuetude.

A Benefit Ticket for Henry Fielding designed by his friend, William Hogarth, reproduced from A. M. Boadley's extra illustrated Fitzgerald *Garrick* in the Folger Shakespeare Library.

Henry Giffard's novel proposal to sponsor plays by means of subscriptions, the standard practice for operas. From the *London Daily Post and General Advertiser* of 19 Nov. 1736.

the IVth. The Part of HOTSPUR, by the GENTLEMAN, who perform'd CATO.

PROPOSALS
By Mr. HENRY GIFFARD,
Director of the Theatre-Royal in LINCOLN's-
INN FIELDS.

FOR the better carrying on the said Theatre by SUBSCRIPTION, and Entertaining such Persons of Quality, and others, as shall do him the Honour to become SUBSCRIBERS, at Half the Expence usually attending such Entertainments, *viz.*

CONDITIONS.

I. No less than Twenty Tickets to be subscribed for.

II. Each Subscriber to pay for the { BOX ————— 2 10 0 / PIT ————— 1 10 0 / GALLERY — 1 0 0

III. The Money to be paid upon the Delivery of the said Twenty Tickets.

IV. In order to prevent more Tickets coming at one Time than the House will contain, the Tickets of each Subscriber will be number'd; and only one Ticket will be admitted any one Night In a Week (*Benefits excepted*) which gives the Subscriber the Choice of Six Nights for every Ticket.

V. Subscribers may transfer their Tickets privately, but not by any publick Advertisement; nor will they be allow'd to be sold in the Streets, or at the Doors of the said Theatre, under the Penalty of losing the Benefit of the Tickets so dispos'd of.

VI. Mr. GIFFARD obliges himself to play several Revived and New Plays, and bring out (at least) one New Pantomime Entertainment, and Revive another.

VII. Any Person may subscribe for the Boxes, Pit or Gallery, singly or together.

VIII. No Subscription will be taken in for any other Number of Tickets than Twenty, Forty, Sixty, and so on.

IX. Persons who subscribe for Twenty Tickets bring in but One a Week; Forty, Two a Week; Sixty, Three.; and so on.

Subscribers Tickets to be deliver'd this Day, and To-morrow, at the Theatre; and to commence from, and be admitted on Monday next the 22d Instant.

N.B.: If the Subscription-Money be sent to the Theatre, Tickets will be deliver'd, pursuant to the Proposals, to any Persons without giving in their Names.

SUBSCRIPTIONS *are taken in at* White's *Chocolate-House in* St. James's-Street; Will's *Coffee-House at* Lincoln's-Inn-Back-Gate; Tom's *and* Will's *Coffee-Houses in* Cornhill; *at the* Angel *and* Crown *Tavern in* Whitechapple; *and at the* Theatre.

IF any Captain or Master of a Ship, bound for the East-Indies, Guinea, or Philadelphia, wants a Sober

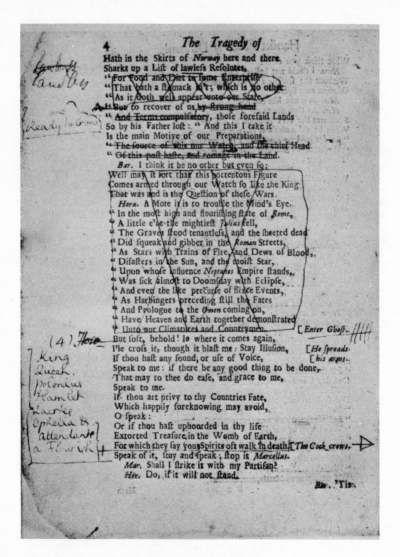

The Tragedy of

4

Hath in the Skirts of *Norway* here and there
Sharkt up a Lift of lawlefs Refolutes,
"For Food and Diet to fome Enterprife
"That hath a ftomack in't, which is no other
"As it doth well appear unto our State,
But to recover of us, by ftrong hand
"And Terms compulfatory, thofe forefaid Lands
So by his Father loft : "And this I take it
Is the main Motive of our Preparations,
"The fource of this our Watch, and the chief Head
"Of this poft-hafte, and romage in the Land.

Bar. I think it be no other but even fo;
Well may it fort that this portentous Figure
Comes arm'd through our Watch fo like the King
That was and is the Queftion of thefe Wars.

Hora. A Mote it is to trouble the Mind's Eye.
"In the moft high and flourifhing ftate of *Rome*,
"A little e'er the mightieft *Julius* fell,
"The Graves ftood tenantlefs, and the fheeted dead
"Did fqueak and gibber in the *Roman* Streets,
"As Stars with Trains of Fire, and Dews of Blood,
"Difafters in the Sun, and the moift Star,
"Upon whofe Influence *Neptunes* Empire ftands,
"Was fick almoft to Doomfday with Eclipfe,
"And even the like precurfe of fierce Events,
"As Harbingers preceding ftill the Fates
"And Prologue to the *Omen* coming on,
"Have Heaven and Earth together demonftrated
"Unto our Climatures and Countrymen.   [*Enter Ghoft.*

But foft, behold! lo where it comes again,
I'le crofs it, though it blaft me : Stay Illufion,   [*He fpreads*
If thou haft any found, or ufe of Voice,   [*his arms.*
Speak to me : if there be any good thing to be done,
That may to thee do eafe, and grace to me,
Speak to me.
If thou art privy to thy Countries Fate,
Which happily foreknowing may avoid,
O fpeak :
Or if thou haft uphoorded in thy life
Extorted Treafure in the Womb of Earth,
For which they fay you Spirits oft walk in death,[*The Cock crows.*
Speak of it, ftay and fpeak ; ftop it *Marcellus.*
Mar. Shall I ftrike it with my Partifan?
Hor. Do, if it will not ftand.

Bar. 'Tis

Hamlet, I, i, 97 ff., as marked by John Ward about 1740 from a 1683 quarto now in the Folger Shakespeare Library. Early eighteenth century managers generally cut the long speeches and kept this play in continuous, rapid movement.

The extent of interest in the sensational story of the real or alleged abduction of Elizabeth Canning is reflected in the title of this score for hornpipes, taken from *Thompson's Compleat Collection of 120 Favourite Hornpipes*, now in the Folger Shakespeare Library.

OVERLEAF:

Ceiling design at Giffard's theatre in Ayliffe Street, Goodman's Fields, from *Garrick Miscellany* in the Folger Shakespeare Library. In the border are shown, reading clockwise, the portraits of Dryden, Betterton, Congreve, and Shakespeare, as painted by William Oram.

| 5 | 4 | 3 | 2 | 1 | 5 | | 10 |

An Exact Representation of the Cieling over the Pit of the
made his first appearance in London (in Publick) O
On the Cieling were painted the Portraits of Shakespeare,
William Cram. The whole length of the building from East
2½ bricks thick the front Wall on the South next Alie Street.
and only 7. Seats. The Color of the Boxes on the inside a ligh
then building called the Royalty Theatre was painted in
and measurement of the Cieling & Boxe &c and the measurement

William Capon pinxt. North Shie

Copied Janr 1831, from the Original

| 20   25   30

in great Allie Street Goodman's fields where Mr Garrick
19th 1741. This Theatre was built by Henry Giffard in 173?
ton. Dryden on the left and Congreve on the Right done by Mr
was 88 feet exactly outside the Walls. 47 feet wide inside the Walls
width of the Pit 30 feet only. The depth to the Orche the 15 feet
he color of pink.   Part of the Scenery for the new Theatre
roof of this House during 1786 at which time I made the Sketch
rea of the Whole House after the fire June 1802. William Capon.

stminster February 1816.

William Capon's drawing of the plan of Goodman's Fields Theatre in Ayliffe Street, with notes by James Winston, reproduced from the *Garrick Miscellany* in the Folger Shakespeare Library. From the dimensions and the number of rows of seats, we can conclude that this theatre was considerably larger than historians of the stage have previously observed.

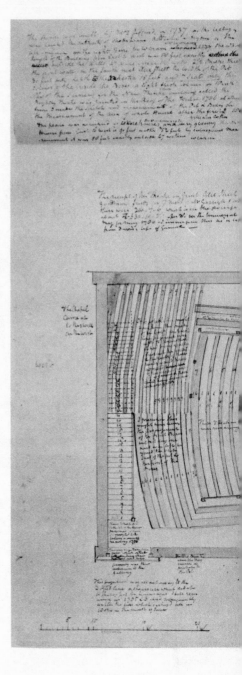

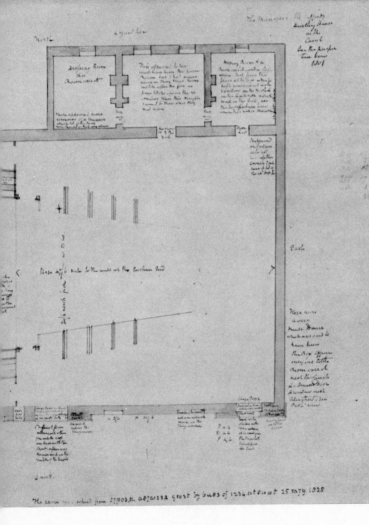

The Coal Black Joak.

Sung in ye Beggars Wedding by Mr. Charke.

Of all the Girls in our Town, or black, or yellow, or fair, or

brown, wth their soft eyes & faces so bright, give me a Girl, that's

blith & gay, as warm as June, & as sweet as May, wth her heart free, &

faithful as Light: What lovely couple then coud be, so happy & so

blest as we, on whom Eternal joys wth smile, & all the fears of

Life beguile, entranc'd in bliss each rapturous Night.

Entr'acte song from *A Collection of Printed and MS. Copies of Eighteenth Century Songs* in the Folger Shakespeare Library.

Theatrical Accommodations and Practices

THE GREATEST space for the audience was in the pit and galleries; many attending, however, desired more conspicuous or more exclusive locations. Naturally, the managers, as well as actors concerned over their forthcoming benefit performances, were equally desirous of extracting the most money possible from the theatre-goers. Reconciliation of these motivations was achieved by creating additional seating arrangements which would be both ostentatious and expensive. The simplest method was to convert some sections of the pit into boxes; the only place for expansion would be to occupy some of the precious space on the apron of the stage. Furthermore, a handful could be squeezed into the orchestra. Consequently, special boxes were constructed on the apron.

The theatres made a practice of being quite specific in their bills about some of these arrangements. For example, at Drury Lane on 19 February 1730 the pit and boxes were put together for a benefit at the customary charge of five shillings; on 3 March 1730 three rows of pit benches were "railed into" the boxes, with the enclosure of two rows a common occurrence; on 25 January 1733 the pit and front boxes were to be "laid together." The custom of augmenting capacity by providing accommodations on the stage, though a source of added income, was also an inconvenience. At *The Man of Taste* (Drury Lane, 25 March 1735) a "few Side-Boxes [were] built on the Stage for the better Accommodations of the Ladies; but no back Seats, to prevent any interruption in the Performance." At *The Relapse* at Drury Lane in the fall of 1729 it was announced that "The Seats upon the Stage will be enclosed." The Goodman's Fields house in Ayliffe Street was very small, and the advent of large crowds prompted Giffard to building not only boxes but also "Balconies on the Stage," (*Daily Advertiser*, 12 September 1733). At Lincoln Inn Fields on 13 May 1731, a benefit notice for Wood, the treasurer, read "Proper Accommodations will be made upon the Stage, by Seats and Scaffolding." For Mrs Oldfield's benefit at Drury Lane on 6 March 1729 there was such an extraordinary demand for places that benches were put on the stage and enclosed to keep the ladies from being cold, and on 20 April 1737 part of the stage was formed into side boxes, primarily for the ladies. The terminology for the building on stage changed later in the period to be called "amphitheatre." Special pains were taken on the night of Mrs Pritchard's benefit at Covent Garden on 23 March 1747: "The Amphitheatre used on the stage at Benefits will be enclosed and divided into three distinct boxes with a ceiling, and illuminated; in the same manner as those in Front of the House." In 1736 and 1737, for some performances of oratorios at Covent Garden, the carpenters floored over the pit and made the whole area into boxes.[87]

But the disadvantages sometimes outweighed the virtues of these arrangements. At Mrs Oldfield's benefit mentioned above, when the stage was narrowed by boxes, it was reported that there was the "greatest Appearance of Ladies of Quality . . . that was ever known, and the House so excessive full, Stage and all, that the Actors had scarce room to perform" (*Universal Spectator*, 8 March 1729). To discourage patrons who wished to be on the stage or in the scenes, Rich announced on 18 April 1735 that the "Performance of Plays being often incommoded by the Number of Persons standing on the Stage," he would take steps to prevent spectators from being there. He was of course unsuccessful in preventing people from obtaining access to the apron, as was every manager before Garrick, and the only recourse was to make as much money as possible from the objectionable practice. The newspaper advertisements for Drury Lane throughout the season of 1742–43 carry the notice that "No Persons will be admitted behind the Scenes, but those that have Silver Tickets" (*London Daily Post and General Advertiser*). Many of the players wanted to continue allowing spectators on the stage, handicaps as they were to the proper movement of the actors; occasionally, as at Covent Garden on 10 January 1739, the dramatist and song writer Henry Carey made a virtue of his self-denial of added income by announcing that at his benefit no benches would be placed on the stage (*London Daily Post and General Advertiser*). Quite clearly most of these special arrangements catered to ladies and gentlemen, especially those who could be induced to pay box prices for the pit enclosed with the more expensive furniture. These boxes were elegantly outfitted, although not all were as fine as the box for royalty on 5 May 1736 at Drury Lane, "handsomely ornamented with white Damask, adorn'd with Silver Laces" (*Daily Advertiser*).

In addition, managers devised means for advance possession of the boxes, particularly on crowded nights, whereby servants could be sent

---

[87] The *Daily Advertiser* of 30 March 1737 reads, "The Pit will be floor'd over and laid to the Boxes."

to hold places. Their employers were requested to send them by three o'clock, the performance beginning at six. It was customary, too, for footmen to hold places in the boxes, even though these unruly servants often caused disturbances. On other occasions, as at Drury Lane on 19 February 1730, when pit and boxes were laid together, no doors (except those to the gallery) were to be opened until four-thirty, thus shortening the time between entrance and curtain. During 1735–36 the King's Opera House regularly announced that the gallery doors would not open until three, the pit and box until four, for a six o'clock production. On 1 September 1737 Drury Lane announced that it had built a new passage into the pit, with a large lobby (containing two fires and benches) for the servants who had been sent to keep places. When a play was doing well, as was *The Historical Register* at the New Haymarket on 21 March 1737, the manager, Henry Fielding, urged his patrons to forehandedness by announcing that "None will be admitted after the House is full; for which Reason, the sooner you come, or secure your Places, the Better." Unfortunately, no one had yet thought of numbering seats as well as tickets to provide our modern methods of reserving seats. In view of Giffard's demonstrated ingenuity and resourcefulness, one wonders whether he was not on the verge of discovering a technique for reserving seats. His newspaper notice announcing a benefit for a player on 28 March 1734 at Goodman's Fields, states, after the customary remark about servants being admitted to keep places on the stage, "and Particular care will be taken to preserve Gentlemen or Ladies Places till their servants come" (*Daily Advertiser*).

After all these measures to increase seating capacity, attract an elite audience, and obtain profits, the manager was confronted with a real problem when a large audience failed to attend. In an informative letter to David Garrick, Mrs Cibber describes what Lacy had done under these circumstances at a benefit production on 9 December 1745: "Drury-Lane Playhouse was not above half full till the latter account; then it was a good house, but not near so great as we had all last winter to the 'Orphan.' He had built up the stage, but as nobody came there, he shut in a flat scene to hide it."[88]

To take proper care of the tender feelings of the social group who took box seats, the managers evolved a new house servant, the "Box bookkeeper," whose business was to receive and record the reservations

---

[88] *The Private Correspondence of David Garrick*, ed. James Boaden, I (London, 1831), 46.

made for the boxes.[89] Accordingly, in the 1730's, the advertisements gave more attention to instructing their patrons how to secure places. The notices generally emphasized that tickets, which had generally become essential for access into the boxes, could be secured in advance at the box office during certain hours or from the box bookkeeper. When Rich opened the Covent Garden theatre he outlined the means of securing places: "All Persons who want Places are desir'd to send to the Stage Door (the Passage from Bow-Street leading to it), where Attendance will be given, and Places kept for the following Nights as Usual" (*Daily Journal*, 6 December 1732).

These offices might be open much of the day, but sometimes, as at the New Haymarket in the winter of 1737, only from ten to two daily. If the office were not in the theatre, the bill gave specific locations where it could be found, as Goodman's Fields did in the fall of 1732 when it announced "Places to be taken at Pidgeons Coffee-house over against the Theatre."

There remained one small area where a few spectators might be seated with great prestige, and this was in the orchestra, often called the "Music Room" (its name at its previous location above the stage). It was here that Voltaire was escorted, book of the play in hand, at Drury Lane in 1726, and that Robert Wilks seated himself to watch the premiere of David Mallet's *Eurydice* after having spoken the prologue.[90] Here too sat old John Rich on the night of 12 February 1747 for the opening night of Benjamin Hoadly's *The Suspicious Husband* at Covent Garden.[91] The orchestra pit occupied a narrow, bow-shaped section extending along only two-thirds of the exterior width of the stage. Eight or ten musicians and their instruments pretty well filled the space.

Since there was so little space, and since neither the manager nor the musicians wanted people in that area, admittance of spectators was regularly forbidden. In the announcement for the production of *Comus* on 6 March 1738 was the statement, "To prevent any Interruption in the Musick, Dancing, Machinery . . . 'tis hoped no Gentleman will take it ill that he cannot be admitted behind the Scenes, or into the Orchestra."[92] Such

[89] Both the Covent Garden and the Drury Lane notices in the spring of 1737 designate this new office. See the *London Daily Post and General Advertiser* of 18 and 23 April, the latter identifying the official at Drury Lane as a Mr Moore.

[90] 22 Feb. 1731. See also a letter from Aaron Hill to Mallet, 23 Feb. 1731—*The Works of Aaron Hill*, IV (London, 1753), 47.

[91] W. J. Lawrence, *Old Theatre Days and Ways* (London, 1935), pp. 241–42.

[92] *The London Daily Post and General Advertiser*; the same note appears in the notices of 8, 9, 10 March, and later.

refusal was not sufficient to end the practice, however, and the following notice was added to all of the advertisements of *The Rural Assembly* in 1742: "The dances depending principally on the Music Room's being kept clear from all Persons but the Performers, 'Tis desir'd that no Gentlemen will take it ill, that they cannot be admitted" (*London Daily Post and General Advertiser*).

Two expressions widely used in the eighteenth-century theatre are often mentioned by historians of the stage but may not be clearly understood by modern readers. They are "Common Prices" and "After Money" (sometimes "Latter Account"). The first alludes to the fact that managers kept increasing admission charges on any pretext—a pantomime, a revival, "new Cloaths and Scenes"—above the common prices, which were, in this period, four shillings for the boxes, two shillings and sixpence in the pit, one shilling, sixpence for the first gallery, and a shilling for the upper gallery. The advanced prices for the same locations were 5*s*., 3*s*., 2*s*., and 1*s*. The second term refers to the money received from persons who came to the theatre at the end of the third act of the main play of the evening and paid only half the admission for their locations in the house. Consequently, when a playbill states that no after money will be taken, the town was on notice that the manager would refuse to permit a person to come in late in the evening to see a new pantomime at half the admission charges. When *The Judgment of Paris* was having a run as an afterpiece in the late winter of 1733 the following notice appeared in nearly every newspaper bill: "N.B. No money under the full Price to be taken during the Time of Performance" (*Daily Post*). On the other hand, if a spectator did not care to stay for the pantomime, he could leave at the end of the main play and obtain a refund of the difference between common prices and whatever he had been charged for his seat, as the two following notices illustrate: "The additional Money to be return'd (if desir'd) to those who go out before the Overture of the Entertainment begins" (*Daily Post*, 12 February 1733), and eleven years later, "Each person who chuses not to stay the Entertainment is desired to take a Ticket at the Door, on delivery of which (if before the Entertainment begins) their Advanced Money will be returned" (*General Advertiser*, 7 December 1744).

The managers also concerned themselves with the comfort and safety of their patrons, but comfort was not easily achieved. When the weather was very warm, the closely packed audience suffered from the heat. On these occasions the managers tried to keep the house cool or delay the time of opening; sometimes they even left off playing until better weather returned. In the early summer of 1733, for example, London was plagued with excessively hot weather, and the New Haymarket, in the midst of a good run of *The Opera of Operas*, announced on 27 June 1733 that it would defer "playing on account of the excessive heat." Productions did not resume until 12 July and then curtain time was set back to seven o'clock. Furthermore, the doors were kept closed until five to prevent the humid air from entering the auditorium. While the New Haymarket management waited for lower temperatures, Covent Garden opened on 29 June, but emphasized in its advertisements: "Care will be taken to keep the house cool."

At other times during the season, patrons complained about the cold and about drafts. Lord Hervey was caustic about the situation at a production of *Porus* at the opera house on 27 November 1731. Though not feeling well, he had gone to the opera and observed the King and Queen clothed in velvet lined with ermine from head to foot to avoid the inconvenience "we freezing plebeians shook under" and noted with satisfaction that Lord Herbert and Lord Albermarle were shivering.[93]

Efforts were made to protect the audience from the cold. On 25 January 1744, the advertisement for the New Theatre, Mayfair, promised that, "in order to make the House warm, there is a new Machine fix'd in the same manner as they have in Russia, & other Theatres in cold Countries to prevent the Gentry from catching cold" (*Daily Advertiser*). And on another January day, Hallam advertised that there would be "a Fire in the Pit to make the House Warm" at the theatre in Lemon Street, Goodman's Fields" (*Daily Advertiser*, 17 January 1746).

A strictly theatrical problem was that of illuminating the stage. Theatres during this period lighted the stage by three means: chandeliers over the inner stage, back of the proscenium, lamps in wall brackets, and footlights. The first and last of these held tallow candles, and the lamps of course burned oil. The date of introducing the footlights is not known, but G. C. D. Odell calls attention to the unmistakable reference in Aaron Hill's *Prompter* of 7 November 1736 to the "Line of Lamps, on the Edge of the Stage."[94] A good many candles must have been used. The inventory of costumes and properties at Covent Garden in 1744 includes 12 pairs of scene ladders with 24 scene blinds and 192 tin candlesticks. From records of payments in the various surviving account books of Lincoln's Inn Fields and Covent Garden, we learn that Rich averaged £2 a day for the candles

93 *Lord Hervey and His Friends*, pp. 114–15.
94 *Shakespeare from Betterton to Irving*, I (New York, 1920), 281.

and about £60 a year for oil. Even so, one may wonder whether the stage was very brightly illuminated. A commentator in the *Daily Advertiser* of 15 August 1744 queries whether Drury Lane and Covent Garden were not too dark. He suggests that a "large lustre hung forwards over the Stage" would have a good effect, and considers that wax candles might give a "clearer and sweeter Light than Tallow." By this I suppose he means that tallow candles created more smoke than wax candles, and that there must have been some stench as well.

Finances

THE OPERA

As was true in the opening decades of the century, Italian opera in the 1730's and 1740's faced problems in financing which differed from those of the playhouses proper; and many of the lessons which might have been learned from the financial disasters of the Royal Academy of Music in the 1720's apparently went unheeded. The first great venture of the Academy ended in deficits in the spring of 1728, and it was a full season before London saw a new operatic enterprise.

The great problem, as before, centered in securing a sufficient subsidy, in addition to subscriptions and box-office receipts, to meet the exceptionally high salaries (high by playhouse standards) which a relatively small number of singers commanded. As was true in the 1720's, opera during most seasons relied upon four principal sources of income: a yearly subsidy from the King, income from a group of yearly subscribers, the box-office receipts from those who did not subscribe, and grants from other opera patrons who at the end of the season contributed the sums necessary to balance the accounts. Although no account books are known to survive to give us an itemized statement of the financial negotiations and problems, some indications of the financial operations can be pieced together from the newspapers and correspondence of the period.

In the nearly twenty years from the autumn of 1729 to the spring of 1747 opera could depend pretty regularly upon an annual subvention of £1,000 from the King, a pattern established in the early years of the Royal Academy of Music. To this support was added, in many seasons, a grant of £250 from the Prince of Wales, and once in a great while the Royal bounty was extended to two competing companies. Although these sums could certainly be put down in a preliminary budget, they were an assistance, not a solution, to the financial problems.

In 1729, when opera resumed, after a season's darkness at the King's Theatre, Heidegger and Handel, who managed the enterprise, again utilized a series of subscriptions, by which the management might know with some certainty the extent of regular financial support. No evidence exists to indicate the number of actual subscribers in these early years, but in

1733–34, when the "Opera of the Nobility" solicited subscriptions, it secured two hundred subscribers at twenty guineas apiece.[95] In 1737–38, when opera was again under financial strain, Heidegger advertised that, as director of opera, he would need an assistance of two hundred subscribers, again at twenty guineas apiece, before he could negotiate with singers for a new season (*Daily Post*, 23 May 1738). This subscription would assure the management of approximately £4,200 for a year's operation. Six years later, when opera had encountered even more desperate fiscal problems, Horace Walpole, writing on 14 August 1743,[96] indicates that thirty individuals had subscribed £50 each for a period of four years, a certain income of £1,200, and there may have been ordinary subscribers at lesser rates.

During the 1730's and 1740's, when Handel was often competing against opera at the King's Theatre, he also used subscriptions to finance his own operas and oratorios. Early in 1743, for example, he appealed to Londoners to pay six guineas which would permit the subscriber to a box ticket at each of six performances; as the current charge for pit or box at this time was half a guinea, Handel simply sought a guarantee, in a sense, of as many advance sales as he could secure. In 1743–44 he varied the subscription to make it four guineas for twelve performances, essentially the same rate per ticket; and in a more ambitious program in 1744–45, he sought eight guineas for twenty-four performances, each subscriber to have a box ticket for each night.[97]

In all of these seasons the response was either sufficient to encourage the management to proceed, or plans were so fully developed that, even if the subscription proved disappointing, it was too late to turn back. In none of these seasons, however, is there much factual information to indicate how much income was received from attendance by nonsubscribers. The reports in the newspapers range from "a thin house" to a superlative £450 at Covent Garden on 19 February 1736 (*London Daily Post and General Advertiser*, 20 February 1736).

The final source of income—payment of deficits by other sponsors of opera—is also not clearly to be seen in the extant records, but the season of 1742–43 offers some instructive indications. Toward the end of the season Horace Walpole became caustically specific concerning the need for underwriting opera, which was then heavily sponsored by Lord

95 Deutsch, *Handel*, p. 341.

96 *The Yale Edition of Horace Walpole's Correspondence*, ed. W. S. Lewis, XVIII (New Haven, 1954), 293–94.

97 See Deutsch, *Handel*, pp. 557–58, 578, 596–97.

Middlesex. Writing on 4 May 1743 to Horace Mann, he pointed out that the yearly deficit for opera was £4,000 to £5,000. By 14 August 1743 he has become indignant that each of the thirty subscribers, who had agreed to pay £50 apiece yearly, had already had to pay an additional £56 in that season alone.[98]

How much was involved financially in a season of opera is never fully indicated in the extant sources. As has already been pointed out, Lord Hervey, writing on 2 November 1734, had heard Heidegger compute the basic expenses of six theatres in London for that season at £76,000.[99] If one calculates the cost of opera on the very conservative assumption that its financing was no more expensive than that of any other theatre, the minimum expense would be £12,300. A writer in the *Grub Street Journal*, 8 April 1736, estimated the charges of the two opera companies at £20,000, a minimum of £10,000 on the average. A news article in the *Ipswich Gazette*, 9 November 1734, reported that opera at the King's Theatre that season was likely to cost a minimum of £22,000, Handel's opera-in-opposition at Covent Garden a basic £9,000. All these figures point to a need for a minimum of £9,000 to £12,000 to meet the basic costs of a season of opera. Since the King's Opera House contracted usually for fifty performances each winter, a minimum budget of £10,000 would represent a nightly cost of £200, a sum nearly four times greater than the nightly charges at the playhouses.

The essential financial problems of the opera companies stemmed from three causes: extremely high salaries for singers, a continuation of the policy which had created deficits for the Royal Academy of Music in the 1720's; lavish productions, especially in scenes and costumes; and dissension, which in the 1730's brought Handel into opposition with the "Opera of the Nobility" and in the 1740's caused Handel to offer oratorios at Covent Garden in opposition to opera at the King's. Although the Royal Academy of Music earlier had been plagued by internal disagreements, these later competitive offerings caused a new and more serious form of financial complication. Since London in the 1720's had found it difficult to support a single opera company in high style, it seemed doubly certain that in the 1730's and 1740's one, if not both, of the competing companies

---

[98] *The Yale Edition of Horace Walpole's Correspondence*, XVIII, 225-26, 293-94. Corroborative testimony comes from the Duke of Bedford's steward; writing his master on 3 June 1743, he states that "The Opera is bankrupt. The Directors have run out £1600 and called this General Meeting to get the consent of the subscribers to take the debt upon themselves.—*Correspondence of John Fourth Duke of Bedford*, ed. Lord John Russell, I (London, 1842), 13.

[99] *Lord Hervey and His Friends*, p. 211.

would have difficulty in sustaining a solvent enterprise. That proved to be the case.

Under the management of the Royal Academy of Music from 1720 to 1728, Italian singers had become accustomed to formidable salaries supplemented by generous gifts at their benefits as well as at other times; in fact, the newspapers occasionally commented satirically upon the ease with which an Italian singer might retire in security after a few lucrative seasons in London. Hence, when Handel and Heidegger in the spring of 1729 began preparations for reviving opera, they established a budget of £4,000 for the five to seven singers, with two at £1,000 each.[100] By 2 July 1729 the *Daily Journal* announced that the new singers had been engaged, and Rolli, writing to Riva on 6 November 1729, indicated that Bernacchi, the highest paid singer, would receive £1,200 for the year; Signora Merighi £900 or £1,000; Signora Strada £600; Fabri £500; with the total reaching nearly the £4,000 allotted for salaries.[101]

In some respects these were more modest salaries than those for the highly favored singers a few years previously, but the tendency was still toward expensive contracts. By the summer of 1730 efforts were made to secure Senesino at 1,200 guineas;[102] his contract finally allotted him 1,400 guineas, the highest salary since the new regime began. Just what the even more popular Farinelli had as his contract in 1734–35 is not clear, but an estimate that the gifts at his benefit on 15 March 1735 would reach £2,000 suggests that adulation from opera lovers made it difficult to write contracts at less than extravagant rates (*Daily Advertiser*, 22 March 1735).

For several years thereafter the newspapers and other contemporary accounts name no specific salaries for opera singers, possibly because the pattern was now taken for granted; but it is probable that a thousand guineas remained the basic contract for a principal performer.[103] Horace Walpole, writing to Horace Mann, 5 November 1741, indicates that much the same level of salaries persisted then: Monticelli and the Visconti at 1,000 guineas apiece; Amorevoli 850 guineas, which Walpole thought not extravagant "at the rate of the great singers"; and the Muscovita 600 guineas, an advance over the payment usually made to the second woman.[104] Signora

---

100 Deutsch, *Handel*, p. 235.

101 *Ibid.*, p. 246. With £4,000 for salaries, £2,200 for scenes, and £1,000 for new compositions, a total of £7,200 would be reached, without reckoning the costs of the musicians, lights, house servants, rents, taxes, and various other necessary charges.

102 *Ibid.*, p. 258.

103 Heidegger's prospectus in the *London Daily Post and General Advertiser* of 25 July 1738 gives this sum as a standard one when he discusses his failure to secure a desired singer.

104 *The Yale Edition of Horace Walpole's Correspondence*, XVII, 191.

Panichi, "the Muscovita," was Lord Middlesex' mistress, so that the arrangement really belongs under the heading of social notes, but the stipend increased the budget by that much more. It was also reported that Giuseppe Tartini had been offered £3,000 but had declined to come to London.[105] All in all, the basic salary roll for singers between 1729 and 1747 probably averaged above £4,000 yearly.

Operatic ventures in this period also continued the artistically laudable practice of presenting fine scenes and providing the chief singers with elegant costumes. In the early months of 1729, when Handel and Heidegger were developing their plans, Heidegger was granted £2,200 to provide "the theatre, the scenery, and the costumes."[106] This was in addition to the fact that the members of the Royal Academy of Music (now inactive as a producer of operas) had granted the two men for five years, apparently without charge, the "scenes, machines, clothes, instruments, furniture, etc."[107] An additional £1,000 was allotted for "composition," i.e., new operas.

That the expenditures by the new regime impressed the public is suggested by a new account in the *Norwich Gazette*, 22 November 1729, that opera in London that winter would be brought on "with great Magnificence, the Cloaths for the Singers, Attendants and Soldiers, being all imbroidered with Silver, and seven Sets of Scenes entirely new." And Rolli, writing to Riva on 11 December 1729, stated that Heidegger had won great praise for his costumes and commendation for his scenery.[108] Quite properly, the management sought to have new scenes and costumes for each new production, a point which the publicity for 1730–31 made: "There are Grand Preparations making at the Opera-House . . . by New Cloaths, Scenes, &c" (*Daily Journal*, 9 October 1730), and the bill for *Porus*, which had its premiere on 2 February 1731, specified that "The Scenes and Habits are all intirely new" (*Daily Journal*, 2 February 1731).

Occasional evidence of the magnificence of the scenes appears in contemporary accounts. For example, *Parnasso in Festa*, prepared in honor of the nuptials of the Prince of Orange and Princess Anne and presented first on 13 March 1734, impressed a correspondent for the *Daily Journal* who had attended the rehearsal: "There is one standing Scene which is Mount Parnassus, on which sit Apollo and the Muses, assisted with other proper Characters, emblematically dress'd, the whole Appearance being

105 Deutsch, *Handel*, pp. 520–21.
106 Rolli to Senesino, 25 Jan. 1729, as quoted by Deutsch, *Handel*, p. 235.
107 Egmont, *Diary*, III, 329.
108 Deutsch, *Handel*, p. 250.

extreamly magnificent." For the festivities attending the marriage of the Prince of Wales to the Princess of Saxe Gotha, in 1736, Handel prepared a new opera and for it "great Numbers of Artificers, as Carpenters, Painters, Engineers, &c." were employed in the preparations. On 12 May 1736 Handel produced *Atalanta*, in honor of the nuptials, and the *London Daily Post and General Advertiser*, 13 May 1736, in its account of the premiere, suggests the care and expense incurred in the decorations.

In which was a new Set of Scenes, painted in Honour of the Happy Union, which took up the full length of the Stage: The Fore-part of the Scene represented an Avenue to the Temple of Hymen. . . . Next was a Triumphal Arch. . . . Thro' the Arch was seen a Pediment, supported by four Columns. . . . At the farther end was a view of Hymen's Temple, and the Wings were adorned with the Loves and Graces bearing Hymenaeal Torches, and putting Fire to Incense in Urns, to be offer'd up upon this joyful Union. The Opera concluded with a Grand Chorus, during which several beautiful Illuminations were display'd.

The large sums invested in salaries, theatre, scenes, and costumes might not have been an excessive financial burden for operas (provided subscribers, subsidies, and contributions to cancel deficits continued), had it not been for the frequent dissensions and rival companies. After four years of the Heidegger-Handel management, disagreements brought a division into one opera company under Handel and another under the sponsorship of the Nobility. The rivalry continued for some time, with both companies laboring under severe financial strains. At the close of 1736–37 the Opera of the Nobility ended its venture. In 1737–38 Heidegger resumed his career as an impresario, with Handel as musical director but not as co-manager. Within a few years, however, Handel and the management at the King's were at odds, and in 1742–43 Handel began a series of oratorios by subscription at Covent Garden; at the end of that season, Horace Walpole, writing on 4 May 1743 to Horace Mann, doubted that the King's could manage another year, because of the "almost certainty of losing between four or five thousand pounds, to which the deficiences of the Opera generally amount now."[109]

On the whole, then, operatic ventures in the 1730's and 1740's repeated many of the financial practices of the first three decades. Relying upon royal subsidies, annual subscriptions, and regular admissions, the management found it difficult to produce operas of a quality and magnificence which it desired; and the combination of high salaries, expensive decorations

[109] *The Yale Edition of Horace Walpole's Correspondence*, XVIII, 225–26.

and scenes, and frequent dissension made it inevitable that deficits would be incurred. Sometimes these meant personal losses, as was true of some of Handel's ventures; sometimes they required a wealthy backer, such as Lord Middlesex in the 1740's, who was able and willing to use his personal fortune to pay the debts of each season.

THE PLAYHOUSES

During the 1730's not only did the scope of operatic enterprise broaden, but more playhouses than ever before were active with full repertories. From the autumn of 1729 to the Licensing Act of 1737 at least three theatres presented full seasons yearly, and sometimes four playhouses actively competed. Nevertheless, our knowledge of the financial affairs of these theatres is very meagre, much less than that for Drury Lane and Lincoln's Inn Fields in the preceding three decades.

The breadth of financial operations in this period has already been indicated in the minimum of £76,000 required for six theatres in the autumn of 1734. Two years later, a writer estimated the receipts at Drury Lane, Covent Garden, and the Haymarket to be £80 (average) at each house, at Goodman's Fields £30 (certainly too low a figure), a total of £270 nightly (*Grub St. Journal*, 8 April 1736).

Yet detailed evidence of the financial operations of the playhouses between 1729 and 1747 is pretty much limited to four account ledgers (two of them incomplete), all for Covent Garden Theatre.[110] As a result, we know relatively little of the salaries, amounts spent on scenes and costumes, on the maintenance and improvements of the other houses: Drury Lane, Haymarket, or Goodman's Fields. The newspapers occasionally allude to prosperity or thin houses at one theatre or another, but detailed figures have not survived.

As they had in the past, the playhouses depended primarily upon box-office receipts for their revenue. At benefits the treasurer deducted a sum sufficient to meet the basic costs, and the theatres had small supple-

---

[110] For 1735–36 there survive in British Museum Egerton 2267 one ledger listing income and part of the expenses and in Add. MSS 32,251 a résumé of a now-lost account book which apparently supplemented the Egerton ledger. For 1740–41 there survives (in the Folger Shakespeare Library) an account book which ends abruptly on 20 April 1741; it lists income and some detailed expenditures. For 1746–47, Egerton MS. 2268 is a complete ledger, but, as was true in many seasons earlier, it records some, not all, of the financial transactions of the theatrical year.

mental income from forfeits, concessions, and, toward the end of this period, the sale of costumes and materials no longer needed in the day-to-day operations.[111]

On one occasion a theatre tried an extensive subscription campaign, probably to secure, as the opera companies did, a certain and predictable revenue. Late in 1736 Henry Giffard, having moved from Goodman's Fields to Lincoln's Inn Fields for that season, solicited subscriptions on this basis: (1) no less than 20 performances to be subscribed for; (2) each subscriber to pay £2 10s. for a box seat, £1 10s. for pit, or £1 for gallery, these charges representing a small discount from the nightly fee; (3) the money to be paid upon the delivery of the twenty tickets; (4) to prevent too many tickets coming in at one time, each ticket was numbered and only one could be admitted each week, giving a subscriber a choice of six nights for each ticket; (5) subscribers could transfer but not sell tickets. Giffard added that he would offer several revivals and new plays, including one pantomime, and that subscribers could purchase twenty, forty, or sixty tickets on the same principle. No information exists to indicate the success of this plan, but the failure of Giffard or other managers to use it later suggests that it did not prove feasible for this type of repertory.

Using the Covent Garden accounts as the example for which the most statistical evidence exists, we discover that Rich derived nearly all of his revenue from the box office. He also secured additional sums from the rental of Lincoln's Inn Fields in 1735–36, but the charge was apparently only that required to operate the house and brought him no profit.[112] He charged his own players from £5 to £50 for the use of Lincoln's Inn Fields, for their own benefit nights, the difference apparently depending, in part, upon whether the player took upon himself all the expense of operation except rent of the theatre. At Covent Garden he usually charged from £40 to £60 against an actor's receipts on his benefit night, though Rich occasionally allowed a lesser charge or even a free benefit by contract. These procedures were a continuation of those practiced in the earlier years of the century by Rich and other managers.

The order of income for Rich during the three seasons for which details exist is: 1735–36, around £13,500 for a full season; 1740–41,

---

[111] For example, in the spring of 1740 Charles Fleetwood, the manager of Drury Lane, put up for sale "the rich Modern and Theatrical Cloaths, lately belonging to the Theatre-Royal in Drury-Lane" (advertised in the *London Daily Post and General Advertiser*, 24 May 1740) and "a further Part of the Rich Wardrobe" (*ibid.*, 28 May 1740). No indication of the revenue from these sales exists.

[112] See British Museum Add. MSS 32,251, pp. 299–308.

approximately £14,325 for 150 acting days or £16,150 for a full season of 170 at the same rate; and 1746–47, approximately £20,285 for 172 acting nights. From each of these figures should be deducted the income (sale of tickets on benefits nights) which accrued to players and not to the treasurer. If these figures are typical, the seasonal trend was toward larger gross income.

Far more detail exists concerning expenditures, since all the available account books register various kinds of payments. As was true earlier in the century, nearly all wages and salaries were paid on an acting basis, i.e., payable only on the nights the house had a performance. Wages were paid to such diverse employees as actors, musicians, singers, the treasurer, bill setters, barbers, charwomen, sweepers, doorkeepers, boxkeepers, and the lampman. There were occasional exceptions. In 1735–36, for example, Stephens, who had been something of a sensation in Shakespearean roles the preceding season, had a contract for £200,[113] and Mrs Horton had one for £250. On the other hand, materials and supplies were often paid on contract; for example, on 27 December 1740 Rich paid "Mr Palmer and Mr Port for lighting and furnishing the Lamps" a bill of £62 6s. 6d. Taxes were usually settled on a quarterly, semi-annual, or annual basis.

The most illuminating figures for the major types of expenditures are a comparison between 1740–41 and 1746–47:

	1740–41	1746–47
Renters' shares	?	ca. £1,300
Salary List	£6,104	7,379
Scenes and Machines	100	253
Wardrobe	522	1,064
Heating	62	100
Lighting	85	350
Repairs and Upkeep	769	488
Printing, Advertising	?	52
Taxes	80	?
Property rental	215	165
Music	206	ca. 680
Number of performances	(150)	(170)

It is clear that these sums offer only a tentative inconclusive suggestion of the nature and kinds of expenses. The vagueness of many entries makes

113 Rich apparently still kept a careful scrutiny over expenses, for he charged Stephens 10s. 6d. for the loss of a "Crutch stick."

it impossible to know under which heading some charges properly belong, and the great difference in the two sets of figures in the cost for lighting is probably due to the fact that the two account books record the payments differently and that each ledger is only one of several kept during a season.

Finally, as was true earlier in the century, the profit and loss figures are beclouded. One reason is that Rich, the manager, regularly took a set sum for himself each night as either his salary or reimbursement for the use of his Patent. In 1735–36 the figure was £3 6s. 8d., and in a season of 170 nights these payments would amount to approximately £650. In addition, all the ledgers abound with additional payments to Rich, some of which may represent reimbursement to him for bills he paid out of hand or they may represent borrowings for his personal use. In addition, he frequently received payments representing his share in the profits of a pantomime. In 1735–36, for example, he received at least £190 for three benefit performances of *Merlin*.

Only later in the century, when more account books are extant for both Drury Lane and Covent Garden, is it possible to arrive at somewhat definitive conclusions on the prosperity of the playhouses.

An additional though minor source of income would seem to be the revenue obtained from the sale of libretti, books of the play, and playbills, save that the extant treasurer's account books contain no entries of such receipts. Concerning productions of oratorios, Winton Dean states that "a new libretto was put out for nearly every revival, and in some cases for each performance."[114] These sold for a shilling, as did copies of the play offered at the door of the theatres. From allusions in various prologues and epilogues we know that the orange women peddled playbills throughout the theatre.[115] The prompter made up these bills, they were the property of the management, and notations of expenditure for the printing appear in theatre account books throughout the entire century, yet these same account books, as stated above, yield no receipts from this source. It seems incredible that John Rich permitted these girls a clear profit.

A much more considerable loss of income came from the dishonesty of the doorkeepers, boxkeepers, and gatherers. In an advertisement of 5 April 1736, for the little theatre in the Haymarket, Henry Fielding explicitly mentions "the Cheats of Doorkeepers" (*Daily Advertiser*). Three years earlier, Handel had been criticised for changing the procedure of ticket

---

[114] *Handel's Dramatic Oratorios and Masques* (London, 1959), p. 96.
[115] For an explicit statement, see Tate Wilkinson, *Memoirs of His Own Life*, I (Dublin, 1791), 22.

sales so that the tickets were issued to the subscribers only on the day of each performance at a new office established for that purpose, as well as for discharging some doorkeepers and hiring new employees of his own choice, whereupon the *Craftsman* of 7 April 1733 (a Tory paper with which Handel was in no way connected) printed a long article explaining that the management was being cheated by the doorkeepers. The eminent stage historian W. J. Lawrence gives a detailed and amusing account of the methods of collusion between doorkeepers and gatherers, together with records of the amounts of the large estates left by some of these house servants at their death.[116]

Management retaliated by creating a new position, that of the numberer. In an elevated box, this official counted the spectators, particularly in the higher-priced locations, until the end of the main play.[117] Thomas Arne was the numberer at Drury Lane for much of the period under consideration. Even so, various incidents occurred to suggest that chicanery was still prevalent. The relatively large sums received by the boxkeepers and treasurers on their annual benefit nights and the discrepancy manifested in the records between the small number of tickets sold at the door on such nights and the high proportion of advance ticket sales by these house servants (in contrast to the normal ratio on benefit nights for the players) certainly invite suspicion. A prominent actor might advertise his coming benefit night in several newspapers, leave tickets at a dozen coffee houses, and canvass among his acquaintances in London society without achieving half the advance sale obtained by a gatherer or boxkeeper. Furthermore, the player could depend upon the normal sale of tickets at the door on the night of performance to approximate or go beyond the house charges fixed by the manager. Yet a glance at the receipts of certain house servants at springtime benefits recorded in the Calendar of performances will show only a few tickets sold at the door and large proceeds from the advance ticket sale. At the benefit for Wood, Covent Garden treasurer, on 1 May 1733, the Account Books show only £31 5s. taken in at the door but £244 7s. in tickets, a total of £275 12s. The significance of this imbalance of ticket money becomes clear when one remembers not only that Covent Garden was, in eighteenth-century terms, a £220 house and lacked the capacity to hold a larger audience, but also that one of the most lucrative benefits

---

[116] *Old Theatre Days and Ways*, pp. 87–92. See also W. J. Lawrence, *The Elizabethan Playhouse and Other Studies* (Philadelphia, 1913), pp. 97, 105, 109, 111–13.

[117] Lawrence, *Old Theatre Days and Ways*, p. 208, calls attention to Thomas Arne's testimony at Macklin's trial (for killing Thomas Hallam) that he had made up his accounts at 8 P.M. and, with his responsibilities ended, had gone to the greenroom.

known at the time, Garrick's night in the spring of 1747, fourteen years later, brought in a pound less, £274. Of course, courtesy and efficiency of the boxkeepers and the treasurer in arranging for seats and holding places were probably being rewarded, but one wonders how many people had been admitted without charge all winter.

Administration and Management

A GALAXY OF PROMOTERS

"I ENDEAVOUR'D to make myself acquainted with the MANAGEMENT of the THEATRE (*which has many parts*)," wrote Theophilus Cibber in the fall of 1733, when he led the Drury Lane players over to the New Haymarket.[118] Cibber was not able to follow his sage precept, the truth of which is exemplified by studying the active and resourceful careers of the various managers of the London theatres as they assumed their varied responsibilities.

Not the least interesting aspect of the history of the theatre during this period is the record of the managers of the different companies. Most of them were close students of the theatre and of contemporary taste, and they distinguished themselves by their experimental activities. Some were concerned with introducing new acting styles, especially Aaron Hill and Charles Macklin, who, well in advance of theatrical customs of the age, were ready to make revolutionary changes of all sorts. Others, like Giffard, William Hallam, and Fielding were prepared to make gradual or radical changes in the repertory. Theophilus Cibber was interested in using the stage traditions he had absorbed as a member of an acting family and was eager to present new kinds of plays to a London audience. Giffard developed what is today called public relations. Far more sensational was Foote as a promoter, with his new techniques in advertising, his establishment of the matinee, and his personalized satires. All were better equipped than Rich, Highmore, or Fleetwood to cast a play; most were as shrewd as Rich in estimating contemporary taste and were prevented only by the enforcement of the Licensing Act from making still further contributions to the development of the London stage.

Much of the art of management could be observed at the new theatre in Goodman's Fields. Thomas Odell, who opened the first Goodman's Fields house, soon relinquished control of the company to the Irish actor Henry Giffard. For a period of about ten years between 1731 and 1743, Giffard managed a regular troupe at either Goodman's Fields or Lincoln's

118 See *A Letter from Theophilus Cibber, Comedian, to John Highmore* (1733). Pamphlet in British Museum.

Inn Fields. During only six of those years was he in charge of the players at a theatre over which he exercised complete control through ownership. Yet in this brief time, he achieved immediate respect and recognition from his contemporaries and trained a considerable number of players who were later successful at the patent houses. Examination of the calendar of performances at Drury Lane years later under Garrick will show that a large number of the players were the actors and actresses who had been trained as Garrick had under Henry Giffard. A glance at the rosters of player personnel at Goodman's Fields during the 1730's will also show that Giffard employed a large number of performers during a season, regularly changing his casting until he had a good production. He moved boldly too. In addition to working with beginning players, he attracted numerous actors from the Drury Lane and Covent Garden theatres, and not only players but scene designers, composers, and a prompter. (See the Calendar of performances at Goodman's Fields in 1731–32, 1735–36, and 1740–41.)

Still, his most enduring accomplishment was that of giving his young players a thorough apprenticeship in the techniques of acting, thorough rehearsals, and a systematic regimen of production, a training that was to be reflected in their later careers. He took great pains to work with Garrick on the road, taking him in a summer company where Garrick played under the name of Lyddal (the maiden name of Giffard's wife) before presenting him on the London stage. Henry Woodward got his early training at Goodman's Fields, and was with Giffard for five years before he went to Drury Lane in 1737. He was later to display his talents there or at Covent Garden for exactly forty seasons. Dennis Delane engaged in four apprentice seasons under Giffard, to emerge as a leading man at Drury Lane or Covent Garden from 1735 to 1750. James Rosco, Charles Blakes, William Havard, John Dunstall, Thomas Mozeen, and Richard Yates were other actors who were trained under Giffard and went on into careers of twenty to thirty years at the patent houses; Mrs Dunstall, Jane Hippisley (later Mrs Green), and Miss Bradshaw were among the actresses who started under Giffard. The record of this latter group of actors and actresses is possibly more significant than that of the others. We don't know how much Giffard taught Garrick; he may have helped him, but Garrick would have been the greatest actor of the century anyhow. It is probable that Delane, Yates, and Woodward would have succeeded regardless of where they started acting, but it is highly improbable that the others would have held the stage at the major theatres at all without the apprenticeship under Giffard. The case of William Havard is possibly the most instructive. After seven years with Giffard, he went to Drury Lane, where, with the exception of the one season at Covent Garden, he was to play for thirty years. Now Havard was no more than a competent actor, but his long tenure accrued because he was a trained, disciplined player. He had learned his profession at a house where the leading players acted 130 to 140 nights in a season, had to be ready to go on stage at all times under a variety of circumstances, with a wide variety of repertory, and get along with the rest of the company.

Giffard also made certain changes in the repertory. In his selection of the season's offerings, he displayed many of the characteristics exemplified with greater talent and more fame in later years by David Garrick. That is, during the years of Giffard's control of a company, he broke from the normal patterns of the older theatres to produce a much higher percentage of contemporary drama than was offered by Rich or by the Drury Lane managers. He dropped Etherege and Wycherley and offered new plays or early eighteenth-century comedies by Farquhar and Mrs Centlivre. In 1741 he was quick to capitalize upon the success and fame of Richardson's *Pamela* by having it adapted into a play for Goodman's Fields. At the same time, he often played more Shakespeare than did the large houses, and he revived Shakespearean plays rather than presenting only the adapted versions of those plays, particularly in 1740–41.

Since Giffard lacked the colorful, truculent personality of Foote and did not engage in belligerent defiance of the established theatres or of the Licensing Act, his career did not provide sensational episodes to be related by the late eighteenth-century memorialists and tended to be forgotten as time went by. Consequently, historians of the stage have not always noticed what an efficient promoter he was or his real skill in the art of gracious public relations. He began his management in the fall of 1731 with a production of the new play of the previous summer, Lillo's *London Merchant*, a drama which had almost instantaneously achieved moral status, and he succeeded in getting a run of a few nights. On 15 October he was able to have it bespoken by several "eminent Merchants." For three other representations of this play later in the season he secured the same sponsorship.

Giffard's display of loyalty to the Crown was carefully demonstrated. An amusing sidelight of the early eighteenth-century troupes was their reputation for maintaining party allegiances. With leaders like Dogget and Cibber, the Drury Lane company was staunchly Hanoverian. But a number of incidents suggested that the Lincoln's Inn Fields players were at least "Opposition," if not downright Jacobite.[119] Giffard took great

[119] See the discussion of this matter in the Introduction to Part 2.

pains to establish himself on the side of authority, in the very years that Fielding was goading and taunting the Walpole administration with his satires at the New Haymarket. On 11 October 1731 Giffard spoke "a new Prologue in Anniversary of His Majesties Coronation," and followed this stroke on 30 October by giving "a very handsome Entertainment on the Anniversary of His Majesty's Birthday . . . when their Majesties Healths, those of the Royal Family and Ministry, were frequently drunk" (*Daily Advertiser*). A year later, 11 October 1732, he gave an even larger party for a great crowd in the streets in honor of the King, and reaped a harvest of newspaper notices.

All London theatres played *Tamerlane* on the anniversary of William III's birthday, 4 November, but Giffard, this season, underscored his political allegiance by composing and speaking an epilogue in praise of William III. The *Daily Advertiser* of 6 November called attention to such orthodoxy and printed the epilogue, as it did again on 1 March 1733, for the "Anniversary of Her Majesty's Birthday, the following Prologue in Honour thereof was spoke by Mr Giffard, Master of the New Theatre in Goodman's Fields."

Giffard outdid himself a year later, when the royal wedding between the Princess Anne and the Prince of Orange took place.[120] He had been busily arranging special entertainments at his theatre that would remind audiences of the great social event, and now he gave a celebration.

Amongst the many Rejoicings made on Account of the Royal Nuptials, the New Theatre in Goodman's Fields, was remarkably distinguish'd; on Thursday Night Mr Giffard order'd 12 triumphal Arches to be erected before the House, which were finely illuminated, a large Bonfire to be made, Fireworks to be play'd off, and Plenty of Drink given to the Populace. And on Friday he invited his whole Company to a very grand Entertainment Prepared for 'em in the Play-house, where their Majesties, his Royal Highness the Prince of Wales, the Prince and Princess of Orange, the Royal Family, Success in Trade, Prosperity to the City of London, and many other Loyal Healths were drank; during which time the Arches were again illuminated, Fireworks play'd off, and the Night concluded with a Ball: In short, the whole was conducted in the genteelest manner, and the utmost Demonstrations of Joy express'd on the Occasion.—*Daily Advertiser*, 18 March 1734

This assiduous attention to the royal family finally obtained recognition. In the winter of 1735–36, he had produced a spectacular entertainment called *King Arthur* and it had met with remarkable success. On 21 January

120 For a full account of theatrical events in connection with this marriage, see Emmett L. Avery, "A Royal Wedding Royally Confounded," *Western Humanities Review*, X (1956), 153–64.

1736, the twenty-eighth night of the run, "Mr Giffard, of Goodman's Fields, being introduc'd by the Right Hon. the Earl of Grantham, had the Honour of presenting a Manuscript of King Arthur . . . as it is now acted . . . to her Majesty, which she was pleas'd to receive most graciously" (*Daily Advertiser*). Authorities like Sir John Barnard might press for an act to terminate the new theatrical companies, but Giffard was building support where Odell had encountered attacks.

He was a good business man as well. His theatre was small, and a full house at common prices would scarcely yield £70. As his varied productions kept drawing crowds, he brought a few more people into the house at larger prices by building a balcony on the stage, admission four shillings. This arrangement must have proved successful, for he followed it by raising the price of balconies and boxes on the stage to five shillings.[121]

Giffard continued his attempts at getting plays bespoken and drawing women to the theatre. The practice of having plays bespoken and of advertising them in the bills as "By the Desire of several Persons of Quality" was by no means Giffard's invention. It had been practiced by every eighteenth-century theatrical manager. But the slight attention given to Goodman's Fields by Genest has prevented stage historians from noticing the ways in which Giffard expanded this practice. If one will examine the record of performances of Goodman's Fields in the 1731-32 season, he will note that out of the 167 nights the house was open, 53 of the productions were bespoken. Giffard started humbly. On 20 nights he was able to advertise that the play was offered "By Desire of some Ladies." As the season wore on, he was able to announce that the play was by desire of some "Ladies of Distinction," and still later "Ladies of Quality," so that in thirty of the bills for the season he had been able use the word "Ladies" in connection with the bespeaking of the night's production. Proof that Giffard was very attentive to getting this support comes from a notice appended to his bill for Monday 20 November 1732: "N.B. Mr Giffard hopes that the Gentleman who bespoke the Spanish Fryar, for Tomorrow, will not take it ill, that Hamlet will be perform'd because the Ladies, whom he mention'd have since sent to him for that Play—but he shall be very glad to oblige him any other day."

He very soon established his reputation as a theatrical manager. Amidst the numerous attacks being made on mismanagement in the *Prompter*, Aaron Hill would turn to praise of Giffard's methods and practices. A long communication to the *Daily Courant* of 25 December 1732, somewhat hostile towards the new theatres and sympathetic towards Drury Lane,

[121] *Daily Advertiser*, 11 Feb. 1734, *et seq.*

concedes that "when People of Distinction condescend to see a Play, they must travel for it as far as Goodman's Fields." Three years later, the anonymous author of a pamphlet, again sympathetic to the patent houses, writes, "I will grant them this, that it [Goodman's Fields] is perhaps the *best-managed* of any others at present."[122]

An excellent example of the kinds of problems that rose to perplex a manager can be seen in an examination of the exasperating delays upsetting production schedules in the season of 1733–34, when all the managers were preparing special entertainments in connection with the impending marriage of the Prince of Orange and the Princess Anne. Announcement of this coming wedding had naturally set the managers to contemplating ways to celebrate the nuptials and win new spectators, but the season must have been a series of frustrations for all concerned. The prince became ill, the wedding was postponed several times, and the ceremony did not occur until 14 March 1734. In the meantime, each manager had to decide whether to produce his special event, already fully prepared, or hold it until the wedding became an actuality. In fact, the managers' decision was to do both; they kept some nuptial entertainments going throughout the season and brought on new ones at propitious moments. Among the special numbers were *The Happy Nuptials*, and *Britannia* at Goodman's Fields; *Bacchus and Ariadne* and a *Nuptial Masque* set by Galliard at Covent Garden; *Aurora's Nuptials*, with music by J. F. Lampe, at Drury Lane; *The New Festival* at the New Haymarket; and *Parnasso in Festa* at the King's Haymarket. Each of these was splendidly got up, and in spite of the delays and vexations consequent upon changed plans, the managers profited from the large crowds that attended.

Giffard was very fond of announcing that a part was being played by someone who had never appeared upon the stage before. Once again, such wording and such a device were no inventions of Giffard; these notices are frequent in the bills for all theatres. But a close study of Giffard's newspaper notices will show that he seems to have engaged in this practice more than any previous manager.[123] For this, he had his reward: on the night of 19 October 1741 Giffard used this formula to announce the first appearance of David Garrick in an acting role.

A few productions at the New Haymarket, at York Buildings, and a single season of authority at both Drury Lane and the Queen's Opera

---

122 *A Seasonable Examination of the Pleas and Pretences of, & Subscribers to Playhouses* (1735), p. 14.
123 Six of Giffard's advertisements in the fall of 1736 announce a different "young Gentleman who never appeared on any stage."

House earlier in the century make up the managerial career of Aaron Hill, a devoted student of almost every aspect of the theatre. Nevertheless, in his brief tenure at Drury Lane he had introduced the double-feature program,[124] and for Queen's he had sponsored Italian opera by inviting the newcomer Handel to compose an opera (*Rinaldo*). The subsequent success of Italian opera did not close his mind, for in the 1730's he was strongly urging the revival of the older native dramatic opera which it had displaced. His most famous pupil was Susanna Arne Cibber, whom he had patiently and skillfully coached to become a tragedienne. Hill's prefaces and periodical essays contain analyses of drama, and theories of acting, staging, repertory, and company management. Nevertheless, it is more instructive to turn from the theory of Hill to the practice of the manager of the New Haymarket in the 1730's—Henry Fielding.

More critics than Hill bemoaned the debasement of the stage by the use of pantomimes and called upon the managers to repudiate these spectacles. Fielding was practical. If pantomime were to be withdrawn, it would have to be replaced by some other form of entertainment that would attract crowds to the theatre. His solution was to create innovations in procedure and to supply personal, topical satire for content. Those who picture Henry Fielding as himself a Squire Allworthy, mild and benevolent, will not recognize the portrait of the manager of the New Haymarket that emerges in the Calendar of performances for the 1730's. Instead will be seen a bold and shrewd contriver intent on being a trouble maker, a promoter who did not scruple at persuading Charlotte Charke to play a role which ridiculed her father, Colley Cibber, who was ready to cry "Foul Blow" upon any setback, and who was both sensitive toward criticism and ready to take extraordinary measures to secure publicity.

His experiments were numerous and lively. From the text of his own plays, we know that he used the curtain between acts and sometimes between scenes, changed the lighting system, and revived induction scenes. As has been shown earlier, he continued production on days when acting was forbidden, performing not only on Lenten Wednesdays and Fridays, but also during Passion Week itself. A striking innovation was his device

---

[124] Dorothy Brewster, *Aaron Hill* (New York, 1913), p. 142. Leo Hughes, in his excellent study *A Century of English Farce* (Princeton, 1956), pp. 82–83, believes that the double-feature was begun during the 1703–4 season. Nevertheless, the newspaper bills for these early years show a wide extent of experimentation, with managers presenting a single scene from some drama or opera after the main production, in a trial and error fashion. Such expedients and improvisations differ from the conscious planning of Aaron Hill in scheduling two complete plays, a long one and a short one, to form the evening's entertainment.

of offering two new plays on the same night. In his brief reign as "Grand Mogul" he brought out an unusually large number of new plays, and for stock he included only very recent drama. Students of living drama, plays as they are actually produced on the stage, should make a careful examination of Fielding's programs, especially in his last season at the New Haymarket, the spring of 1737.[125]

Four more entrepreneurs were to follow Fielding as directors of the little theatre in the Haymarket in the few years remaining before mid-century. All were actor-managers. The briefest tenure was that of Charlotte Charke. Though she had been exposed to a great deal of theatre lore at Drury Lane, she was too emotionally undisciplined to manage a company, and her venture was as unsuccessful as both earlier and later efforts at other theatres. Her brother, Theophilus Cibber, possessed some ability as a manager and even more as a student of popular taste. When he came to manage a troupe at the Haymarket, in 1744, his selection of plays demonstrates his judgment in sounding popular taste. He revived *Romeo and Juliet* and *Cymbeline*, the former to large and enthusiastic crowds, the latter to the magistrates and deputies, who closed his house. The choice of these plays was perfectly tuned to desires of audiences in mid-eighteenth-century London. Booth as Cato, Booth as Brutus had once drawn the plaudits, but now audiences wanted to see charming young actresses lean out of balconies and awaken in underground vaults.

The next manager, Charles Macklin, is significant because of his endeavours to supplant the older school of acting by a new style, called, of course, "natural" in its day. He wished to make other changes too, both in costume and in principles of staging. Forced by the magistrates to desist, he was unable to supply the new actors trained in the style that Garrick endorsed.

Foote was the most successful manager of the group. The law overcame Giffard, despite his ingratiatory abilities in public relations, but Foote achieved a patent. From the Whig view of progress, this result made Giffard a failure and Foote a success. However, the training that Foote as a director could give was valuable only to one kind of actor, the low comedian such as Shuter and Weston. He fitted into the Haymarket tradition, however, in that he produced a new kind of play, an odd sort of burlesque with mimicry. Here his influence on actors was harmful, as it led them to spend a disproportionate amount of time and effort on "take-off" and mimicry. He

[125] See the informative article by Emmett L. Avery, "Fielding's Last Season with the Haymarket Theatre," *Modern Philology*, XXXVI (1939), 283–92.

was a shrewd promoter, getting a lot of advertising for his matinees and new productions, and his evasions of the Licensing Act.

Over at the New Wells in Goodman's Fields, the actor-manager William Hallam deserves credit because of his intense desire to stage legitimate drama. He had been operating the New Wells as a pantomime and variety house until 1743; then in the fall of that year, he shifted to regular plays, presenting the usual double-feature of a full-length play followed by a pantomime. He had nineteen singers and dancers for these pantomimes. In his second season the troupe played to thin houses, and one would have supposed that Hallam would revert to the previous programs at the Wells. Instead, in the fall of 1746, he elected a bold and unconventional program, by engaging only a few dancers but doubling the number of actors and actresses. With a company of fifty players he was able to stage popular plays, and had the personnel to cast *The Tempest*, *1 Henry IV*, and *Richard III*. Then came the surprising managerial policy: pantomime was discontinued. Instead he offered the most popular farces of the eighteenth century, a different one each week, as afterpieces. In view of the demonstrated preference of the audiences at the large theatres for pantomimes, his own long experience in producing pantomimes, and the growing enforcement of the Licensing Act, it is remarkable to observe Hallam staging legitimate drama exclusively. No extant records show what Hallam's receipts were under this new policy, but remarks in the press indicate that attendance was holding up very well at the end of the season; the house was shut down by the magistrates and not by failure at the box office. Hallam's overhead was certainly low, with his decrease in the number of dances; yet with fifty players he could and did exercise wide variety of choice in the selection of plays to be offered. Drury Lane had only eight and Covent Garden only three more actors and actresses in this season of 1746–47 than had Hallam at Goodman's Fields. When his productions were finally stopped by the law, he aided Lewis Hallam in taking players to tour the new towns in the American colonies along the Atlantic seaboard to produce British drama there.

Edward Pinchbeck was a skillful promoter, as evidenced by his advertising devices, yet his observation led him to conclusions directly contrary to those of the Hallams. Managing the theatre in James Street for many years, he had produced regular dramas occasionally, but relied upon pantomime as a staple. Even this entertainment palled on Pinchbeck; he preferred machines. Again and again, as can be seen in the Calendar of performances, he advertized "Grand Machinery" to show the siege of Cartagena or some other topical event. When, near mid-century, he observed that the Licensing Act was going to be enforced strictly, he did not even try for a license but gave up the James Street house.

DRURY LANE

The efficient and stable management in effect for so many years at Drury Lane finally came to an end, and in the 1730's disintegrated into almost complete chaos amid an extended public discussion of the proper conduct of a theatrical enterprise. The crisis did not come at once; a number of events were necessary to disrupt the excellent organization of the triumvirate, Wilks, Booth, and Cibber.

The death of Sir Richard Steele in 1729 must certainly have reminded the managers of Drury Lane that the Royal patent vested in him was scheduled to expire three years after his death. Application was made for a new patent granted directly to the triumvirate. Royal approval was forthcoming, and a new patent was granted to "Robert Wilks, Colley Cibber, Barton Booth . . . their Heirs, Executors, Administrators, and Assigns" to be effective on 3 July 1732.[126] Dissolution of the partnership began immediately, for on 13 July Barton Booth sold half of his share to a young man, stage-struck and wealthy, named John Highmore, reputedly for the sum of £2,500.[127] The next step in reorganization came at the beginning of the theatrical season, when Colley Cibber assigned his share and his authority in the management to his son Theophilus, on a term basis from September to 1 June 1733.[128] Wilks had been ill and died on 27 September, so that the fall productions opened with young Cibber, Booth, and the newcomer Highmore as the managers. To this group was added the painter John Ellys, to whom Mary Wilks apparently assigned half of her share on 31 October.[129] It was a season when the best kind of leadership was necessary, as the novelty of the two new theatres in Covent Garden and Goodman's Fields provided sharp competition; instead, the new managers were constantly embroiled in disputes smoothed over or adjudicated by the restraining

[126] Daily Post, 27 April 1732; A Bill for Restraining the Number of Houses for Playing of Interludes (1735), British Museum 11795K31; "The Case of the Patentees," in the Daily Post of 4 June 1733. The effective date was 1 September, according to Genest's quotation from Wilks's will.—Genest, Some Account of the English Stage, III, 336.

[127] Benjamin Victor, A History of the Theatres of London and Dublin, I (London, 1761), 7.

[128] St. James's Evening Post, 31 Oct. 1732; A Letter from Theophilus Cibber . . . to John Highmore.

[129] Both names appear in "The Case of the Patentees," Daily Post, 4 June 1733. See also St. James's Evening Post, 31 Oct. 1732.

influence of Booth. Old Colley Cibber must have observed all this; at any rate, he withdrew before there could be any financial loss by selling his entire share "of the Cloaths, Scenes, and Patent" to John Highmore for three thousand guineas.[130] Booth had also been ill, and he died on 10 May. With his calming influence removed, the crisis of administrative control was precipitated. The first move was that of the patentees, now Mary Wilks, Hester Booth, John Ellys, and John Highmore, who locked the actors out on 26 May and took possession of the properties at the theatre to prevent what they considered an attempt on the part of the actors, headed by Theophilus Cibber, to gain the house for themselves. On 4 June the patentees published in the *Daily Post* a statement of their case. They pointed out that Drury Lane had been leased from the Duke of Bedford and that the renters had been paid 12s. per acting night, without any disagreement between renters and managers until some of the performers lately had begun to treat with some of the renters to secure Drury Lane for themselves. To prove that the players had not suffered under the management, the owners pointed out the respectable salaries being paid the actors and stressed that wages and incidental costs brought a daily expense of £49. Touching upon a matter which became a center of debate, they stated that the late patent issued to Wilks, Booth, and Cibber was so unusual that "there is no other Instance of Actors being at the Head of His Majesty's Company of Comedians; and, it is believed, that the like will never be done again, till there shall be another Set of equal Merit in their Performances with them to recommend them to the like Favour."

Shortly thereafter two views of the controversy appeared in the *Grub Street Journal*, 7 June 1733, each discussing the relation of actor to management. Philo-Dramaticus developed the thesis that "It hath been always thought essential to the preservation of the stage, and the encouragement of authors, to have the management of the theater committed to proper persons, who had given some public proof of their capacity to judge what would be most instructive or agreeable to the taste of an English audience." Whether the new patentees possessed these qualities he left to the decision of the public, but he asserted that Steele thought it "advisable, and in no way unworthy of him, to join with those who were professed players" (i.e., Wilks, Booth, and Cibber) because "they were all eminent in their professions as actors." As for the new owners, who possessed no professional ability, "their care and caution will naturally be employed to make their purchase turn to the most *advantage* to themselves, and not to the reputation,

[130] Victor, *A History of the Theatres*, I, 6–11, and *Fog's Journal*, 24 March 1733.

interest, or encouragement of their own company, or the authors. They will certainly allow as small an income as possible, even to the best performers." It was unjust, "that the useless and unprofitable members of any society, should feed upon the profits arising from the excellencies of all the rest"; and he concluded by asking, "What case can be more distressful than that of the players under the present management?"

In the same issue Musaeus argued against the stand of the malcontent players. He maintained that Wilks, Booth, and Cibber were examples of the "insolence of stage-tyrants," especially in their treatment of contemporary dramatists, and that, when the new patentees undertook "with the utmost diligence to regulate the conduct of the theatre, to remedy all abuses, and remove all just occasion of complaint," they met with an insurrection from players who apparently were content if paid their stipends during the seasons when the actor-managers had divided the profits at the end of the year but who acted as if they had become slaves if they were to receive the same salaries while seeing the profits divided among the new patentees. In his view, Theophilus Cibber, seeking power, called for a rebellion and proposed a company in which each performer was to have a salary equal to his previous one, all were to share in the profits in proportion to their pay, all were to be managers by having equal votes in council and sitting in equal judgment upon authors. "Like the drunken sailors in the play, they are *all* to be *Viceroys*, PISTOL [T. Cibber] desired only to be *viceroy over them*."

No theatrical event involving principles of management created so much public discussion in the first forty years of the century as this quarrel. Actors, managers, editors, spectators, correspondents in the newspapers— nearly everyone took a hand in it. It resulted in a defection of the players headed by young Cibber in the fall of 1733 to act at the New Haymarket in opposition to Drury Lane under Highmore. Years later Cibber told how he and his companions "found a happy Asylum . . . protected by a generous Town, against the despotic Power of some petulant, capricious, unskilful, indolent and oppressive Patentees."[131] A letter to the *Daily Journal*, 26 September 1733, pointed out that the Drury Lane patent, once divided among three actor-managers, now existed in six shares, and might it not branch into twelve, "and those into twelve more, and every one of them or their Assigns, have a right of gathering together, forming, entertaining, governing, privileging, and keeping a Company of Comedians . . . but this may show how far a Patent may be misused." The basis for this *reductio*

[131] *Two Dissertations on the Theatres* (London, 1756), p. 19.

ad absurdum was probably the recent news of Hester Booth's sale of her remaining half-share to the manager of the Goodman's Fields theatre, Henry Giffard, in mid-September.[132]

Young Cibber ingeniously tried an historical line of legal defense by appealing to Charles Lee, Master of the Revels, thereby reviving the controversy over the relative authority of the Lord Chamberlain and the Master of the Revels that had erupted in the 1660's. A communication to the *Daily Post* of 29 September 1733 insisted that Lee, by virtue of his office, "has an equal Right to Licence the Acting of Play's." Lee's patent was searched, but the text does not specify plays, and Cibber had no legal support here, although his bills styled the company as "The Comedians of His Majesty's Revels." In turn, Highmore also tried for a legal ruling. A suit to have two members of the Haymarket rebels and, for good measure, two more from Goodman's Fields, declared vagrants under the statute of 12 Anne failed on 5 November 1733 because of a disagreement over what terms should appear in the summons by which to apprehend the players (*London Evening Post*, 3 November 1733).

Meanwhile, the revolters had been building another line of defense against Highmore's lawsuit; they had been cultivating the good will of the trustees and renters of Drury Lane. Consequently, on 13 November, "the lord chief justice York . . . determin'd in favour of the Hay-Market company," on the ground that "the company of the Hay-market took a lease of the two trustees appointed by the thirty-six Sharers of Drury-Lane house; but the trustees being willing that the said lease should be good both in law and equity, consulted the said sharers; and twenty-seven out of the thirty-six agreed to the said lease (*London Evening Post*). Harper was acquitted on 28 November, and Highmore had lost out all around (*London Evening Post*).

The unfortunate Highmore and John Ellys struggled through the season the best they could. The remaining owner, Giffard, was busy with his own theatre, although he sometimes acted at Drury Lane. Only a few actors had remained loyal, particularly Kitty Clive and Macklin; otherwise, a weird assortment of minor players appeared on the boards there this season. The Royal family tended to support the patentees, but for the Prince of Wales who, with some of the nobility, went to the little Haymarket. As the season wore on, Highmore found himself losing £50 to £60 a week. Eventually, he gave up and entered into negotiations with another wealthy

132 *London Evening Post*, 18 Sept. See also Henry Carey's Preface to *The Honest Yorkshireman* (1736), and Victor, *A History of the Theatres*, I, 10–11.

amateur, Charles Fleetwood, to whom he sold his shares of the patent before 2 February 1734 (*Daily Courant*, 2 February 1734).

The rebels at the Haymarket made their triumphant return to the Theatre Royal on 8 March, upsetting the schedule of benefits arranged for the loyal players (*Daily Advertiser*, 9 March 1734). It was only a partial victory; Highmore had sold out, but young Cibber had also lost control. It was now Fleetwood's theatre, and would continue such for the next ten years. Although the fashion among stage historians has been to dismiss Fleetwood, almost as if he were nonexistent, or at best an absentee proprietor, the fact remains that he was the manager for almost eleven years, and numerous primary sources indicate that he took active control of affairs at the theatre. He may have appointed Charles Macklin stage manager, but this was no more than good sense for a man without experience in the theatre, as Fleetwood was. However, whenever troubles arose, he was present in person and was assuming the responsibilities that went with managership. The language of a controversy over a dancer's failure to perform at Drury Lane on 24 February 1735 sounds as if Fleetwood were *de facto* manager of the company, as the affair was reported by the *Daily Journal*. So too, in the fall of that year, the *Daily Advertiser* of 10 November reports that Fleetwood had personally engaged old Colley Cibber to act in a few plays. Treasurers' account books are lacking, but from the full programs offered over entire seasons in the 1730's and from the salaries reported to have been paid to the players, Drury Lane was very much a going concern under Fleetwood, and in some years may even have been quite prosperous.

In the next decade, however, Fleetwood seems to have neglected his personal supervision, turning over the players to Macklin and finances to Pierson, the treasurer. At any rate trouble came in the 1742–43 season, when Fleetwood's financial arrangements with his actors had been so unstable that salaries were not being paid regularly and the players were being treated with insolence by Pierson. The resentment was such that Garrick refused to play on the night of Pierson's benefit, 7 April 1743. Finally, the leading players formed together under Garrick and Macklin, determining to secede, as they had in 1733, and seek a license to perform at the New Haymarket. In the flush of their anger, they signed an agreement not to return to Fleetwood without the consent of *all* who were taking part in the revolt. The Lord Chamberlain refused them a license, Fleetwood drew in players from Giffard's disbanded company to form a new troupe, and the opening of the fall season of 1743–44 found a number of the rebels in financial distress. Fleetwood wanted Garrick to return, as the chief drawing card in the profession, and ascribed the revolt to Macklin, refusing to accept him under any terms. If Garrick and Macklin went to Dublin, as they once proposed, the remaining ten players would be stranded, since Fleetwood held firm. In December, Garrick at last returned to the fold, he said, for the sake of the remaining players, though Macklin was left without a place in either theatre. At this distance in time and space, it is difficult to assess the claims of either Garrick or Macklin equitably. Garrick had reneged on an agreement, but the circumstances had changed sharply after the seceders had made the resolution to hold together. Fleetwood was enraged by the ingratitude of Macklin, whose life he had saved after Macklin killed Hallam, and consequently, there was no way in which Garrick could help Macklin. Garrick went so far as to offer Macklin six guineas a week, in the hope that time would ease resentments, and Macklin might be engaged again. But Macklin responded in a petty and unreasonable way to this and every other proposal Garrick made. Garrick wanted to solve the problem; Macklin wanted to prove himself justified on every point. Their dispute is put forth in three contemporary documents (as well as in later biographies): *The Case of Charles Macklin, Comedian*, published on 5 December 1743; *Mr Garrick's Answer to Mr Macklin's Case*, 8 December; and *A Reply to Mr Garrick's Answer to the Case of Charles Macklin*, 12 December. In the exchange, Garrick seems to have been generous, Macklin contentious. Both stand upon technicalities relative to their own "solemn engagement to each other," and both become vituperative.

The group-secession brought about qualms in the public concerning the detrimental effects of concerted action, as is apparent in the pamphlet *Theatrical Correspondence in Death: An Epistle from Mrs Oldfield in the Shades to Mrs Bracegirdle* (1743), while expressing the ultra-conservative point of view, through the supposed mouths of old players, of the "humble servant" concept of actors, and of the decayed state of theatrical management. Another essay included a list of the actors' salaries, to show what large stipends the rebellious players had been receiving. In due time, Kitty Clive replied by denying the validity of the figures cited. Charges and counter-charges appeared in pamphlets, newspapers, and magazines. Possibly what damaged Fleetwood and Pierson most was the pamphlet *Queries to be answered by the Manager of Drury Lane Theatre* (1743), wherein thirty-four rhetorical questions were skillfully put forth to damn the operations of the manager and the treasurer. Fleetwood may have arranged a reply, for answers (with even more specious rhetoric) appeared in the tract *Queries upon Queries* (1743). It reveals, however, Fleetwood's abiding anger against

Macklin, upon whose shoulders he lays the blame for nearly all the mis-management.

Query No. 34 of the previous pamphlet does suggest the decay of management. It reads:

Have not the hardships of all who have belonged to him, particularly the lower sort of people been innumerable? Have not the dressers and others at 1 shilling or 18 pence per night been unpaid fifteen or sixteen weeks together? Have not collections been made among the actors to prevent some from starving, and to bury others? Has not his treasurer insolently refused to pay them their due, and laughed at their distresses? Have not the doors of the theatre been kept shut at Benefit Nights till near five o'clock, in order to get money for coals, candles, etc., from the persons concerned, tho' large arrears were due to 'em? Was not word sent to Mr Berry at a time when nobody expected his life, that the doors shou'd not be open'd, unless the whole charge of his benefit was paid, a thing most unprecen-dented? Are not Mr Mills and Mrs Butler in a most melancholy situation upon his account? Was not one arrested for £500, and the other forc'd to keep her chamber four months, for fear of being arrested too? And are they not liable to a debt of above a thousand pounds which he had covenanted to pay long before this? Has he not drove some of the poorer people to beg their bread for want of the smallest part of their just debts, and does he think upon publishing the many calamitous cases of particular persons, that the publick will be surpriz'd at the present struggle of the actors against such a manager?

Management indeed had many parts. The lesser personnel did have to be paid and looked after if the actresses were to have costumes ready, if newly-painted flat scenes were ready to fit in the scene grooves, and if all members of the company were to be available when the casting of a play required them. Fleetwood won the immediate conflict. Macklin and William Mills were blacklisted. (Clive too was banned, but had powerful friends.) Upon Garrick's agreement to return, the other seceders were allowed to come back in December. The players had been worsted, but most observers could see that the operation of Drury Lane had declined to a pitiful state of mismanagement and negligence. So badly had things gone that Fleetwood had mortgaged the patent for £3,000 and gotten £7,000 under separate lien on the costumes, scenes, and properties.[133]

The end was near. What drove him out was the response to his increase in prices at the beginning of the 1744–45 season. Audiences rioted on 17 and 19 November, whereupon Fleetwood offered the patent for sale.

[133] R. W. Buss, *Charles Fleetwood* (London, 1915), p. 4.

The bankers Richard Green and Morton Amber (who already had a successor in mind) bought him out, paying £3,200 for the patent and guaranteeing him £600 yearly for life.[134]

Negotiations proceeded swiftly. On 20 November Fleetwood had appealed to the public through the columns of the *General Advertiser*, where a constable's affidavit shows him still manager; on 19 December Macklin's name was in the advertisements to play at Drury Lane. Between those dates, the change of ownership must have taken place.

The bankers' candidate was James Lacy, a veteran of Fielding's company at the New Haymarket, later a most successful promoter at Ranelegh, and currently under-manager for Rich at Covent Garden. Vigorous and experienced as Lacy was, he entered management at a bad hour. The rebellion in Scotland of 1745 carried his banker-sponsors into bankruptcy, and the general agitation diminished theatre attendance for a time at all three London theatres. A hardened entrepreneur, Lacy watched Rich hire Garrick for Covent Garden to play with Quin and draw tremendous crowds during the 1746-47 season, and then moved, during the spring, over the ruins of the bankers, beyond the role of manager to invite David Garrick into partnership and purchase of full ownership. The renewal of Drury Lane and the years of great success lay just ahead of them.

STAGE MANAGERS AND PROMPTERS

The passing of the actor-managers (Wilks, Booth, Cibber), the general apathy toward legitimate drama on the part of John Rich, and the appearance of wealthy amateurs as owners of the theatres led to a division of authority and duties in the production schedule by the creation of another officer called the stage manager or under-manager. At Drury Lane Theophilus Cibber served in this capacity for a time, and while he eventually became a nuisance to the other members his work was quite efficient. In the spring of 1733, when the house had been losing money, he devised and got up a successful pantomime *The Harlot's Progress; or, The Ridotto al'Fresco* (31 March) on which he had devoted a great deal of time and pains in preparation.[135] A remarkable feature of this piece is that it places a Jewish merchant in a favorable light, treating him not with sympathy but with respect as a pillar of trade. Young Cibber's conduct with regard to his

---

[134] *Ibid.* See also Victor, *A History of the Theatres*, I, 68–69; *Gazette*, 24 Dec. 1745.
[135] See *A Letter from Theophilus Cibber . . . to John Highmore*.

wife and one Sloper, her admirer, was so contemptible and disgusting that everyone from his contemporaries to the present has either ignored him or polished him off with a deprecatory phrase. Hence, no proper study has been made of his career in the theatre. Cibber anticipated by many years the interest in the Scotch folk ballads that William Collins was to call for and Bishop Percy to produce, for he had revised Allan Ramsay's *The Gentle Shepherd* and produced it on the Drury Lane stage. It was Cibber who had first brought out Lillo's domestic tragedy *The London Merchant* when in charge of the Drury Lane summer company in 1731. Later, when he was manager or co-manager of the seceders at the New Haymarket in 1733–34, he had shown his knowledge of theatrical tradition by offering Part I and Part II of Shakespeare's *Henry IV* on consecutive nights.

An amusing example of his ingenuity occurred during one season when he was engaged by John Rich. He proposed to Rich that the company revive *The Rehearsal* so that he could play Bayes. Rich demurred: Colley Cibber had been a great success, and the crowd would remember this to make invidious comparisons; if so, money would be lost. Young Cibber then suggested "a ludicrous Spectacle" to be inserted into the play, "to reinforce Bayes's troops, and, with a new set of *Hobby Horses*, raise two new Regiments, who should Exercise in martial Order upon the Stage, and by their capering and prancing like manag'd War-Horses, divert the Multitude."[136] Rich consented, and the hobby-horses appeared, not only at that revival, but at every other theatre that offered the Duke of Buckingham's burlesque well on into the last half of the century. When Cibber left, Macklin served as stage manager at Drury Lane for seven or eight years. From a statement in 1743, Fleetwood indicates that much of the responsibility of management had been given over to Macklin.[137]

The stage manager or under-manager for Rich was James Quin until the fall of 1734, when Quin went over to Drury Lane.[138] After that, Rich paid Lacy Ryan a guinea a week to assist with managing.[139] Contemporary opinion was that Ryan produced the plays and Rich the pantomimes. From the treasurer's account book, it is clear that Ryan gave out the free orders (i.e., passes) on nights when papering the house was felt to be sound policy. Ryan was still manager in the 1740–41 season,[140] but shortly

---

136 *An Apology for the Life of Mr. T. C., Comedian*, p. 123.

137 *Queries upon Queries* (1743).

138 *An Apology for the Life of Mr. T. C., Comedian*, p. 72.

139 British Museum Add. MSS 32,251, fol. 299.

140 H. W. Pedicord, "Rylands English MS 1111," *Bulletin of the John Rylands Library*, XXXVII (March 1955), 507.

afterwards, so Victor tells us, Rich made James Lacy his stage manager at Covent Garden.[141]

As time went on, increasing responsibilities were assigned to the house prompter. Aside from the duties during a performance, to be related under Production, the prompter drafted the playbills and had charge of their distribution.[142] He often conducted routine rehearsals and kept track of the players reporting to the theatre so that he could inform the manager whether any last minute change in casting was necessary. He also came to have considerable authority with regard to the timing of the evening's program—main play, afterpiece, music, and entr'actes. Sometimes he was sent forward to "front" for the management, and explain a delay in performance or the absence of an advertised dancer. A responsible prompter was a great asset to a theatre, the prompters in this period outlasting all managers save John Rich. John Stede was Rich's prompter at both Lincoln's Inn Fields and Covent Garden for twenty years, until he was finally superseded by the actor Harrington. At Drury Lane, William Rufus Chetwood held the post for an even longer time. His successor, Richard Cross, was given some authority in choosing the plays to be offered. Managers occasionally felt it expedient to give out large numbers of free passes on certain nights, to initiate the success of a new production, or to give the impression of crowded houses. Cross's duty was to keep track of the times when the house was papered and to record gross receipts to aid in determining forthcoming programs.[143] Cross, incidentally, becomes one of the most important primary sources for stage history, from the beginning of his tenure as prompter well into the later period of Garrick's ownership, through the preservation and survival of his notes, or "diaries."

THE OPERA

The dissension among the singers and among their supporters in the Academy, bad management, and the effective satire on opera in *The Beggar's Opera* have led to the popular view that the opera somehow disappeared in the second quarter of the century. On the contrary, interest in opera was a sign of taste, and King and Court supported the operas financially,

---

[141] *A History of the Theatres*, p. 66.

[142] W. R. Chetwood, *A General History of the Stage* (London, 1749), p. 59.

[143] Pedicord, "Rylands English MS 1111," p. 515. See also H. W. Pedicord, "Course of Plays, 1740–42; An Early Diary of Richard Cross, Prompter to the Theatres," *Bulletin of the John Rylands Library*, XL (March 1958), 1–46.

although the dissensions, the bad management, and the satires and attacks were to continue and perhaps increase as the years passed. The first attempt to re-establish the production of operas came in January of 1729, when Heidegger and Handel planned to work in partnership, hoping to achieve a more efficient form of management than the Academy. The two enlisted the support of the Academy, however, and on 18 January 1729 the Earl of Egmont records that he and Robin Moore attended a meeting of the Academy, where the members agreed to prosecute those subscribers still in arrears and to permit Heidegger and Handel to carry on production "without disturbance" for five years, lending them the scenes, machines, costumes, instruments and furniture belonging to the Academy.[144] Heidegger wanted to obtain Cuzzoni and Faustina again, and the King promised to pay their salaries, but Handel preferred a system of changing singers so that he could compose new works for new performers. This plan received Royal approval; Handel was allotted a thousand pounds for himself and four thousand to secure the singers.[145] Accordingly, Handel set off for Italy and returned at the beginning of July, having contracted with three men and four women.[146]

The preparations for a new season, which opened on 2 December 1729, suggest the same lavish expenditures which characterized the Academy's program: "the Cloaths, for the Singers, Attendants, and Soldiers, being all embroider'd with Silver, and Seven Sets of Scenes entirely New" (*Daily Journal*, 17 November 1729). As before, the principle of operation was the subscription, with both pit and boxes at 10s. 6d. supplemented by Royal subsidy.[147] Yet many of the old difficulties remained. Lord Hervey reported that even before the opening Signora Strada and Signora Merighi were quarreling over their respective billings.[148] The year was unsuccessful, with the total number of productions falling short of what had been promised the subscribers. But Handel persuaded Senesino to return the following autumn, and the scheduled program for 1730–31 was given in full, to better audiences. The productions of the next year were expanded to include Handel's new oratorio *Esther;* and contemporary notices again indicate good attendance during the year. The activities of the English

<hr />

144 Egmont, *Diary*, III, 329.

145 Letters of Rolli to Senesino, 25 Jan. and 4 Feb. 1729, as quoted by Deutsch, *Handel*, pp. 235–38.

146 *Brice's Weekly Journal*, 4 July 1729.

147 The King provided £1,000.—*Calendar of Treasury Books and Papers, 1729–30*, I (London, 1897), 416, 580.

148 *Lord Hervey and His Friends*, p. 41.

opera company at Lincoln's Inn Fields provided considerable competition during 1732–33, and Handel apparently decided to switch from operas to oratorios in the future. Meanwhile, he was experiencing difficulties in the daily operation of the opera house. As described earlier under Finances, Handel's new practice of releasing tickets only on the day of performance alienated many of Handel's supporters among the aristocracy. Furthermore, there were repeated charges of the great composer's highhanded ways of treating people as well as his troubles with Senesino. Whatever the cause, a number of the noblemen who had previously sponsored Handel now gathered in the spring of 1733, at a meeting presided over by the Prince of Wales, to plan a rival enterprise for the production of opera.[149]

This clique of the nobility engaged most of the singers from the previous season, and Handel was forced to secure new singers for the fall of 1733, performers who were not established in the musical world, and it is not surprising to learn that attendance fell off rapidly. With possibly two hundred subscribers to the new opera company, Handel and Heidegger did not obtain as many advance subscriptions as before.[150] As the season wore on, audiences were small, pamphlets and letters to periodicals aired the controversies, the partnership between the two managers was ended, and Handel was in financial distress. It is interesting to note that in the fall of 1734, George II ordered his customary subvention of £1,000 pounds to be paid directly to Handel, the only time the king was to make such an explicit designation of payment.[151]

In the fall of 1734, then, Porpora, the new manager for the rival company, moved into the King's Opera House with a distinguished group of singers led by Farinelli. Handel moved to Covent Garden where he staged oratorios, but his fortunes were at low ebb. However, in spite of the temporary success achieved mainly through the vogue of Farinelli, London could not support two rival ventures, and in the spring of 1737 the rivalry ceased. Heidegger collected new performers and was the manager as the operas began in the fall of 1737, but the closing of all theatres upon the death of the Queen curtailed his plans, and he came to a new agreement with Handel on order to re-open in January 1738. Handel composed a new opera, *Faramondo*, and the two promoters got through the season fairly well, although the forced curtailment of the season prevented them from

149 See Deutsch, *Handel*, p. 304.

150 *Ibid.*, p. 341, quoting a private dispatch to the King of Prussia.

151 See the *Calendar of Treasury Books and Papers, 1731–34*, II (London, 1898), 580, and the order of payment itself, signed by Sir Robert Walpole to "Mr Hendell." In other years the money was paid to Heidegger or to the sponsoring Academy.

offering all the performances promised to the subscribers. This failure adversely affected the campaign for subscribers in the spring, and by 26 July 1738 Heidegger published a letter in the *Daily Post* stating that not enough subscriptions had come in to finance the operations of the coming season and announcing his withdrawal. Consequently, the opera house was dark during the 1738–39 season, save for those few nights when Handel rented it for the production of some oratorios.

In fact, three seasons were to pass before another opera was heard at King's, the longest silence since Italian opera had been introduced into England. Giovanni Pescetti had attempted to produce opera over at the little theatre in the Haymarket during the season of 1739–40, but with meagre results. Handel had now turned his full attention to his oratorios, offering his last opera, *Deidamia*, in the 1740–41 season at Lincoln's Inn Fields. Finally, in 1741, new financial support was found, and Lord Middlesex became the impresario until 1748. He started well, bringing Galuppi in as resident composer and Ameconi as scene designer, and making Francesco Vanneschi stage manager. For three years, a full program was given, but the financial losses were very heavy, and no operas were given in 1744–45. After a late start in the next season, Lord Middlesex renewed his endeavors and by keeping the house open almost until summer was able to eke out forty-six performances. With fresh backers, he started an extensive campaign for subscriptions, brought in new singers and dancers, and achieved a fairly successful season at last.[152]

---

152 Burney, *A General History of Music*, IV, 451–55; Deutsch, *Handel*, pp. 520 ff.; and see the separate Introductions for these years in the Theatrical Seasons.

Advertising

THE VOLUMINOUS amount of information available today concerning the programs offered by the Drury Lane and Covent Garden theatres and the individuals who took part in them arises chiefly from the fact that the managers advertised continuously in the newspapers; this practice, however, was followed only irregularly by the promoters at the smaller houses, especially after the Licensing Act. On the other hand, if it were not for the information appearing in the papers concerning the smaller theatres, we would know next to nothing about the activities of these places of entertainment or even that such existed. Established theatres, with a long record of continuity, with careful treasurers and prompters and with historically minded managers like Kemble, accumulated and preserved their records. But smaller companies, even though effectively organized and led by a competent director, had no permanent place for a repository; and such account books as were undoubtedly kept are no longer extant.

Some companies entered advertisements of performances regularly, and occasionally specified for the reader which newspapers would carry their official notices. Thus, when crowded audiences greeted the opening performances of Theophilus Cibber's revival of *Romeo and Juliet* at the New Haymarket in 1744, Cibber notified the public that "the Plays [would] be advertised in the *Daily Post*, the *Daily Advertiser*, and the *General Advertiser*. . . . The large Play Bills and Hand Play Bills will be posted and delivered out on the days of Performance only" (*Daily Advertiser*, 6 October).

In fact, by the early 1730's, Londoners had to consult two, and sometimes three, papers to learn the offerings at all the playhouses. In January 1730, for example, the Drury Lane notices appeared in the *Daily Post* and *Daily Courant;* the Haymarket advertised in the *Daily Post* only; opera notices and Lincoln's Inn Fields and Goodman's Fields bills appeared in both the *Daily Courant* and *Daily Journal*, with benefit notices for all houses being carried in various weekly and bi-weekly papers. In 1731 the *Daily Advertiser* began to carry bills for the opera house and eventually for several theatres, but its special feature was a box listing of all performances in London each day. Hence, newspaper advertising expanded considerably during this period. In certain seasons, such as the spring of 1737 and the fall of 1743, theatrical advertising and theatrical news occupied a considerable section of an entire paper.

A manager prepared his advertisements for the papers in two ways: the daily paid notice (program, cast, time, prices) and what came to be known as the "puff." That is, as time went on, ingenious entrepreneurs used devices whereby their notices could be inserted into the news columns. One method was the letter to the editor. On the first page of the newspaper would appear a letter fitted out with the proper accoutrements of date, place, salutation, and signature. The author would say that he had gone out of curiosity to a performance of such-and-such a play (naming the drama, the afterpieces, and the entertainments) and was agreeably surprised at the fine fireworks at the end of the show or the remarkable Bohemian dancer; he would recommend it to all. This device was widely used by the promoters of the various Wells. During Foote's first term as manager of the New Haymarket, all his notices except those for benefit performances appeared in the news columns of the *Daily Advertiser*.

Macklin's use of this device was quite clever. When he started rehearsals of *Othello* in January 1744, he opened his advertising campaign for the actual production by inserting anonymously in the *Daily Advertiser* and in the *General Advertiser* of 23 February an insulting letter which sneered at his interpretation of Iago. (Except for a letter by John Hill, this letter remains our only immediate contemporary proof of Macklin's acting that role.) The writer wondered how Macklin was preparing himself for this part and accused him of having consorted with Jews to perfect his interpretation of Shylock. Interest in the performance was immediately stirred.

Samuel Foote made extensive use of this kind of advertising. In his first two seasons at the Haymarket dozens of items, letters, remarks, and the like concerning Foote appear in the papers. The publisher's own file of the *General Advertiser* survives, in the British Museum, and on it, carefully marked, are the itemized charges for each day's advertisements. Across Foote's notices is the revealing notation "2s.," the price Foote had paid Woodfall for his publicity.

In addition, Foote "planted" letters designed to arouse genuine replies. On 20 April 1747, at the beginning of the season at the New Haymarket, the *Daily Advertiser* carried an angry response in which Foote is threatened with horsewhipping if he puts on his show. On the next day Orator Henley paid two shillings for a notice in the *General Advertiser* entitled "Foote a Fool," in which he attacked Foote in his usual vigorous and coarse manner. Henley normally advertised only in the *Daily Advertiser*; by being trapped into attacking Foote in the other paper he simply saved Foote two shillings. Edward Pinchbeck, wounded by Foote's success, carried double-sized advertisements warning the public not to be led away from his own genuine auction by Foote's "Auction." In this case, it might be said that Pinchbeck tried to capitalize on Foote's notoriety; even so, the notices provided additional publicity for Foote's Haymarket matinees.

Another indication that these letters were really sponsored advertisements is that they were often repeated day after day. Designating a new entertainment at the New Wells in Lemon Street as "a new Mine of Pleasure," a letter appearing on 1 May 1747 in the *General Advertiser* was reprinted daily until 13 May.

The eighteenth century called this a puff. Middleton, promoter of a booth in Mayfair in 1745, becomes somewhat self-conscious after announcing a revival of "the late facetious Mr Pinkethman's diverting Droll . . . not acted these thirty Years" and concludes: "This is no Puff." And an irate businessman, wishing to market a product, writes to the editor of the *Daily Advertiser*: "You can oblige me if you let me know the lowest Price of a good Puff."

In the compilation of this stage history, the editors have had to learn to discard as unreliable hundreds of newspaper notices through recognizing them as puffs. Note the cynicism of the following comment made in the *Grub St. Journal*, 20 July 1732, upon an extract it had printed: "'We hear the whole performance of the Beggar's Opera (which was acted last Tuesday for the first time at the Theatre Royal in Drury-lane by the summer Company) met with great applause; there was a very handsome audience, &c. Daily Post July 13.' *This puffing was not occasioned by the* great applause, *nor by the crouding of the Audience, which might be very* handsome, *tho' not very numerous.*"

Nevertheless, the reader has some safeguards in trusting data from these notices, the chief one being the intimate connection between the London theatres and the public. Let the advertised fireworks be omitted or the "Grand Machine" fail to be shown, and a prompt apology will be made in the papers the next day, the editor himself sometimes interjecting sympathetically an explanatory account. Thus Fleetwood on 7 December 1734 published an apology in which he alludes to the audience being "incens'd at their Disappointment in Mr Poitier and Mlle Roland's not

Dancing, as their Names were in the Bills for that Day" (*London Daily Post and General Advertiser*). On 14 January 1747 Mlle Violante did not appear for her dance on that night at Drury Lane, as advertised in the bills. From the *General Advertiser* two days later we learn that the audience became noisy and complained of her failure to appear; she was forced to publish an apology.[153] The failure of Mme Chateauneuf to perform at Drury Lane on 23 January 1740 when her name was in the newspaper bill to dance in a new ballet brought on one of the most purely wanton riots experienced by that theatre. At the end of the ballet, when most of the audience were leaving, some men seated in the boxes "pulled up the Seats and Flooring of the same, tore down the Hangings, broke down the Partitions, all the Glasses and Sconces; the King's Arms over the middle front Box was pulled down and broke to pieces; they also destroy'd the Harpsichord, Bass Viol, and other Instruments in the Orchestra; the Curtain they cut to pieces with their Swords, forc'd their way into the lesser-Green-Room, where they broke the Glasses" (*Daily Advertiser*, 25 January).

Promoters of sporadic productions at the little theatres did not insert their bills in the papers with any degree of regularity, often advertising only for benefit performances. Occasionally notice will be made, for example, that benefit tickets for "The Orphan Wednesday last will be taken, the house being crowded," when no previous newspaper notice for a Wednesday performance in the previous week had appeared. All of the nine advertised performances at the James Street Theatre, spaced through the season of 1748–49, are for benefit performances. Since Hallam's company had stopped performing in the spring of 1747, leaving most of the players out of work, and since the names of most of Hallam's troupe appear on these nine recorded benefit nights, it could well be that there were additional surreptitious performances. Robert Morris, a colonial visitor, speaks of attending performances at the New Haymarket in the fall of 1735 when the newspapers carried no notices of acting at that house.[154]

Bills for the organized, established companies contained the titles of the mainpieces and afterpieces, details of entertainments of singing and dancing, the time, place, hour, prices, and the cast. Announcements of irregular productions often lack these full details, but attempt to compensate by giving a partial synopsis of the main play. Coincident with the Jacobite

153 See the advertisement for Drury Lane in the *General Advertiser* of 14 Jan. and the letter of apology on 16 Jan.

154 Beverly McAnear (ed.), "An American in London," *Pennsylvania Magazine of History and Biography*, LIV (July 1940), 376.

uprising in 1745, Hallam announced *The Massacre of Paris*, giving a synopsis of nearly two hundred words. Hallam depended on topical interest and not upon the names of his players to draw a crowd. Such bills also depended heavily upon allusion. The following bill for a stage adaption of Smollett's *Roderick Random* will serve as an excellent example of "synopsis" advertising and will also show that a production at a small theatre or booth did not preserve the customary sharp distinctions of main play, afterpieces, and entertainments recognized at Covent Garden and Drury Lane.

At Bridges, Cross, Burton, and Vaughan's Great Theatrical Booth in the George Inn Yard . . . will be presented an Historical Drama never acted before, call'd The Northern Heroes, or, The Bloody Contest between Charles xii, King of Sweden, and Peter the Great, Czar of Muscovy, with the Loves of Count Gillensternia, a Swedish General and the fair Elimira, a Russian Princess, Containing the most remarkable Events of that Time; and concluding with the Memorable Battle of Pultova, and Charles's Retreat into the Turkish Dominions. Interspers'd with a Comic Interlude (never perform'd before) called the Volunteers; or the Adventures of Roderick Random and his Friend Strap. Also the Comical Humours and Amours of Corporal Garbage and Serjeant Slim, with Vanspriggen the Swedish Sutler's Widow; the merry Pranks of her foolish son Janny, and several other diverting Incidents.[155]

In this connection it is quite puzzling to note Hussey's refraining from naming the "Historical Piece written by Shakespear" shown at his booth during Bartholomew Fair in 1746, the actual performance corroborated in a later notice in the *Daily Advertiser*, where a writer tells us that "Shakespear was followed justly." One would assume that the current wave of Shakespearean popularity would cause the promoter to use the title because of its familiarity.

Various devices were used to attract attention. On one occasion a manager publicly announced that he was giving away free tickets. The *Daily Advertiser* of 26 April 1736 advertisement for Goodman's Fields announces *The Conscious Lovers* for 30 April and concludes: "in Honour of the approaching Royal Wedding; on which Occasion Mr Giffard will speak a new Prologue, and distribute a number of Tickets to Ladies and Gentlemen, Gratis, and no Money will be receiv'd that Night." A cliché evidently supposed to possess great appeal to prospective audiences was the statement that the lead performer had never acted before. Giffard tried hard to capitalize upon such interest again when he took his troupe to Lincoln's Inn Fields in 1742. Of the fifty performances advertised, eight

[155] *General Advertiser*, 24 Aug. 1748.

announced a gentleman or gentlewoman "who never appear'd on any Stage before" as well as three anonymous "Gentlemen." But no more Garricks emerged. Only two of the players thus announced—Miss Bradshaw and Hayman—secured engagements at the major theatres. Nevertheless, for as long as performances continued at the minor theatres, a steady sequence of advertisements gave notice of the projected appearance of "Richard III—a Gentleman, first appearance on any Stage."

In addition to the newspaper notices, promoters used posters and handbills. In fact, since many productions were hurriedly got together, they often had to rely upon handbills instead of advertisements in the newspapers. Actors carried these handbills from house to house and left copies in the taverns and coffeehouses. The custom was so general that an exception is mentioned: a newspaper bill for a performance at James Street in 1744 notes: "There will be no posting bills." Giffard, on the other hand, found a novel touch in advertising, in the spring of 1734, by posting bills "four feet in length, daily upon the gates and other noted places of the metropolis."[156] The eye catching handbills were sometimes in red, sometimes in black, and sometimes in red-and-black, as the Covent Garden bill of 19 March 1737, and at least once, on blue paper, used by Mrs Charke for announcing a performance on 29 April 1734 at the Tennis Court in James Street (*Daily Advertiser*, 29 April).

The most interesting theatrical advertisements during the period were those announcing the New Haymarket productions in the spring of 1736 and 1737. The combination of topical allusion, satire, and ingenuity would suggest the Dean of St. Patrick's as the author, did we not know that they were really composed in the fertile mind of Henry Fielding. Visiting potentates, aldermanic disputes, debates in the House of Commons, royal appointments to "places," details in John Rich's last pantomime, and adaptations of Shakespeare are but a few of the current events glanced at by Fielding as he invited a London audience to attend the production of "the Grand Mogul's Company of Comedians." His novel advertising drew him free publicity from the *Daily Post* and *Craftsman* in January 1736–37, when both papers repeatedly alluded to his coming duel with pantomime and politics. Wilbur Cross has given a vivid account of this subject, though there is no substitute for reading the notices themselves in the seasons when Fielding was active at the New Haymarket.[157] One such bill provides this announcement of the premiere of *A Rehearsal of Kings*.

156 *London Magazine* (March 1734), p. 105.
157 *The History of Henry Fielding*, I (New Haven, 1918), 207–37.

Never Acted before

By a Company of Comedians from the Clouds, late Servants to their thrice renown'd Majesties

KOULY KAN and THEODORE

AT the NEW THEATRE in the HAY-MARKET, on *Wednesday the 9th of March*, will be presented a new Dramatic Comi-Tragical Satire of Three Acts, entitled

A REHEARSAL of KINGS

OR,

The Projecting Gingerbread-Baker:
With the unheard-of Catastrophe of

MACPLUNDEREAN, *King of* ROGUSMANIA:

And the ignorable Fall of

Baron TROMPERLAND, *King of* CLOUTS.

The principal Characters are,

Mynheer Maggot, Mynheer Wiserman, King Rogusmania, King of Clouts, King Bombardino, King Pamper-Gusto, King Lexoneris, King Taxybundus, three Wandering Kings, Sardonides, Bandequimonti and Crimerowky, two Queens incog. Plutonibus and Companardicoff, Don Resinando's Ghost, and the Ghost of a Dutch Statesman.

With new Scenes, Habits, and proper Decorations. To which will be added a new Farce of one Act, call'd

Sir PEEVY PET.

Boxes 5*s*., Pit 3*s*., Gallery 2*s*.

1st N.B. To prevent the Imposition of Box-keepers, Gentlemen and Ladies are humbly desir'd to take Tickets at the Office, or send for them to the Theatre, where Attendance will be given every Day, and Places may be taken.

2d N.B. Considering the extraordinary Expence that must necessarily attend equipping so many Monarchs of different Nations, the Proprietor hopes the Town will not take Umbrage at the Prices being rais'd.

3d N.B. The Proprietor begs leave to enter his Caveat against all (what Names soever distinguish'd) who may *hire*, or be *hir'd*, to do the Drudgery of Hissing, Catcalling, &c and entreats the Town would discourage, as much as in them lies, a Practice at once so scandalous and prejudicial to Author, Player, and every Fair Theatre Adventure.—*Daily Advertiser*, 23 February 1737.

One sign of a theatre's financial welfare was the degree of consistency in placing newspaper advertisements. If all went well, as at Goodman's Fields in the 1730's or during Garrick's famous season there, the bills were complete, the prices remained constant, and the notices appeared regularly. But when the audiences were small these patterns were broken. Casts might or might not be given, and changes were made in the prices. The major theatres experienced the greatest difficulties whenever they attempted to change prices; even riots followed. Hence it can be assumed that the impresario of a small theatre would not change his box office charges without urgent reasons, especially if his production were enjoying a degree of stability. When Hallam's company at Goodman's Fields commenced to draw poor houses in the middle of the 1745–46 season, their troubles were immediately reflected in contradictory bills, numerous cast changes, and experiments with admission charges. The house had opened in the fall with prices the same as the previous season: boxes 2s. 6d., pit and first gallery 1s. 6d., and upper gallery 1s. On 17 December the prices were raised to 3s., 2s., 1s. Then real confusion began, for Hallam started varying the admission to different locations within the theatre. In ensuing notices, the box seats vary from two shillings to half a crown to three and even four shillings; pit prices alternated between 1s. 6d. and 2s.; and in the first gallery between 1s. and 2s. Then chaos. Advertisements in one newspaper showed one set of prices and in another a different set for the various accommodations. By the end of the season this particular confusion was cleared up, but the bills for the last seventeen performances at this theatre carried the same admission charges only twice.

The Benefit Performance

NEWLY established companies generally followed the standard practices for benefit performances prevailing at the patent houses. The benefit season for members of the company started in the spring; charity benefits occurred at any time during the year; and an author's first benefit came on the third night of the production. For example, Henry Giffard's troupe in Goodman's Fields for the season of 1741–42 began the player's benefits on 15 March. The dates had been set long in advance, and announcements had appeared in a variety of newspapers. The opening benefit was for Mrs Giffard, the next was Garrick's, then Yates's, and a few others. For them, seats were built on the stage in the form of an amphitheatre, just as was being done for the leading performers at Drury Lane and Covent Garden during the same season.

After these, interspersed with regular performances for the house, began the partial or shared benefits for the lesser actors and actresses. Sometimes two players shared a benefit; on other nights six or seven might have tickets. In due course and rank came the benefits for the treasurer, the prompter, the boxkeepers, numberers, doorkeepers, and the rest of the house servants. Finally, there was one for some playwright, now in financial difficulties, or for an old actor who had lost regular employment. This spring it was for Thomas Walker, the original Macheath in *The Beggar's Opera*, now without any engagement.

Throughout the entire season five benefit nights had been offered for "Tradesmen in Distress," for "A Gentleman with a large Family under Misfortunes," and for "Mrs Loder, a Widow in Distress, having four Children unprovided for" (*London Daily Post and General Advertiser*, 21 December 1741). Such charity performances were arranged by every group of players that made any pretense to being an organized company. Even in late January 1746, when the troupe at Goodman's Fields was about to disband because of small audiences, the manager offered a number of benefit nights for widows, tradesmen, or parents of large families—all in distress, of course. A generous response could often be depended upon for such sufferers, or for "A Brave Soldier who suffered extremely at the Battle of Dettinggen." Generous responses led to a practice of running many benefit performances by groups in one-night stands at small theatres. Mrs Daniel, in announcing her benefit on 22 February 1743, at James Street, says, "The Performance will be carried on by Persons used to the Stage, and not by People unacquainted with it, as has too often been practiced in Benefits at the same Theatre" (*Daily Advertiser*).

The most publicized benefit during the year was of a new sort. In the spring of 1738 three musicians had seen the orphaned children of the impoverished and recently deceased oboist J. C. Kytch working as stable boys in the Haymarket and had founded an organization to provide financial protection for retired musicians and their families. On 23 April 1738 those desiring to become subscribers for "The Fund for the Support of Decayed Musicians and Their Families" met at the Crown and Anchor Tavern, elected governors, and completed their organization.[158] They decided to hold a benefit concert to raise money, and the first was given on 20 March 1739 at the King's Opera House, with Dryden's *Alexander's Feast* as the main production. In the following year the serenata *Acis and Galatea* was the featured performance, and as the years passed the event became a regularly scheduled concert. The prices for pit and box seats were half a guinea; a full house would consequently return a large sum. The initial announcement appeared a month or six weeks in advance of the performance, and great activity in soliciting with tickets ensued. The full program, carrying the songs, the singers, and the composers, occupied more space than did any notice for the regular theatres, and it appeared in all the daily papers. Not only did the singers engaged at the Opera House participate but also the various other important singers and musicians who were in London at the time. The program in the bills contains such a long list of airs, arias, duets, and choruses that it begins to resemble those folio programs given audiences at nineteenth-century theatres. Subscribers were instructed not to use their season tickets, and every effort was made to clear as large a sum as possible for the beneficiaries. At the end of the advertisements, as a sort of report in good faith to the public, was an accounting of the expenditures from the fund during the past years, properly attested by the governors. From these notices, we learn that approximately four to six hundred pounds was taken in at the annual performance.

Authors were still not paid by the managers for their play manuscripts. Their rewards, if any, came from a benefit on the third, sixth, and ninth nights of the performance of their new drama, though some variations

158 Deutsch, *Handel*, p. 457.

in practice existed. At a small theatre the author might have a benefit on the second, or even the first night of his new play. Some dramatists— Aaron Hill, for example—might attract contemporary acclaim by letting someone else have a benefit on one of the author's third nights. (The players were not, as a rule, permitted to schedule a new play of the current season.) James Miller, by an unusual arrangement, was allotted an additional benefit on the twelfth night of the original run of his play *The Mother-in-Law*.

Leading players and dramatists gained support from fashionable society, and often played to packed houses on the benefit night, though neither source was as lucrative as it was for the imported opera singers. Performers having such social contacts and anticipating support included their residence address in the newspaper announcement of the benefit production, so that "Persons of Quality" would know where to send their servants to secure tickets (and add an appropriate bonus). In fact, in the 1730's a considerable increase occurred in the practice of the players listing their residence in the advance bills. The interest of the aristocracy, and even royalty, is further shown by their individual gifts. George II gave Farinelli £200 on his benefit night. Reporting on Miss Holliday's night at Lincoln's Inn Fields 6 May 1731, the *Gentleman's Magazine* noted that she "received from the Royal Family, over and above the usual Present, a large Gold Metal, weighing about 50 Guineas, with the Bust of her Majesty as Electress of Hanover on each side." At the special benefit for the aged John Dennis on 18 December 1733, for which Alexander Pope had written a special prologue, the Prince of Wales sent twenty guineas to Dennis (*Daily Advertiser*, 19 December). After Lacy Ryan had been brutally attacked and seriously injured by a robber, and of course in no condition to engage in personal solicitation for his benefit night on 24 March 1735, the *Daily Post and General Advertiser* reported that "Sir William Saunders engaged for Ryan near a *fourth Part* of his Audience."[159]

Three years earlier a writer who had written a scandalmongering play, *Alexis's Paradise; or, A Trip to the Garden of Love at Vaux-hall*, left England one jump ahead of a warrant for his arrest, leaving the backers of his intended production in the lurch. The *Daily Advertiser* reported that one person had already paid "the Author 25 Guineas." Even under close

---

[159] From the use of the word *Audience* rather than *Tickets*, one may assume that Sir William actually went around among his own social class and turned out a crowd instead of just asking them to contribute money for Ryan's needs. The customary method of aiding a player on his benefit performance was to buy more tickets than the purchaser intended to use.

competitive circumstances many of the benefits for actors were played to packed houses. James Quin drew £206 9s. 6d. on his benefit night, 19 March 1731, at the Lincoln's Inn Fields Theatre, the same night of Mrs Oldfield's benefit, "By Command," at Drury Lane, with the King, Queen, Prince of Wales, and three Princesses present as patrons for Mrs Oldfield. On 11 March 1731, at Lincoln's Inn Fields, Mrs Younger received £209 2s. On 23 April of the same season and at the same house, John Hippisley got £212 4s. on a night when Drury Lane and Goodman's Fields were both open and Henry Fielding's *Tragedy of Tragedies* was being performed at the New Haymarket. The popular singer Leveridge received £235 for his benefit night on 16 April 1730 at Lincoln's Inn Fields. At all of these performances, and certainly at Leveridge's, many persons must have contributed more than the face value of the tickets, as the house did not hold £235. Years later, Ryan received £256 10s. 6d. on his night at Covent Garden on 30 March 1747; Mrs Cibber even more, £267 6s., on 4 April.[160] Not all of these totals, of course, represented clear profits. The deduction of house charges reduced the figure considerably. The daily overhead had increased by the end of this period from £50–£60 to £60–£63 at Covent Garden.[161]

Favourites of the town, such as Garrick, Macklin, Mrs Woffington, and Mrs Pritchard, at Drury Lane in 1742–43, might be engaged for a free benefit in addition to their salary, in which case no house charges were deducted. But treasurers were ruthless with lesser players. The performer was held financially responsible for the house charges, regardless of what money came in. He might be diligent, courteous, and industrious, going from home to home of the nobility, and leaving tickets at popular taverns, coffeehouses, and bookstalls; he might have inserted advertisements in both daily and weekly papers in advance; but let the weather be bad or a political storm break, he still would have to deposit the amount necessary to cover the overhead costs. A manager might give a widow a second chance at a charitable benefit if such a disaster occurred on the assigned night, as Fleetwood did for Mrs Harper in the spring of 1742 at Drury Lane, but he rarely did so for a player.

As the number of players and house servants increased, the practice developed of giving the lesser members of the organization half the value of the tickets they sold. The strictest record was kept of these salaries, as can be seen from the extant Covent Garden Account Books.

160 Covent Garden Account Books, British Museum Egerton MS. 2268.

161 In 1747, as shown by the Covent Garden Account Books, Egerton MS. 2268. The charges were not always the same for each recipient; in 1736 Rich charged Stoppelaer and Mullart £50, but required £60 of (either) other actors.

Even the best established members of a company could not feel safe until the evening was over and the cash in hand. When Garrick fell ill in the winter of 1746–47, the principal actors and actresses at Covent Garden all postponed their previously scheduled benefits. Even Quin and Mrs Cibber were depending on the great actor's attraction to bring a large audience and financial success for the season.[162]

Treasurer's books are not extant for any of the theatres in Goodman's Fields or the New Haymarket, but from newspaper notices a day or so after a benefit stating that the house had been filled, or from theatrical bills notifying ticket-holders that they would be admitted at a later performance, we can assume numerous successful nights. Sometimes, of course, the venture was a failure, as may be inferred from the notice on 13 October 1747 by the summer company at Richmond: "By particular Desire (being positively the last Time of performing), Miss Morrison having had a very bad Success in her first Benefit." We must suppose that this was but "Hope's delusive Mine," this late in the season for a summer company. Hope and only hope was the generating force for many of the isolated benefits for isolated actors at the little houses, booths, and great rooms. After 1742, an unhappy procession of actors in jail arranged for benefits, in frantic attempts to raise cash. Bennet notes on his bill of 25 September 1746, "This Benefit chiefly design'd for the Use of my Creditors." This grim observation was echoed by Richard Starkey, "late of Goodman's Fields Wells, now a Prisoner in the Fleet," in trying for a benefit on 29 January 1747, and by poor Bullock, so many years a mainstay for John Rich, but now taking a benefit while confined in the Fleet Prison and by both William Mills and Theophilus Cibber in the spring of 1746.

Benefit programs were arranged by the beneficiary, always provided he could persuade the actors of his choice to comply, and they were designed to please "the Town" or to demonstrate the best abilities of the beneficiary. An interesting study could be made of the plays, farces, ballad operas, and specialty acts chosen on benefit nights in London theatres throughout the eighteenth century to learn the degree of their correlation with the pattern of offerings in the regular season. Pantomimes would have to be excepted, of course; for a manager would not allow members of his company to utilize the house machinery for staging a pantomime that was not bringing financial rewards to the owner or manager. Kitty Clive sponsored high comedy intermixed with considerable singing, when her turn came to choose the

[162] See the newspaper advertisements in the *General Advertiser* in late March for the nervous tone of the wording in the bills.

program. For her benefit night in 1740, she played Millamant in *The Way of the World* and sang "Love's but the frailty of the mind" to a new setting composed for her by Handel (John Eccles had originally set the piece for Mrs Bracegirdle's voice).[163] In 1746 she revived *Marriage a la Mode*, "not acted these 30 Years," with the insertion of additional songs, as well as entr'acte singing by other members of the company. The next year she brought out *The Wild Goose Chase*, "By Mr Beaumont and Fletcher, never acted there," thereby superseding its adaptation by Farquhar, *The Inconstant*, a stock play up until that time. But other players often made unfortunate choices. Shuter and Theophilus Cibber, usually quite astute in playing to audiences, had no judgment concerning themselves, and would act leading roles in tragedies at their benefits. This stupidity was not overlooked by critics in the audience. Nevertheless, after giving due allowance for such examples, a study of the selection of pieces on benefit nights gives a valuable clue to trends in taste.

Of those persons receiving a full benefit, the programs of the house servants are also significant. The advertisements for the benefit nights of Chetwood, Stede, or Cross show us what those prompters probably thought the house should be offering every night. The most variegated program at the Goodman's Fields Theatre during the 1741–42 season was one arranged by the prompter Beckham for his own benefit. *Oroonoko* was the main piece. At the end of Act I was dancing by David ap-Shinkin; after Act II, another dance, *The Welsh Buffoon*, by the son and daughter of David ap-Shinkin; after Act III, Miss Medina was to sing "Can Love be Controul'd?" and Mrs Bishop a concert air from *Alexander's Feast*; after Act IV a pantomimic dance, *The Two Millers and the Courtezan*, done by the two Masters and Miss Granier; at the end of the play a "Preamble on the Kettle-Drums" by Jos. Woodbridge, "who never perform'd upon that Stage before," and, in conclusion, Handel's *Water Musick* by the orchestra. Then David Garrick would act in *The Schoolboy* for the afterpiece. After Act I came a new Scots dance by Master and Miss Polly Granier and others. At the end of the play, "The Coronation Anthem *Long Live the King* (never performed there before) set to Musick by Mr Handel with an additional Band" (*London Daily Post and General Advertiser*, 22 April 1742). Beckham placed tickets for this performance at four of the leading coffeehouses and taverns in the city, as well as at Dodsley's own shop.

The great number of benefits and their advance notices prompted a widespread forging of benefit tickets. On 7 March 1743, the *Daily Post*

[163] Deutsch, *Handel*, p. 470.

notes that a Mrs Penny was committed to Bridewell for selling counterfeit tickets to Drury Lane, especially for "Mrs Clive's Benefit to come." All through the season warnings were issued concerning forged tickets. Similarly, two years earlier a frequent notice stated: "No Tickets will be admitted that are sold at the Door of the Theatre by Orange Women."[164]

Even at the small theatres the players had trouble with forgers or scalpers. Mrs Freeman was forced on 3 March 1742 to announce that "Tickets bought out Side of the Door will not be admitted" at her benefit that night in Lincoln's Inn Fields. She had been going from door to door peddling her tickets, and someone must have forged a block for use at the door of the theatre. The distinctive financial feature of a benefit night was that if it were at all successful the audience had secured tickets in advance, rather than paying at the office, at the entrance, or in the theatre, as at regular performances.[165]

All in all, the benefit performance became a gala affair at the regular theatres. The recipient was something of an entrepreneur himself, with his selection of the play and afterpiece to be offered, his arrangements with colleagues to obtain featured dancers, singers, and specialty performers, and his methods of advertising. Many actors had distinctive tickets created for their benefit nights, varying in size and design, from small paper cards to large forms made from metal plates engraved by Hogarth. Several histories of the drama have reproduced specimens of these tickets, so that they should be well known. A specially elaborate one was announced by John Roberts for his coming night on 2 May 1737 at the New Haymarket: "Tickets (containing the Prologue to the Register, by way of Ode to the New Year, with the Musick engrav'd on a Copper Plate) may be had of Henry Roberts, Engraver, at the Star over against the Vine Tavern in Hilborn, and at the Theatre" (*Daily Advertiser*). Another interesting ticket was provided by the popular singer Richard Leveridge, now about seventy-five years old, for his benefit on 14 May 1745 at Drury Lane: "The Tickets for the Play, with the Musical Notes Printed on them, may be had at Mr Leveridge's Lodgings."[166]

[164] *Daily Advertiser*, 21 April 1733. Or tickets could be lost. In an advance bill of 20 Feb. 1736 in the *Daily Advertiser* Hyde warns that box tickets Nos. 208 and 214 had been lost and "will not be accepted." This notice provides indirect testimony to the vigilance of the doorkeepers.

[165] From a notice in the *London Evening Post* of 26 Dec. 1738 it is clear that money was still being collected in the boxes.

[166] From an unidentified newspaper clipping in a collection at the Folger Library.

Costumes

. . . the long applauding note,
At Quin's high plume, or Oldfield's petticoat.
—*Epistle to Augustus*, *ll.* 330–31

SO LITTLE factual information pertaining to the theatrical wardrobe has previously been known and so sarcastic are a few of the contemporary periodical essayists on the topic of actors' costumes that a general impression of shabby dressing on the stage has developed. On a priori grounds alone, one should remember that persons parading in front of an audience in the Augustan period would be handsomely, if not elaborately, dressed, and that the journalists were only ridiculing a lapse that fell short of contemporary standards. What made Hogarth's *Strolling Actors in a Barn* comic was not that the players lacked costumes (for plenty are shown), but that the costumes are out of style. Fortunately, conjecture is no longer needed in view of the various treasurer's account books and inventories now known and described in the other introductions to this history.

To the large and expensive wardrobe that John Rich had accumulated by 1729, parsimonious though he was accused of being, he steadily added and made replacements, season by season. As the 1735–36 season at Covent Garden got underway, he purchased a suit of "Scarlet and Silver" for Lacy Ryan, at £25 4s., and a "Coat and Breeches of Cloth laced with Gold & a Green Silk Waistcoat," for Bridgwater, at £15.[167] On 4 December, he got "2 rich Suites of Clothes" for Mrs Porter, and on 7 February 1736, "A blew Cloath Coat faced with Scarlet & a Wastcoat ditto trimmed with Gold and a dark brown Velvet Coat embroidered with Silver and an Orange col[oure]d Wastcoat embroidered with Silk and Silver," at £43. Feathers and cloth materials were secured at various times. In the 1740–41 season Rich seemed to be busy replenishing the stock of "Waistcoats." On 18 November he paid £12 for "an Embroider'd Waistcoat for Mrs Woffington," and went

---

[167] All of these entries are taken from a summary by Joseph Haslewood of the treasurer's account book for Covent Garden in 1735–36, now in the Latreille MS., British Museum Add. MSS 32, 251 fol. 299. See also Miss Sybil Rosenfeld's article, "The Wardrobes of Lincoln's Inn Fields and Covent Garden," *Theatre Notebook*, v (Oct. 1950), 15–19.

on to purchase six more for other players.[168] On 19 September he paid £13 for brocaded silk to make a suit for Mrs Horton. Later, he paid twelve guineas for a "Robe de Chambre Trimm'd with Silver" to be used by Mrs Porter, though we do not usually think of this great tragedienne in association with bedroom scenes. Throughout the season there were purchases of dancing pumps, feathers, and mantuas. And for an unnamed actor a new pair of buckskin breeches is procured.

In 1744 Rich itemized his wardrobe at Covent Garden to form the basis of a mortgage. Excerpts from the complete inventory were printed by Saxe-Wyndham in his *Annals of Covent Garden*.[169] His selections demonstrate well the properties used for staging, but do not adequately represent the enormous extent of the wardrobe, and the problem it was then creating of storage. Full details of the inventory, now in the British Museum, defy summary.[170] Rich kept twenty-six compartments in his "Great Wardrobe" filled. Each compartment was identified by a capital letter. "K" is as representative as any: "a Pluto's shape . . . Volpone's black shape, plus dress wrapt in a yellow tabby Turkish vest. Volpone's old blue, plus jacket and breeches . . . the fool's dress. Falstaffe's new dress, Justice Shallow's ditto. Falstaff's old dress, 2 old jackets of Falstaff's, Sir Hugh Evans dress ditto. Disguise of white sattin. Jack Rugby's coat, 2 buff coats, 2 white high-crowned hats, 1 black ditto. Mr Slender's coat and waistcoat. Sir Hugh's old black bugle coat. Hearn the hunter's."

In addition, sixty items, including a quantity of wigs, were stowed in the "chest by the fire" and in "Drawers by the fire"; one hundred more in the "press without the wardrobe," in the "trunk by the stairs," in the "press by the door of the wardrobe"; and upstairs over the wardrobe, there were Aboan's new linen dress in *Oroonoko* and all the slaves' linen dresses, besides "8 witch's hats, 6 antic dancing dresses, 49 feathers taken off dancers's hips, a white sattin coat painted *Joy to Great Caesar*," and Sir Peter Pride's hat and plume. The woman's wardrobe was nearly as complicated, containing twelve regular compartments, supplemented by three drawers by the door, several presses, and a deal box "in Mrs Horton's room."

Rich's purchases in the season of 1746–47 added much more to his considerable stock.[171] Most of the money went towards dress goods and lace, as will be seen from his list.

[168] From one of the treasurer's account books of Covent Garden, 1740–41, at the Folger Library.
[169] II, 309–14.
[170] Add. MSS 12201, foll. 1–73.
[171] Covent Garden, Account Books, British Museum Egerton MS. 2268.

	NUMBER	£ s. d.
Men's suits (complete)	6	52 13 0
Men's coats and waistcoats	6	69 0 0
Women's suits (complete)	6	75 2 0
Hooped petticoat	1	0 14 0
Gloves (for Garrick)	6 pair	0 7 6
Hats (men's) gold open lace	1	2 12 0
Yard goods		
Cotton		10 0 0
Silk		264 0 0
Wool		153 0 0
Linen		84 0 0
Trimming		
Gold, Siver, Copper Lace		238 0 0
Night robe	1	3 0 0
Hose		14 0 0
Total		£966 0 6

The absence of similar inventories or accounts for the other theatres prevents us from knowing the extent of their wardrobes. According to Giffard's deposition in 1735, during an early attempt at a statute limiting the number of theatres, he spent several thousands pounds in equipping his house, some of which must have gone to the wardrobe.

There are no newspaper advertisements of any booth for Yeates at Southwark Fair in September 1741, and without separate information we would have no record of performance. A mishap, however, becomes news, in the following entry from the *London Daily Post* of 11 September: "Yesterday betwixt One and Two in the Morning, some Rogues broke into the Booth of the younger Yeates, in Southwark Fair, and stripped his Wardrobe of Cloaths to the Value of near Forty Pounds so that he was for some time incapacitated from acting yesterday."

A letter from the librettist Rolli of mid-December 1729 to Riva gives interesting testimony documenting the historical costumes, though this is not the point of the letter; Rolli writes, "There is a certain Bertolli, a Roman Girl, who plays men's parts. Oh! my dear Riva, if you could only see her perspiring under her helmet."[172]

Innovations made by Mlle Salle in 1734 and 1735 had mixed effects. For the premiere of a ballet of her own composition, *Pigmalion*, she replaced

---

[172] At the performance of the opera *Lotario*, an arrangement of Antonio Salvi's *Adelaide*. Signora Bertolli, a mezzo-soprano, sang the role of Idelberto. See Deutsch, *Handel*, pp. 248–49.

the traditional cumbersome panniered dress by simple classical draperies and wore her own hair, flowing and unloosened. The numerous repetitions of this piece and the extravagant gifts at her benefit later in the spring would suggest that the audience was not displeased by the new costumes.[173] On the other hand, when Handel's new opera *Alcina* appeared on 16 April 1735, there was a different response to Marie Salle's costume worn for the ballet on that night. Deutsch cites the London correspondent of the *Mercure de France* for the following description: "She ventured to appear without skirt, without a dress, in her natural hair, and with no ornament on her head. She wore nothing in addition to her bodice and under petticoat but a simple robe of muslin arranged in drapery after the model of a Greek costume."[174] Her appearance was greeted with hisses; she danced after the play on the following night and never returned to England.[175] We can assume a strongly hostile demonstration took place, but we cannot be certain of the main cause. She had been a favorite of the London audiences, since she had danced as a child in 1716; consequently, the audience must have been upset by something. One view is that the Porpora faction supporting opera at the King's had arranged a claque and was entirely responsible for the demonstration. S. W. E. Vince, however, suggests that the audience response was spontaneous, and he is supported by the appearance very shortly of two bits of verse of epigram that allude unfavorably to Salle's costume.[176]

---

[173] The first night was on 14 Jan. 1734 at Covent Garden, and the ballet was repeated about 18 times before her benefit on 21 March. See S. W. E. Vince, "Marie Salle, 1707-56," *Theatre Notebook*, XII (Autumn 1957), 7-14.

[174] Deutsch, *Handel*, p. 387, gives his source as Grove's *Dictionary*, 1st ed., I, 131.

[175] Deutsch, *Handel*, p. 386, and Vince, "Marie Salle," pp. 7-14.

[176] Vince, "Marie Salle," pp. 7-14, cites E. Dacier, *Mlle Salle* (Paris, 1909); for the verses, see Deutsch, *Handel*, p. 387.

Scenery

Back fly the scenes, and enter foot and horse.
—*Epistle to Augustus, l.* 314

BAROQUE scenes flourished on the London stage in the second quarter of the century, eliciting the admiration or provoking the witticisms of the spectators. Lengthy accounts of these ornate and elaborate scenes were written by various foreign visitors, who were especially awed by them. At the Drury Lane theatre the principal scene designers were John DeVoto and Hayman. DeVoto also designed scenes at Goodman's Fields and at the New Wells, for William Hallam, years later. One significant device of scene design was the development of what Aaron Hill called "slanted scenes."[177] For the production of Hill's *Merope*, writes Kalman Burnim, "the temple was represented by wings and shutter; some of the side wings depicted columns and painted people who seemed to stand between the columns. So skilfully were these wings to be painted that the people on them would be scarcely distinguishable from the real life in the forward area and around the altar."[178] What had emerged were techniques of painting angular asymmetrical perspective. "With the *scena per angolo*," continues Burnim, "which Gerdinando [Bibiena] had introduced in Italy during the last decade of the seventeenth century, he departed from the central axis, and substituted a more flexible scheme, resulting in the impression of diagonal placement of scenic architecture, and opening the stage to previously undreamed of loftiness and vastness."[179] These scenic arrangements used for operatic productions in Italy were familiar to London audiences of the public theatres, for John DeVoto had been employing these techniques. The scenegraphic sketches by DeVoto that survive reveal his affinity and talent for the *scena per angolo*, and E. Croft-Murray points out that DeVoto's earliest known drawing for the stage, dated about 1719, employs the technique.[180]

Once of Giffard's most ambitious productions at Goodman's Fields was the pantomime *King Arthur*, for which DeVoto was the scene designer. It

---

[177] In a letter to Garrick of 11 July 1749.—*Works*, II, 376–77.
[178] "Some Notes on Aaron Hill and Stage Scenery," *Theatre Notebook*, XII (Autumn 1957), 31.
[179] *Ibid.*, p. 30.
[180] *John Devoto*, Society for Theatre Research, Pamphlet Series, No. 2 (London, 1953), pp. 7–8.

was brought out on 17 December 1735, "magnificently decorated with Cloaths, Scenes, and Machines" (*Daily Advertiser*). As the piece continued for a long run, DeVoto created some new scenes for it, for the performance of 23 January 1736, one "representing the exact views of the Hermitage and Merlin's Cave, as . . . in the Royal Garden of Richmond" (*Daily Advertiser*). The scenes became the talk of the town and were so greatly admired that "Mr DeVoto, who made the Draughts, has had several copies bespoke by the Nobility" (*London Daily Post and General Advertiser*). We do not have to depend exclusively on newspaper accounts of the scenes in the piece. Fortunately, Thomas Gray attended an early performance and wrote Walpole on 3 January:

The frost scene is excessive fine; the first scene of it is only a cascade that seems frozen, with the Genius of Winter asleep and wrapped in furs, who upon the approach of Cupid, after much quivering and shaking, sings the finest song in the play. Just after, the scene opens, and shows a view of arched rocks covered with ice and snow to the end of the stage between the arches are upon pedestals of snow eight images of old men and women that seem frozen into statues, with icicles hanging about them and almost hid in frost, and from the end come singers.[181]

DeVoto's work on this piece illustrates a growing tendency toward rather elaborate scenes and props depicting specific places. On 22 May 1736, Hayman, now the designer and painter at Drury Lane, brought out "A new Entertainment after the Manner of Spring Garden, Vauxhall, with a new Scene representing the Place" (*London Daily Post and General Advertiser*). So in addition to spectacular eye-appeal was added the pleasure of recognition. Yes, the theatre has always been the home of illusion, so the scene painter's fancy continued to give local habitation on canvas to imagined scenes from the poet's descriptions, as did Hayman in this instance. Earlier that season, Drury Lane had brought out *The Fall of Phaeton* with scenes by Hayman which were much admired (*London Daily Post and General Advertiser*, 28 February).

In recent years attention has been drawn to another experimental scene designer, Thomas Lediard, who created some magnificent settings for continental productions. His principal work in England was with the offering of *Brittania* at the New Haymarket on 16 November 1732, the advertisement emphasizing the key word—transparent—in his theory. "With the Representation of a TRANSPARENT THEATRE, Curiously Illuminated, and adorn'd with a great Number of Emblems, Motto's,

---

[181] *The Yale Edition of Horace Walpole's Correspondence*, XIII, 98.

Devices, and Inscriptions; and embellish'd with Machines, in a manner entirely new" (*Daily Advertiser*). The descriptions, too long to give here, are accessible. Richard Southern has thus analyzed Lediard's effects:

> Thus we may suppose that even such special scenes as Lediard's were somewhat shadowy to see; and, in this case, opportunity might well have been taken to treat such pieces of scenery as came against brightly-lit surfaces in some form of translucent material, so that some effect might be borrowed from the light behind, *through* the scene itself. Upon such translucent passages, painting would be executed in transparent colours, or in opaque paint where a detail was required to have more or less the effect of a silhouette against the ground. Something of the effect of stained glass would result, but not too conspicuously, since the front of the pieces would also receive a quota of light.[182]

Productions at Covent Garden also used elaborate scenery. Two quite graphic accounts are preserved of the staging of the opera *Atalanta* at that theatre on 12 May 1736. The *London Daily Post and General Advertiser* describes the scenes and decorations witnessed by a large audience.

> A new Set of Scenes painted in Honour to this Happy Union, which took up the full length of the stage: The Fore-part of the Scene represented an Avenue to the Temple of Hyman, adorn'd with Figures of several Heathen Deities. Next was a Triumphal Arch on the Top of which were the Arms of their Royal Highnesses, over which was placed a Princely Coronet. Under the Arch was the Figure of *Fame*, on a Cloud, sounding the Praises of this Happy Pair. The Names *Frederick* and *Augusta* appear'd above in transparent Characters.
>
> Thro' the Arch was seen a Pediment supported by four Colums, on which stood two Cupids embracing, and supporting the Feathers, in a Princely Coronet, the Royal Ensign of the Prince of Wales. At the further End was a View of *Hymen's* Temple, and the Wings were adorn'd with the Loves and Graces bearing Hymeneal Torches, and putting Fire to Incense in Urns, to be offered up upon this joyful Union. The Opera concluded with a Grade Chorus, during which several beautiful Illuminations were display'd.

On 11 June Thomas Gray wrote to Horace Walpole a more vivid account of the same productions.

> There are only four men and two women in it. The first is a common scene of a wood, and does not change at all till the end of the last act, when there appears the Temple of Hymen with illuminations; there is a row of blue fires burning in

182 "Lediard and Early 18th Century Scene Design," pp. 49–54.

order along the ascent to the temple; a fountain of fire spouts up out of the ground to the ceiling, and two more cross each other obliquely from the sides of the stage; on the top is a wheel that whirls always about, and throws out a shower of gold-colour, silver and blue fiery rain.[183]

These detailed and graphic portrayals give us some notion of "the manifold and complex devices that once made the stage one of the largest and most elaborate tools employed in the expression of any art."[184]

[183] *The Tale Edition of Horace Walpole's Correspondence*, XIII, 102.
[184] Southern, *Oxford Companion to the Theatre*, s.v. "Scenery."

SIR,

HAVING had some Acquaintance for more than forty Years with the Theatre, I cannot avoid offering a few Remarks on the present Revolution in that *important* State. I know not by what Fatality it has happen'd, but during this Period of Time, there has subsisted among the Players almost a constant Opposition to the *Interest* and *Power* of a Manager. Whether the *Dignity* of the Characters they represent on the Stage, is apt to intoxicate them with too great an Opinion of their *own*, I will not determine, but it is certain they no sooner commence *imaginary Princes*, but they begin to think themselves intitled to the Revenues and Authority of *real ones*; no Reward is thought equal to their Deserts, and nothing but Sovereignty itself can satisfy their Ambition. The *extravagant Demands* and *aspiring Views* of one of these Gentlemen at present, sufficiently justify this Observation, who though in his *Infancy* on the Stage, is already grasping at the Reins of its Government, and is modest enough to think that Reward which has sometimes crowned a twenty Years Labour and Success of the most eminent Performers, already due to his *Minority* of Merit. In a Time when the Stage was in its most flourishing Condition, when the inimitable Performances of a *Betterton, Wilks, Cibber, Estcourt, Mills,* and *Oldfield,* dignified the Theatre, their Advantages were little more than *one Third* of what accrued to an equal Number of modern Performers last Season; and least the Enormity of this Difference should be suspected, it may not be improper to give an Estimate of the Salaries and Benefits as they stood in the Year 1708 and 9, and the Year 1742 and 3, computed at 200 Days playing, is as follows:

In the Year 1708 and 9.	l.	s.	d.	l.	s.	d.
Mr. Wilks's Salary for Acting and Management,	250	0	0			
By a Benefit, paying Charges,	90	14	0			
				340	14	0
Mr. Betterton's Salary, at 4 l. per Week, and 1 l. per Week his Wife, tho' she did not act,	166	13	4			
By a Benefit, paying Charges,	76	4	0			
				242	17	4
Mr. Estcourt's Salary, at 5 l. per Week,	166	13	4			
By a Benefit, paying Charges,	51	8	0			
				218	1	4
Mr. Cibber's Salary, at 5 l. per Week,	166	13	4			
By a Benefit, paying Charges,	51	0	0			
				217	13	4
Mr. Mills senior's Salary, at 4 l. per Week,	133	6	8			
By a Benefit, paying Charges,	58	1	0			
				191	7	8
Mrs. Oldfield's Salary, at 4 l. a Week,	133	6	8			
By a Benefit, paying Charges,	62	7	0			
Cloaths,	13	5	9			
				208	19	5
				1419	13	1

In the Year 1742 and 3.	l.	s.	d.	l.	s.	d.
Mr. Garrick's Salary for acting only,	630					
By two clear Benefits, and one paying 50 l.	500					
				1130	0	0
Mr. Macklin's Salary, at 9 l. 9 s. per Week, and 6 l. 6 s. per Week certain, for his Wife, who acted a few Times,	525					
By his clear Benefit, and her's, paying 50 l.	230					
				755	0	0
Mrs. Woffington's Salary, at 7 l. 10 s. per Week certain,	250					
By a clear Benefit,	180					
Cloaths,	50					
				480	0	0
Mrs. Pritchard's Salary, at 7 l. 10 s. per Week certain,	250					
By a clear Benefit,	180					
Cloaths,	50					
				480	0	0
Mr. Mills junior's Salary, at 6 l. per Week certain,	200					
By a Benefit, paying 25 l.	140					
				340	0	0
Mrs. Clive's Salary, at 15 l. 15 s. per Week certain,	525					
By a clear Benefit,	220					
Cloaths,	50					
Ticket at her Benefit, as per Agreement,	21					
				816	0	0
				4001	0	0
				1419	13	1
				2581	6	11

N. B. The Benefits are computed by the Account of the House, and no Computation made of Gold Tickets, which are sometimes very considerable.

Will not any one who sees this Comparison, be at a Loss to account for the *Reason* of the Difference? Can they impute it to a *Superiority* of Merit in the present Performers? Or can they imagine the Receipts of the Theatre in any Proportion *equal* to the Advance of the Salaries? However, at the latter End of *Booth, Wilks,* and *Cibber's* Time, when the Receipts were equal to the present, they never receiv'd more than 10 l. per Week each, for *Acting and Management;* and Mrs. *Oldfield's* highest Salary was 300 l. for the Season. How then shall we account for these exorbitant Demands of the present Actors, but at the Expence of their *Modesty?* Or how can any endeavour to countenance them, but as the Expence of their *Understanding?* I am, *&c.*

——1743.——

One of the many letters to the editor arising from the dispute between the players and the manager of the Drury Lane Theatre in 1743. From a clipping in the Folger Shakespeare Library.

Dear Sir.   Tuesday Morning.
                                    19 D[e]r 1741

I suppose You must have heard by this
Time of my playing King Richard at
Goodman's Fields & suppose You are Appren-
sive I design to continue on y[e] Stage — I have
troubled You with an Acc[t]. of my Intention.

You must know that Since I have been
in Business (The Wine Trade I mean) I have
run out almost half my Fortune & Tho' to
this Day I don't owe Any thing yet y[e]
Terible prospect of running it all out ma[de]
Me think of Something to redeem it — My
Mind lead me to y[e] Stage, w[ch] from being
very Young I found Myself very much
inclining too & have been very unhappy
that I could not come upon it before

The only thing that gives me pain upon ye occasion is that My Friends I suppose will look very cool upon Me particularly ye chief of 'em, those at Carshalton — but do as I do, I am wholly bent upon ye Thing & Make very near 300 £ annum of It — as My Brother will settle at Lichfield I design to throw up ye Wine Business as soon as I can conveniently. & I desire You'll let My Uncle know — if you should want to speak with Me ye Stage Door will be always open to you or any other part of ye house, for I am Manager with Mr Giffard & you may always command

y^r most humble Servant
D: Garrick

A letter from David Garrick concerning his first London performance, in *Richard III*, on 19 October 1741, reproduced from the collection of Garrick letters at the Folger Shakespeare Library.

Façade of James Street Tennis Court, which was used for plays and puppet shows throughout the first half of the eighteenth century. From London County Council *Survey of London* (1940), Vol. xx.

Score of minuet danced by Mlle Violette, later the wife of David Garrick, reproduced from extra illustrated copy of Boaden's *Private Correspondence of David Garrick* (1831) in the Folger Shakespeare Library. Colley Cibber's play, *The Refusal*, was scheduled for performance on the night of Mlle Violette's first appearance.

A popular entr'acte and benefit night song, from the collection of eighteenth-century songs in the Folger Shakespeare Library.

THE
MUSICK
IN THE
MASQUE
OF
COMUS.

Written by *MILTON*.

As it was Perform'd at the THEATRE-ROYAL in *Drury-Lane*.

Compoſed by

THOMAS AUGUSTINÈ ARNE.

OPERA PRIMA.

LONDON;
Printed by WILLIAM SMITH, at the Muſick-Shop in *Middle-Row*, neat *Holborn-Bars*; and ſold
by the Author at his Houſe Nº 17, in *Craven-Buildings, Drury-Lane*.

Title page to the music for the production of Dr. Dalton's arrangement of *Comus*,
from a copy in the Folger Shakespeare Library.

A BILL *for Reſtraining the Number of Houſes for Playing of Interludes, and for the better Regulating Common Players of Interludes.*

Ɯhereas his Majeſty King *Charles* the Second, did, by Letters Patent, bearing Date the twenty-fifth Day of *April,* in the Year of his Reign, give and grant unto *Thomas Killigrew,* his Heirs and Aſſigns, full Power, Licence and Authority of erecting one Theatre or Play-houſe, and of keeping Players and other Perſons for acting Tragedies, Comedies, Plays, Operas, and other Entertainments of the Stage, with ſeveral Powers and Proviſoes therein mentioned.

And whereas his ſaid Majeſty, did by other Letters Patent, bearing Date the fifteenth Day of *January,* in the fourteenth Year of his Reign, give and grant unto Sir *William Davenant,* his Heirs and Aſſigns, the like full Power, Licence and Authority of erecting one Theatre or Play-houſe, and of keeping Players and other Perſons for acting Tragedies, Comedies, Plays, Operas, and other Entertainments of the Stage, with the like Powers and Proviſoes; by both which Letters Patents aforeſaid, it is declared and enjoined, that all Companies of Players

A   other

The famous Licensing Act of 1737, a statute that exerted almost incalculable influence on the course of the English theatre.

Actors and Acting

WITH the increase in the number of theatres, the newly established companies provided an opportunity for more actors and actresses. Experienced players came to London from Ireland and from the strolling companies. New players began apprenticeships, and the companies were soon filled. The expansion in numbers is striking. Before the premiere of *The Beggar's Opera*, the two companies had a total of 130. In the season of 1729–30 over 250 named players and dancers were listed in the bills, and throughout the next seven years there would be upwards of 300 whose names were advertised during the season.

The older companies had expanded slightly at the beginning of this period and were to level off for the rest of the half-century. The total average figure for players, singers, and dancers attached to Drury Lane was very steady; in eighteen years between 1729 and the spring of 1747 the average was 74. The largest number employed was 90 in 1741–42, if we disregard the unusual circumstances of the departure and return of the seceders in 1733–34. Covent Garden consistently ran slightly higher, employing about 80 members each year, with the highest total—98—in 1741–42. Of these totals, about 35 were men and 20 were women, among the players, a slight increase in the proportion of actresses over that of earlier years. Drury Lane generally had about 25 dancers and Covent Garden 30. Totals for the smaller companies with large and frequent turnover cannot be analyzed very readily, as it is impossible to determine how many players were engaged by the company during a given week. Giffard's acting company was generally about the size of the Drury Lane troupe. The remainder of the engaged personnel were singers, many of whom, like Beard and Leveridge, would take regular parts in plays. Fielding's troupe at the New Haymarket was small, because he needed no dancers for pantomimes, but he advertised the names of about forty to fifty players each season. Few of the new actors had the polish of the regular troupers at Drury Lane, and many needed several years of training before they would become professionally competent, yet these totals are still remarkable and manifest an awakened interest in the theatre.

The second opportunity provided by the expansion of theatrical activity emerged from the free enterprise that existed when four managers needed players. An actor now had a chance to try out at more than one theatre. The laws of supply and demand were restored, and a dissatisfied player could move around with some freedom. Histories of the drama record numerous examples in the 1720's and after the Licensing Act of 1737 of players being officially restrained from going to another theatre or being ordered to return to one theatre or even of being blacklisted by the cartel between Rich and the Drury Lane managers and not permitted any chance of being engaged. But in 1732, Thurmond apparently weary of the management practices of Theophilus Cibber, John Ellys, and the inexperienced patentee John Highmore, simply moved over to Goodman's Fields, taking his pantomimes along with him. Giffard already had a choreographer, Holt, but welcomed Thurmond, for having the veteran Thurmond's presence simply meant that Giffard could arrange more entertainments. During this same season at least a dozen players shifted from one company to another. Mrs Thurmond, Robert Wetherilt and his wife, and Corey also left Drury Lane to join Giffard; and Bullock, Hulett, and Penkethman came to him from Rich's company. The itinerant Stoppelaer played at both Drury Lane and Goodman's Fields throughout the entire winter. Other players moved back and forth between the four companies, with the two Mullarts, the leading players at the New Haymarket, leaving that house to be engaged at Drury Lane. This was, from everyone's view except that of the managers, an exceedingly healthy state of affairs.

A third opportunity for the players, and one that was to have important consequences for the next few decades, was that the new managers were seriously engaged in providing actors with a professional training. When Drury Lane was in the hands of people who knew very little about the training of players, such as Highmore, Ellys, and Fleetwood, and when Covent Garden was run by a man who knew his profits came from the pantomimes and who was openly contemptuous of the problems of casting a play, a novice might expect very little help unless one of the stage managers like Lacy Ryan or Charles Macklin took some special pains with him. In contrast, a beginning player at the New Haymarket or the new theatres in Goodman's Fields came under the tutelage of Henry Giffard, Henry Fielding, or William Hallam, all of whom, as we have seen in the section on management, worked closely with their players. At these smaller houses, too, a player learned co-operation with other members of the troupe.

Players who couldn't get along with other members of a company caused a great deal of trouble both for themselves and the management. When a feud erupted, as the famous quarrel between Mme Roland and the Ballet Master Desnoyer in 1739 at Drury Lane, everyone lost by it. The danseuse had refused to dance with Desnoyer anymore—the reason? He refused to rehearse new dances at her lodgings. From the series of charges and countercharges aired in the *London Daily Post and General Advertiser*, we learn that new dances were rehearsed on the stage, the contemporary readers learned that Mme Roland's salary was paid to a dancer named Poitier, and Fleetwood learned more about the hazards of managing a theatrical troupe. From bickering like this to serious quarrels, and even the tragedy of Macklin's killing one of the Hallam tribe, some historians of the drama, dwelling on these sensational episodes, give the impression that the Greenroom was a perpetual battlefield. Close study of the information extant about the day by day life of the players reduces the spice yet yields conclusions of no less interest to the serious study of drama. Over a long period of time, the members of the different companies carried on the duties of their exacting profession in a fairly harmonious way. Even the bitter quarrel in 1736 between Mrs Cibber and Kitty Clive over claiming the role of Polly in *The Beggar's Opera*, a conflict which quickly broke into the newspapers, provides facts to demonstrate normal co-operativeness of the players. A writer in the *Grub St. Journal* (30 December 1736), lists twenty-six examples of similar cruxes in immediately recent seasons, where two players wanted the same role which both had enacted in one of the theatres. The result, continued the journalist, was that John Mills willingly yielded Volpone and Cato to Quin, and Hamlet to Milward; William Mills surrendered Dominic in *The Spanish Fryar* to Quin; Harper gave up his favorite role of Falstaff to Quin; Miller turned Abel Drugger over to T. Cibber; and Mrs Thurmond gave Desdemona to Mrs Cibber, etc., "entirely to promote the general Interest of the Theatre." In a word, of the last twenty-seven conflicts over casting among the leading members of the company, there had been only one controversy, or refusal to subordinate self-interest to the good of the theatre. Not that there was no aggravation! Theophilus Cibber must have been a constant nuisance. Another writer in the *Grub St. Journal* complains that T. Cibber "is apt to spoil a Scene in the Alchymist by playing with a phial in his dumb shew."[185] More serious, Cibber frequently broke a fundamental law of the theatre, by failing to show up at curtain time. Liquor was the most frequent cause, but pique at the manage-

[185] 1 July 1736.

ment or at another player and occasionally being impounded in jail by a bailiff were contributory factors. I will give one example, chiefly to show the dangerous consequences of such dereliction upon production. On opening night of the 1737–38 season at Drury Lane, the company learned just before the play started that Cibber was "ill" at Kingston. He was scheduled to play Tom in *The Conscious Lovers*. There was no alternative; Macklin went on stage and read the part. The audience was naturally displeased and hissed him. Macklin read the part "tolerably well," until the audience relented and finally applauded him.[186] Thus the company got through the evening, but Cibber was fast wearing out his welcome with the management, a fact he never seemed to grasp years later, when no manager would engage him. There were sharp clashes from time to time. The enigmatic note in a treasurer's book "Jack Ray damn'd by Quin, in Bardolph, this night [next word illegible] at Rehearsal" suggests a harsh episode. Not two weeks later, there was a "Quarrel between Quin and Mrs Cibber about the Dressing in ye Green Room."[187] But in turning to evidence from another treasurer's book, we learn that on 22 January 1735 Hippisley gave a big party for the entire company. The reason for the entry arises from the fact that on 13 October Rich decided to pay Hippisley's expenses for the occasion, £11 10s. 11d.[188]

The status of the profession was moderately elevated. Harper's successful defense against the charge of vagrancy elicited favorable comment and was considered something of a milestone. The support given to the theatre by the London merchants in 1735 (described under Playhouses) and the diminution of the clerical attacks that had so greatly harrassed the players in the age of Queen Anne are noticeable improvements. Such figures as James Quin, Colley Cibber, Mrs Porter and Mrs Clive, among others, were accepted by society, with several players belonging to exclusive clubs.[189] Scandal about the private lives of the actresses still continued, for complete respectability had not yet been reached. One comedienne, however, operated within the law and under the sanction of the wedding sacrament. Her maiden name was Elizabeth Grace and her first marriage was to a man named Barnes; after which, she married Christopher Martin, Richard Elrington, a Mr Workman, and finally Richard Wilson. C. Beecher Hogan, to whom I am indebted for this delightful biographic sketch, makes no

---

[186] British Museum Egerton MS. 2320.

[187] *Ibid.* Entries are dated 22 Sept. and 6 Oct. 1737.

[188] British Museum Add. MSS 32,251.

[189] Aline Mackenzie Taylor, "The Patrimony of James Quin," *Tulane Studies in English*, VIII (1958), 55–106.

mention of any further company she may have had in her youth. Covent Garden audiences first saw her on 30 November 1733 as the Hostess, Dame Quickly, in *1 Henry IV*, a part that she continued to enact through the performance of 27 January 1741. At this remote distance and time, we may conjecture that she was properly cast in this role.

Salaries for actors improved throughout the second quarter of the century, especially for the leading players. In 1732–33 at Drury Lane we find Theophilus Cibber, John Mills, Johnson, Miller, and Mrs Heron all drawing £5 a week, as well as what they could make on their benefit nights, or about £180 for the season (*Daily Post*, 4 June 1733). In 1735–36, at Covent Garden, Mrs Horton drew £250 for the year, Stephens, £200, Hippisley, £180, and seven or eight players around £150.[190] By the 1742–43 season, salaries were alleged to be up to seven guineas for leading players, and twice this sum for stars like Kitty Clive and Garrick. Kitty Clive denied this, and the source is journalistic articles, not treasurer's books.

Yet an actor's listed salary is only a statistic; what the members of a company actually received might amount to a much different total. A leading performer's scale might be a guinea a night, but if management were negligent so that a full schedule of plays was not offered, or in such financial difficulty that the treasurer could not pay the full stipend due, a player was in hard straits. Thus Mrs Cibber to Garrick late in January 1746: "It is surprising Drury Lane goes on acting; one night with another to be sure, they have not received above 40 pounds; the actors are paid only three nights a week; though they play every night."[191] If the performers failed to receive their contracted salary, they often had to borrow money where they could. On the other hand, if a player were negligent and missed rehearsals, part of his salary was withheld in fines. The worst blow to all theatrical financial security was to have a theatre closed. The death of Queen Caroline in November 1737 kept the theatres dark until January, the longest enforced cessation of acting since the death of William III.

THE WHEEL OF FORTUNE

After the Licensing Act, actors were shut off from their previous opportunities at different theatres. There was the interlude from 1740 to 1743,

190 British Museum, Add. MSS 32,251.
191 *Private Correspondence of David Garrick*, I, 49.

when Giffard re-opened Goodman's Fields; and a few players found room with Hallam's New Wells in the winter seasons from 1744 to 1747. After that, to play in London, an actor needed an engagement at one of the patent houses. As one examines the lists of new performers at the smaller theatres before evasion of the Licensing Act was strictly enforced, he observes the vicissitudes of a player's life. Some, like Mrs Pritchard, spent only a brief time in apprenticeship before reaching fame and fortune. Others came up slowly and stayed in the main theatres for a long time; others came up as slowly, only to lose their engagements after a brief tryout. Not many of the players at the minor theatres had the ability to hold their own at the patent houses. Others had careers which resembled the wheel of fortune, sometimes playing before large audiences at Drury Lane, then performing at one-night stands in concert halls and booths, where the constables might stop the show at any moment. There was, then, toward the end of the period covered by this introduction, a steady rotating of players listed in any one notice for any one theatre. Like Chaucer's buckets in the well, some were on their way up and others on their way down.

Some made the ascent very rapidly. Garrick spent but one season at Goodman's Fields before going on to become the greatest actor of the age. Fanny Barton Abington appeared for only one summer at the New Haymarket before going on to her successful career at Drury Lane. Robert Baddeley, too, spent but one season with Foote before entering into his long tenure at Drury Lane. Mrs Elmy performed only a few times at the New Haymarket in 1744 before she secured an engagement first at Drury Lane and later at Covent Garden as a leading actress. Not all who rose so quickly were able to sustain their early promise. An actor named Samuel Stephens started at the top, taking the role of Othello for his first appearance at Covent Garden on 19 October 1734. He was an immediate favorite, and in the next season drew a higher salary than any other man in the company, £200. But he faded. By 14 March 1736, the role had been taken from him and given to Delane. Stephens stayed with the company for several more years, and reduced to bit parts, before he was finally dropped. On 14 February 1743, Giffard announced "Macheath by a Gentleman who never appeared on any Stage before." This gentleman, Hayman, was immediately signed by John Rich for Covent Garden. After the third season his name was dropped from the rolls. We do not hear of him again at any of the theatres.

Other players had to spend more time in apprenticeship before their talent was observed. John Lee got his training from Hallam at Goodman's Fields. When this troupe was disbanded, he was engaged by Foote. In the fall of 1747 he was engaged at Drury Lane, and he played there or at Covent Garden continuously through 1766, not leaving the stage completely until 1777. The famous low comedian, Ned Shuter, had an erratic beginning. He had made his debut at Richmond in 1744 and appeared once at Covent Garden in the following season, but was not engaged, nor did a single night's performance at Drury Lane secure him an appointment. In 1746 Hallam took him on at Goodman's Fields, where he played regularly. In the following year he began to play for Foote until he was noticed by Garrick and signed for Drury Lane, where he played until 1753, when he went to Covent Garden to spend twenty-two seasons. His colleague Costollo had to wait a longer time and play in more companies before he could reach old Drury, appearing at the New Wells, Mayfair, dancing at Southwark Fair, acting for Hallam three years, and then becoming a leading member of Foote's troupe at the New Haymarket. After his performance in Foote's *The Knights*, Garrick brought him to Drury Lane, where he stayed until 1766. John Dunstall and his wife both acted for years at the fairs and in Giffard's company at Goodman's Fields, before he started his thirty-three year career at Covent Garden and before she secured engagements at both the major theatres.

Others underwent long apprenticeships and then could not hold a position at the patent theatres when the opportunity arrived. Starting in 1740, Mrs Bambridge had played at the various minor houses, getting into the Goodman's Fields company in 1741. Then her name appears in the notices for booths at the fairs. By December 1744 she was a member of Hallam's company. For the next four years she played in isolated performances at the New Haymarket and various small houses. Finally, in 1749 she was engaged by Rich, but was dropped in her second season; in 1752 she obtained a second chance at Covent Garden but after two seasons she was again released.

Playing side by side with these performers at the small theatres and in one-night stands were those actors who had been released by the major companies. The two Misses Scott had performed at Drury Lane for some years and then appeared at the Lemon Street theatre in Goodman's Fields. Shortly afterward, they staged an independent benefit and stated their woes in the newspaper advertisement, complaining of "having been discharged from the Drury Lane playhouse by the Manager, without being told, or even permitted to ask why he did so."

Somewhat pathetic is the case of Miss Karver, when she offered a benefit performance on 14 February 1759, "who sang some years ago at

Drury Lane, since at Mr Foote's theatre in the Haymarket." So she had indeed. And behind her tenure at Drury Lane was the promising start she had made in the 1730's, when she had created the role of Maria in Lillo's *Fatal Curiosity*. The actress Mrs Daniel made the rounds in the 1740's, playing at most of the small houses and great rooms. Earlier she had been at Drury Lane, and in 1746 at Covent Garden, but the next year she was released, and returned to the small theatres, playing one-night stands at James Street, the New Haymarket, and the New Wells, Clerkenwell.

The best known example of a falling career is that of Charlotte Charke. No account of her career will be given here, but it is difficult to think of a person who had a more promising start or who had more sponsorship than did this daughter of Colley Cibber. Here was an actress who made her debut on the Drury Lane stage and who was the daughter of the manager. From that house she deserted to the New Haymarket. In time she descended from performing in regular companies to announcing one-night stands in various houses; then from regular acting to managing puppet shows. When she did act in a play, at one of the various booths or wells, she was announced for Lothario, Macheath, Marplot, or other male roles.[192]

Of more varied interest are the careers of those players like Charles Macklin who went up and down the ladder of success not once but several times. His story is too well known to be included here, as is that of Theophilus Cibber, whose progress was the most erratic of all, ruining every advantage and alienating every manager he ever had. Some lesser-known actors also experienced their share of the viccissitudes of theatrical fortune. A performer named Phillips had been appearing in pantomimes at both patent houses, but without a continuing engagement he had gone into Giffard's company in 1740. When Giffard closed down, Phillips turned to managing a booth at Southwark. Financial difficulties forced him to leave the country; so he played in Dublin for two years. His return to England is announced in the advertisement for a benefit arranged for himself and his wife, to be offered on 10 February 1746 at Goodman's Fields, for the "Entertainment of the Turkish Ambassador" (*General Advertiser*). Phillips, "late Harlequin of Drury Lane, his first in this Kingdom for three years," would dance a "Sailor's Hornpipe" after Act I, present "A Quaker's Sermon on the Viola" after Act II, "Portray a Drunken Peasant" after Act III, and at the end of the play put on a pantomime dance called

---

[192] Curiously enough, she apparently remarried. A notice in the *General Advertiser* of 3 June 1746 for a production at the New Wells, London Spa, Clerkenwell, reads: "Occasional epilogue written and spoken by Mrs. Sacheverel, late Mrs Charke."

"Harlequin and Clown." There was but one drawback: "being under confinement in the King's Bench, he has not at present an opportunity to wait on such Gentlemen and Ladies, as he may hopes to esteem his well wishers. But in order to render Mrs Phillips's Entertainment as agreeable as possible to the Publick, Mr Phillips will be there on that Night. Tickets at Mrs Phillips Lodgings at Mrs Norman's in Ayliffe Street, and of Mr Phillips in the King's Bench Prison, Southwark." We may wonder what the Turkish Ambassador thought. At any rate, the benefit drew enough to discharge his debts and let him begin a series of performances in defiance of the Licensing Act at the Bowling Green in Southwark. An unexpected circumstance rescued him. The fiasco of the Bottle-Conjurer's hoax at the Haymarket in 1749 gave his fertile mind a subject for a new pantomime: and that spring he is entered on the payroll of Covent Garden, playing "Don Jumpedo" jumping down his own throat to great applause and consequent newspaper publicity.

With Garrick at the Goodman's Fields theatre in the fall of 1741 was the veteran actor William Paget. He had had his day. Entering the Drury Lane company in 1731, he had enacted Falstaff on 17 May 1734, and London audiences had for fifteen years seen him in the role of Caliban. Later he had played in each of the four companies in London before the Licensing Act. But when Goodman's Fields was forced to close a second time, in 1742, Paget was one of the many sufferers. He sent out advance notices of a benefit performance for himself to be given on 9 November 1742 at James Street, by several former members of Giffard's company. He added that he was out of work and needed the money. The performance was not given, and the next word from Paget appears in the *Daily Advertiser* two weeks later, emanating from his new address, the Fleet Prison. From there he announced that his benefit would be held on 25 November— "Tickets may be had of Mr Paget in the Fleet Prison . . . who has no other Method of getting susistence in his Confinement." He may not have received enough to get out of prison at that time, for his name does not appear again in theatrical advertisements until September 1744, when he played for Theophilus Cibber at the Shakespearean revival at the New Haymarket. After this, he secured steady employment for three years at Goodman's Fields. On 6 April 1747 he took a benefit at which he introduced one of his small sons as Falstaff's page and the other as Tom Thumb in the afterpiece, "The whole to conclude with an Epilogue of Thanks written by Mr Paget and spoken by him and his two Children." The prices that night were only three, two, and one shillings, so that his gain could not have been very large. But things were looking up for Paget; that fall he would be engaged by John Rich and return once again to a Theatre-Royal.

THE STRENUOUS DEMANDS OF ACTING

By the middle of the twentieth century it was normal routine for a prominent figure in the entertainment field to appear in a radio program, a television show, and in a theatre during the same evening. In the early nineteenth century the practice of requiring an actor to appear on stage at two different theatres was widespread. Managers, like Elliston, who controlled two theatres regularly arranged programs wherein certain performers were forced to shuttle back and forth between the two houses, quickly changing costume in their hansom. Historians of the stage who have commented on this practice have not been aware that it existed as far back as the second quarter of the eighteenth century. That unscrupulous entrepreneur John Rich provides our first known example of shuttling on the English stage.

Immediately after Rich had moved his company of comedians into his new theatre in Covent Garden in December 1732 one of his first productions achieved a run. The success of Miss Hannah Norsa in the role of Polly on 16 December caused *The Beggar's Opera* to be held over through 10 January. This highly successful series afforded Rich an opportunity to try a novel experiment. Having in his troupe a total of seventy-eight actors and dancers, some of the best known of whom, like Quin, were not in the cast of Gay's comedy, and still renting his old theatre in Lincoln's Inn Fields, he decided to use all of his forces in capturing the holiday crowds. On 23 December, he advertised a performance of *Tunbridge Walks*, to be followed by the pantomime *Harlequin Doctor Faustus*, for the coming Tuesday, 26 December, at Lincoln's Inn Fields. The main play was a drawing-room comedy with a short cast, but the pantomime offered as an afterpiece required fourteen dancers. Parts in the advertised casts were assigned much in the manner they had been at the last performance of these pieces before the company had moved. Such casting, however, left some great, if not insuperable, difficulties if Rich hoped to begin both programs on time and run them off smoothly. In this advance notice, Chapman was down for the Beggar at Covent Garden, with Milward as the Player, and Mrs Forrester as Jenny Diver; yet all three were in the bill for *Tunbridge*

Walks. Nor did the manager's problems end there; the entertainments at both theatres were to be accounted for. Here, too, some players and dancers were announced for both theatres. The changes in the cast listed in the advertisement on the day of performance, 26 December, indicate that Rich was fully cognizant of these conflicts. He now listed three of the younger members of his company to take the places of Chapman, Milward, and Mrs Forrester in *The Beggar's Opera.* But those persons who were to perform at Covent Garden in Gay's play and also dance in the afterpiece at the other theatre found their names left in the bills. On the next day Rich repeated the experiment, announcing *Venice Preserv'd*, a play which required over twenty players, and *Apollo and Daphne*, a pantomime that needed twenty-one dancers, for the Lincoln's Inn Theatre, Gay's ballad opera still continuing at Covent Garden. On this night seven actors and dancers had to perform at both houses. From Rich's account books we know that both plays were performed. On 26 December, Rich had taken in £93 7s. 6d. at Covent Garden and £65 12s. at his old house; on 27 December, £76 12s. 6d. at the new theatre, £53 11s. 6d. at the old. On 1 January Rich offered programs at both houses again. By now he had returned Chapman to his original role as the beggar in Gay's play, yet required him to enact Southampton in *The Unhappy Favourite* at Lincoln's Inn Fields. Here unusual agility was required. Southampton does not appear at the beginning of Banks's tragedy, but even so, Chapman had to put in his appearance as the Beggar in the introduction to *The Beggar's Opera*, leave the theatre by the stage entrance into Box Street, hasten across Russel Street, and out Duke Street, until he reached Portugal Row, into which the stage entrance of Lincoln's Inn Fields theatre opened, a half mile away. After playing there, he would have to return for the concluding episode in *The Beggar's Opera*, at which time several of its participants would have to leave immediately to dance in *The Rape of Proserpine* at the old theatre. On this night the crowd at Lincoln's Inn Fields was larger than at Covent Garden, with £112 13s. at the former to £70 17s. 6d. at the latter. Rich dropped these arduous demands on his company after the holidays, but revived his experiments on Easter Monday and Tuesday. His account books indicate that he was unable to carry out this exacting schedule on the second of these nights. For this second performance, five of Rich's actors had to play in the main piece at one theatre and in the afterpiece at the other; ten dancers had to perform in entr'actes at one house and in the pantomime at the other.[193]

193 For full details, see A. H. Scouten and Leo Hughes, "John Rich and the Holiday Seasons of 1732–33," *The Review of English Studies*, XXI (1945), 46–52.

Rich's difficult schedule ended with this season, but records of actors performing at two theatres on the same evening appear quite steadily. On Wednesday 21 January 1747, Kitty Clive was listed to play Miss Notable in *The Lady's Last Stake*, the main piece at Drury Lane, and was also billed to appear that night as Lucy in *The Virgin Unmask'd*, the afterpiece at the New Theatre on the Bowling Green, across the river in Southwark, a production for the benefit of Harlequin Phillips. Both theatres began their main play at six o'clock (*General Advertiser*). The main piece, *The Orphan*, at Southwark probably required somewhat more time to run off than did Cibber's comedy. On 12 December 1744, Thomas Lowe was scheduled to sing at some unspecified time during the program at Drury Lane; he was also advertised to appear at seven o'clock at the Swan Tavern in Cornhill, where he was to sing for the benefit of his friend the musician Burk Thumoth (*General Advertiser*). The announcement of Theobald's *Happy Captive*, opening at the New Haymarket on 16 April 1741 reads, "We are oblig'd to begin exactly at six o'clock, some of the Performers being afterwards wanted at the other Theatres." On 14 March 1743, Jack, Joseph, and Polly Granier are advertised to dance at the New Wells in Goodman's Fields, where the performance began at five o'clock, and they are also billed to dance at the end of the third act of the main play at Lincoln's Inn Fields, as well as at the end of the play. Giffard's company started their play at six o'clock, so it was possible for the Graniers to get across town and reach Lincoln's Inn Fields in time. On 7 April 1742 Beckham, the prompter, held his benefit night at Lincoln's Inn Fields and announced that Dove would play a part in the main production, *The Relapse*. Dove was at that time dancing regularly at the New Wells, Clerkenwell, and his name was in the advertisements to perform that day at the Wells. Where it was at least possible for Rich's players and dancers to make the half-mile trip between the two theatres involved, Dove had a long distance to go through the city to perform at both the places where he was scheduled. The London Spa is well to the north of eighteenth-century London. The dancer Carney was also listed by Beckham to perform with Giffard's company on the same night. Carney was a member of Hallam's troupe at the New Wells in Goodman's Fields, and his name was in the bills to dance on that night. However, since the program began at five, he probably had time enough to reach Giffard's house, where he was not scheduled to appear until the end of the main play, when he would dance a minuet.

Moving from one booth to the other at the same fair was much easier. The dancer Bambridge played Barberino in *Devil of a Duke* at Hippisley and Chapman's booth at the George Inn Yard and also acted the Cardinal in the ancient droll *Fair Rosamund* at Adam Hallam's booth in West Smithfield, being advertised for both roles throughout the duration of Bartholomew Fair in 1742. At the same time Johnson performed in the pantomime used as afterpiece at Hippisley and Chapman's Booth and took a role in the main piece at Phillips and Yeates's Booth opposite the Hospital Gate in West Smithfield.

Another demand on actors that required some alertness was the old practice of doubling roles. As the companies enlarged, the practice seemed to have been ended for a time, but Henry Fielding, with a relatively small number of competent actors, revived the practice for his burlesque and satirical pieces at the New Haymarket in the 1730's. Examples were rare at the other three theatres, though Pinkethman doubled Polonius and the first Gravedigger in *Hamlet* on 20 April 1730 at Goodman's Fields, until about 1742, when players at all of the theatres began doubling parts for a time. Much of the doubling came in the women's parts in *The Beggar's Opera* and in lesser parts in Shakespearean plays. With the greatly increased number of players engaged by the companies, there was no longer any real need for this ancient custom.

Repertory

OF THE lively and full programs offered by the London theatres in the second quarter of the century, a significant aspect is the infusion of novel types of drama and a remarkable increase in the total number of new plays. Before examining these new kinds of dramatic entertainment, it will be helpful to recall in briefest outline a span of theatrical history in order to show some of the reasons for this rejuvenation and development. After the Restoration in 1660, several companies acted plays for the first three or four years. The patents granted by Charles II established a monopoly of two theatres that continued until 1682, when the two companies were united. In 1695, Betterton led a group of players away from Drury Lane, and two competing companies appeared from that year until 1710, albeit irregularly in 1707–10. During the next four years, again only one troupe was active in London. Little wonder, in the absence of competition, that this company avoided producing new plays and omitted afterpieces or entertainments.[194]

When Rich opened the little theatre in Lincoln's Inn Fields, these conditions changed, in that both companies began to produce a double feature, i.e., a program that consisted of a main play and an afterpiece, together with accepting a few new plays for presentation. Even so, as Emmett Avery has shown (in the Introduction to Part 2), scarcely enough customers could be found to support two theatres. The weaker of the two was the troupe at the new house; and to draw more patrons, John Rich changed the customary type or production, displacing the main play and afterpiece by staging a short play of the kind used for afterpieces and following that by a pantomime. Famous players and close attention to the technical aspects of production kept the Drury Lane company attractive, though very few new plays were brought out. In fact, Barton Booth "often declared in public company, that he and his partners lost money by new plays; and that, if he were not obliged to it, he would seldom give his consent to perform one of them."[195] Booth could afford

---

[194] John Loftis, *Steele at Drury Lane* (Berkeley and Los Angeles, 1952), pp. 127 ff.
[195] Thomas Davies, *Memoirs of the Life of David Garrick*, I (London, 1780), 208.

to talk in such a way so long as Nance Oldfield, Wilks, and Cibber were still helping him attract spectators; nevertheless, this attitude meant slow death for the drama.

In 1728 the entire theatrical situation changed, when Gay's *Beggar's Opera* and the Cibber-Vanbrugh *Provoked Husband* both began long runs. As these two plays continued to be performed night after night to large houses, it soon appeared that a larger audience potential existed than had been supposed by those in control of the theatres. A third house, Potter's little theatre in the Haymarket, had been opened in 1720, but no organized company had yet produced legitimate English drama there.

Different people connected with the theatre interpreted the phenomenon of continuing crowds at two theatres in various ways. As E. M. Gagey points out in his study of the ballad opera, a multitude of writers began to compose imitations of *The Beggar's Opera*, apparently under the supposition that it was this form of drama which the public craved.[196] The managers at Drury Lane brought out a new and expensive pantomime, *Perseus and Andromeda*, and presented it night after night. John Rich did nothing; he may have assumed that money would continue to pour in at the pit and box offices. But over at the new house in the Haymarket a small group of about thirty players began systematic production of plays in the fall of 1728, and by the end of the season they had played 108 times. The significant feature of this troupe's activities is that they chiefly played new works. They put on nine new plays to account for most of their performances. One was the very strange piece *Hurlothrumbo*, written by Samuel Johnson of Cheshire, and acted 29 times that season. The most popular one, however, was a new ballad opera, *The Beggar's Wedding*, with 35 performances. Of the others, one was a tragedy, one another ballad opera, one pastoral comedy, and three were political satires. The piece that would hold the stage for the rest of the century was Colley Cibber's little morality play, *Damon and Phillida*.

In the following season, 1729–30, a fourth company, organized under Thomas Odell, began acting at a new house in Goodman's Fields. By 12 November four companies began daily performances and the theatrical renaissance was beginning, for on 29 November, with *Venice Preserved* at Drury Lane, *1 Henry IV* at Lincoln's Inn Fields, *Tunbridge Walks* at Goodman's Fields, *Flora* at the New Haymarket, and *Tunbridge Walks* at Tony Aston's company near the Opera House, five plays were being offered on the same day for the first time in over a hundred years.

196 *Ballad Opera* (New York, 1937).

An important point to notice about the productions of the new companies is that while many of their players were novices or mediocre strolling players the managers experienced no difficulty in finding authors who would provide new plays for them. At the New Haymarket, of the ninety-eight performances during the season, all but three were devoted to presenting the eleven new plays of the season or to performing those plays which had been first shown during the previous year. The most famous of the new playwrights contributing to this company was Henry Fielding, whose burlesque *Tom Thumb* ran forty-one nights, generally as an afterpiece to his new satire *The Author's Farce*, which achieved forty-two performances. S. Johnson supplied another piece, *The Cheshire Comics*. It is generally correct to say that *Tom Thumb* has never left the stage; nevertheless, the new play this season that has the most significance in an analysis of repertory is a dull, heavy drama called *Fatal Love* by Osborne Sydney Wandesford. Faulty as is the execution of this play, it is a domestic tragedy and a forerunner of the kind of tragedy that Fielding would later produce at this theatre.[197]

Meanwhile, the new company at Goodman's Fields went into full production, gaining the surprising total of 185 performances, just as if they were an old, established company. They too found new authors. For them, Fielding wrote his *Temple Beau*, which was given 13 times, and three other dramatists each had one new play produced. Otherwise, the company played contemporary comedy. On only 37 nights was a tragedy shown. Twelve comedies of manners were played for a total of 75 nights. Four Shakespearean plays were acted a total of 15 nights. Fletcher's *Rule a Wife and Have a Wife* (acted twice) was the only other Elizabethan play. Of the Restoration period, only 4 plays were given: *The Committee*, *The Rover*, *The Orphan*, and *Venice Preserved*. The rest of the productions were of more recent drama. Such an analysis has meaning only in contrast with what was being done elsewhere. At Drury Lane, 4 new plays were also presented, gaining a total of 35 nights; 13 plays composed before 1642 were acted 25 times; 26 Restoration plays in stock made 59 performances. The house was lighted 166 nights; consequently, over half of their main pieces were plays from the Elizabethan and Restoration periods. Of the comedy of manners, Drury Lane audiences saw the plays of Etherege and Wycherley; in tragedy they saw a good many of the older Restoration heroic dramas of Dryden and Lee, none of which was shown at Odell's theatre. The Drury Lane productions differed in yet another way from the programs at Goodman's Fields in that they regularly added a pantomime

197 Nicoll, *A History of English Drama*, II, 119.

or ballad opera after the main play of the evening; the latter house followed in offering some pantomime and some ballad operas, but half of the nights during the season saw a regular play as the evening's entertainment, without any afterpiece.

By the end of that season, a total of 26 new plays had been presented by the different companies. The theatre had indeed come alive. On 48 nights during the season four theatres had been open at the same time; on 36 nights, three theatres and the opera, or a total of 84 nights when a spectator had his choice of four different productions on the same evening.

In the next season, 1730–31, the players at the New Haymarket gave nine new plays and generally acted recent drama for a total of 106 nights. At Goodman's Fields, the programs were much as they had been the year before. Out of 182 acting nights, 113 were given to plays composed in the eighteenth century. Meanwhile, both Drury Lane and Lincoln's Inn Fields increased the number of new plays.

When Giffard took charge of the management, the repertory underwent some changes. In the season of 1732–33, for example, the new Goodman's Fields theatre was open 171 nights. Only two new plays were offered. Many recent ones were still included, with a half dozen performances each of *The Provoked Husband*, *The Beggar's Opera*, and *The London Merchant*. On the other hand, Giffard increased the number of Shakespearean plays. To show how he differed from the customary pattern at Drury Lane and Covent Garden, one can see from the calendar that the former offered 14 nights to Shakespeare and the latter 23, whereas Goodman's Fields acted eight plays for a total of 40 nights. Nor can the impact of this total be dismissed on the grounds that the players were inept; with Delane, Hulett, Rosco, Havard, Mrs Haughton, his own wife and himself, Giffard could go a long way toward casting a Shakespearean play.

Meanwhile two revolutions in musical drama were under way, the first to be an immediate failure, and the second to become a permanent contribution. In the spring of 1732 and in the season of 1732–33, a concerted attempt was made to re-establish English opera. "In March 1732 Thomas Arne (senior), Henry Carey, and J. F. Lampe opened a season at the New Theatre, in the Haymarket and the campaign was continued at other theatres."[198] The new works were not ballad operas, but were operas "after the Italian Manner."[199] The composers were trying to use Italian

---

198 Dean, *Handel's Dramatic Oratorios*, p. 265.
199 This phrase was used on the title pages of the editions and in the newspaper advertisements of the opening performances.

musical forms and conventions, but attempt a more credible plot and use the English language and English singers. The chief productions were *Amelia* on 13 March 1732 (music by Lampe and text by Carey); *Britannia* on 15 November 1732 (music by Lampe and text by Thomas Lediard, whose remarkable scenes for this work, earlier described, remind us of the tremendous effort being made to attain success); *Teraminta* on 20 November 1732 (music by J. C. Smith and text by Carey); *Dione* on 23 February 1733 (music by Lampe); *Rosamund* on 7 March 1733 (music by T. A. Arne, using Addison's libretto); *Ulysses* on 16 April 1733 (music by J. C. Smith and text by Samuel Humphreys); and *The Opera of Operas* on 31 May 1733 (music by T. A. Arne and text by Mrs Eliza Haywood).

A greater composer than any of these was needed to achieve a triumph of English opera, and Aaron Hill immediately appealed to Handel

> to deliver us from our *Italian bondage* . . . I am of opinion, that male and female voices may be found in this kingdom, capable of everything that is requisite; and, I am sure, a species of dramatic Opera might be invented, that, by reconciling reason and dignity, with musick and fine machinery, would charm the *ear*, and hold fast the *heart*, together.
>
> Such an improvement must, at once, be lasting, and profitable, to a very great degree; and would, infallibly, attract an universal regard, and encouragement.[200]

Handel rejected the appeal, with the consequence that English opera was to lie dormant for nearly two centuries afterwards.

However, at the very time of Hill's attempt to enlist him in the cause of reviving English opera, Handel's creative force was engaged in developing an entirely new art form, the dramatic oratorio. In these years, the greatest of these powerful compositions were appearing on the London stage: *Esther, Deborah, Athalia, Saul, Samson, Semele, Joseph and His Brethren, Hercules, Belshazzar,* and *Judas Maccabaeus.* Winton Dean has given a full account and careful revaluation of these works in his Handel's *Dramatic Oratorios and Masks,* a most valuable and appreciative study, so that no further discussion will be made of them here other than to remind the reader of their presence in the theatrical fare of the time.

Turning again to the bustle and turmoil at the New Haymarket, we will observe in the seasons of 1735–36 and 1736–37 some further contributions to the repertory. First, a reference must be made to two well-known facts of literary history; English tragedy was becoming weaker and weaker; and the new and artistic form of drama inherited from the

[200] *Works,* IV, 115–16.

Restoration—the comedy of manners—had run its creative course. The testimony of the contemporary eighteenth-century commentators shows that they recognized this condition as clearly as do later students of the drama. High comedy was still in the dramatic tradition, so that some revival of it would appear years later in Goldsmith and Sheridan; but there was no hope for contemporary tragedy. It was moribund. What the London theatres needed was experimental work toward another kind of tragic drama. Still, the managers of the patent houses offered a standard repertory: they were not conducting experimental theatres like the Provincetown Players in the early twentieth century in the United States. The policy was very properly demonstrated when Cibber allowed the young actors at Drury Lane, acting as a summer company by themselves, to stage Lillo's *London Merchant* on 22 June 1731. After the success of the new play, it was then brought on by the regular Drury Lane company the following season. Nevertheless, young authors who were trying new kinds of drama needed a theatre to produce their plays. What must be kept in mind is that within a few years of each other, four new dramatic forms made their appearance. Handel's dramatic oratorios, John Gay's ballad opera *The Beggar's Opera*, Fielding's satirical and topical comedies such as *Pasquin*, and the clumsy but potentially the most dynamic of all— the *Schicksalstragödie*, such as *The Fatal Curiosity*, *The London Merchant*, and *The Fatal Extravagance*. These plays, crude as they were, pointed directly to the nineteenth-century problem play. With these four types we have a resurgence of contemporary creative genius in the drama.

From this point of view, the situation at the New Haymarket assumes significance. In the season of 1735–36, Fielding's company acted only 95 times, mostly in the spring. Eleven new plays were produced. The best-known was *Pasquin*, acted 39 times in succession and 62 or 63 times in all. Of the rest, two plays illustrated the new tendency of serious drama, the domestic tragedy. One was Mrs Haywood's adaptation of *Arden of Feversham*; the other was Lillo's *Fatal Curiosity*. That these new plays were revitalizing the London stage was evident on every hand. Attending the New Haymarket on the seventeenth night of *Pasquin's* long run, the Earl of Egmont reports a crowded house.[201] On Monday, 29 March, three nights later, the Prince of Wales, with his entourage was at the twentieth consecutive performance. On 2 June, when the rest of the Royal family still in town were at the opera, the youngest princesses slipped off to the New Haymarket to the benefit performance of *Fatal Curiosity* for Lillo. Fielding

201 *Diary*, II, 250.

had taken great pains with the production of this drama. He had made some revisions in fitting it for the stage, he had carefully supervised the rehearsals, drilling the actors in their parts, and he had written the prologue himself.[202]

The spring of 1737 saw an even more exciting period of entertainment. The company at the New Haymarket acted only fifty-eight times, but succeeded in producing fourteen new plays. The most notorious, of course, was Fielding's *Historical Register*. The play which soon entered the repertory at the patent theatres and was to be acted throughout the rest of the century was Carey's *The Dragon of Wantley*, a burlesque on the operas. Most of the other new plays were satires. *Eurydice*, however, points towards Shavian comedy, as Allardyce Nicoll has noted.[203] Of the other plays acted, Lillo's *Fatal Curiosity* was shown eleven times. Fielding never permitted pantomime at his theatre; accordingly, it can be seen that the pattern of dramatic entertainment was much different at the New Haymarket from what was going on anywhere else in London. Fielding made another innovation in repertory by his practice of bringing out two new plays on the same night.

Meanwhile, Giffard was not idle. His company produced five new plays this season, for a total of forty-four nights. Crowds had been attending his programs, too, for he apparently made enough money to pay £1,500 for a one-sixth share of the Drury Lane ownership, and his revival of masques had stimulated great interest. For a performance of the masque *Britannia*, the *Daily Advertiser* commented that "the new Entertainment at Goodman's-fields continues to meet with universal Approbation; 'twas computed that above 300 Persons of all Ranks were oblig'd to return last Night for want of room: the Play was bespoke by several Ladies of Quality, who express'd the utmost Satisfaction at the whole Performance." Thus with five new plays here and fourteen at the New Haymarket, it can be seen that before the passage of the Licensing Act genuine outlets existed for authors who had written new plays, whether these plays were bizarre or conventional. To this total of new plays may be added another, the staging of which throws much light on the contributions of an increased number of theatres to a healthy situation in the drama.

The piece itself is but a trifle and has no intrinsic value. Its title was *The Honest Yorkshireman* and its author Henry Carey. He had written this farce in the summer of 1734 and submitted it to Fleetwood at Drury Lane

[202] Thomas Davies, *Lillo's Dramatic Works*, I (London, 1810), 11. Davies gives this as a personal recollection, stating that he had attended a rehearsal, where he met Lillo for the first time.

[203] Nicoll, *A History of English Drama*, II, 265.

in the fall. That manager kept the manuscript all season and returned it to Carey in the late spring, too late for the playwright to submit it elsewhere. Young Theophilus Cibber requested the piece for the young actors to put on during their projected summer season. Accordingly, Carey's play went into rehearsal and was duly announced for performance. At this juncture, however, we learn that "the Patentee of Drury-lane Theatre has countermanded the Summer playing."[204] The indignant author now rented the Lincoln's Inn Fields house, still under John Rich; and on 7 and 9 July the *Daily Advertiser* carried notices of a premiere on Friday 11 July. However, Carey was baulked again; the bills in the *Daily Advertiser* of 10 July and in the *Craftsman*, No. 471, state that the play would now be performed on 15 July, but at the New Haymarket. Here at last it was produced and surprisingly enough achieved instant popularity. Now the situation was altered and other people wanted the new afterpiece. Carey was able to take the company into the Goodman's Fields theatre for his benefit night, and Giffard produced the little farce about twenty-five times in the following season. Carey earned some money after all, but when his play was printed he described it on the title-page as "refus'd to be Acted at Drury-Lane Playhouse: But now Perform'd at the New Theatre in Goodman's Fields, with great Applause." In the Preface, he tells of his experience at the hands of the patentees, and states his gratitude to young Cibber and to Giffard. This episode has been selected to show the opportunity an author had when there several different theatres in London. Drury Lane and Covent Garden had not staged a single new play in the entire season of 1736–37, in contrast to the nineteen new plays at the other two houses. After the Licensing Act, it might not be so easy to hasten to another theatre, as Henry Carey had been able to do. The story of Fielding's *Don Quixote in England* is better known. Fielding had offered this topical comedy to the Drury Lane management in the fall of 1729, but Booth and Cibber had refused to take it. During the 1733–34 season, Fielding reworked his play into a ballad opera and inserted more contemporary allusions. It was accepted at Drury Lane and put into rehearsal; however, the popularity of the Dutch giant, Mynheer Cajanus, at that house brought about an indefinite postponement. Taking the same players who had rehearsed the piece, Fielding went over to the New Haymarket, where he staged the premiere on 5 April.[205]

204 See Leo Hughes and A. H. Scouten, "The First Season of 'The Honest Yorkshireman,'" *Modern Language Review*, XL (1945), 8–11, for a full account.

205 See Fielding's Preface to *Don Quixote in England* (1734), and the *Daily Advertiser* of 5 April 1734.

At this point objection might be raised that few of these many new plays had great dramatic merit. However, the reader may well consider the close parallel with the situation in the London theatres around 1589, with the same expansion in the number of companies and theatres and the appearance of crude and awkward but potentially significant new types of plays like Kyd's *The Spanish Tragedy*. The increase of theatres and the popularity of the drama soon brought the ablest writers into the theatre. Furthermore, lovers of Elizabethan drama are apt to forget that the great masterpieces of the time constitute only a small fraction of the number of new plays in Sir Walter Greg's handlist.

The great increase in the number of new plays staged in London from 1729 to 1737 not only provided outlets for those authors who had plays; it also stimulated an interest of authors in the drama. Consequently, it is not strange to read in literary histories of the young authors who went up to London with a play in their hip pocket, as did Samuel Johnson, Tobias Smollett, Chatterton, and Smart. Their talents lay in other fields, but their initial attraction to the theatre suggests that had the restrictions of 1737 not been established, more playwrights would have appeared. That Johnson's tragedy *Irene* was eventually produced by Garrick at Drury Lane reminds us that after 1737 a dramatic author needed an influential friend in the theatre to get a play staged.

Another significant aspect of the increased number of theatres in the 1730's is the variety of entertainment open to the London audience. The revival of elaborate masques has already been mentioned. On 22 October 1730, "a Masque was prepared at His Royal Highness' Command, on that occasion by Mr Rich, and performed in His Royal Highness' Gardens at Cue [Kew], which were illuminated with above a thousand Lamps" (*Daily Journal*, 23 October 1730). But a more representative picture can be found by examining the total offerings on a given day at the theatres. On Tuesday, 27 March 1733, the following kinds of entertainment could be found: at Drury Lane, Fielding's adaptation of *The Miser;* at Covent Garden, Kelly's *The Married Philosopher* (the first introduction of the French *drame* or *comodie larmoyante*), with five dances and *The Black Joke;* at Goodman's Fields, *A Bold Stroke for a Wife*, followed by a ballet; at Lincoln's Inn Fields was advertised *Tunbridge Walks* with the pantomime *Perseus and Andromeda;* at the New Haymarket, Fielding's *The Old Debauchees*, with *The Farmer's Son;* at the King's Opera House, the oratorio *Deborah*, where the Earl of Egmont reports "near a hundred performers, among whom about twenty-five singers."[206] Here was certainly a profusion of varied

[206] *Diary*, I, 345.

spectacles. The total attendance on this night can be estimated at about 2,500. From this picture, one inference is clear: London theatres were no longer catering only to a limited group, but were instead attracting the interest of a larger public. Not since the golden years around 1605 and 1608, the apogee of Elizabethan and Jacobean drama, had there been so many as five theatres open on the same day; and the London theatres were now in their fourth season of such activity. Yet London had grown rapidly since the days of the Globe and the Swan. At the most generous estimate, Professor Alfred Harbage calculates a population of about 160,000 in London then.[207] During the period of the union of the companies, 1682–95, there was but one theatre in a city close to a population of a half-million, a theatrical situation true again of 1710–14, when the city was slightly larger. In 1722, the players in Rich's company were suffering because of small attendance. Yet here in Easter Week of 1733, some 2,500 spectators had assembled at the six different houses. Harbage estimated the total attendance at the theatres in 1605 to be about 2.5 per cent of the London population; our conjectured total for 1733 would represent only one-half of 1 per cent of a population now grown to about 675,000.[208] Hence the significance comes from the sharp increase over attendance early in the century and in the Restoration. Furthermore, this estimated attendance would yield a greater total for the week than the 12,000 that Samuel Foote considered to be the extent of the potential London audience in the middle of the century.[209]

On only a few nights were five or six theatres again open simultaneously. Even though enforcement of the Licensing Act was slow and sporadic, conditions changed after 1737. Many of the changes led to improvements in production, but in a survey of the theatres from the point of view of analyzing the repertory, it follows that the development of English drama was prevented by the monopoly of the two patent houses. After 1737, a dramatist would not find another theatre as easily as had Fielding in 1734 and Carey in 1735. If Colman had not produced She Stoops to Conquer after its rejection by Garrick, Goldsmith would have had no other winter theatre to which he could turn. After 1737, a group of actors could not secede and set up for themselves, as the Drury Lane players had done in 1733. When such a move was attempted ten years later, with such prominent

207 Shakespeare's Audience (New York, 1941), pp. 37–38, 171–73.
208 Ibid., p. 41. See also Dorothy George, London Life in the Eighteenth Century (London, 1923), pp. 21–60, and Norman Brett-James, The Growth of Stuart London (London, 1935). Both present charts and conjectures on the size of the London population.
209 A Treatise on the Passions (London, n.d.).

men as Garrick and Macklin as leaders, the rebels found that there was no place to go. Though his own stubborness was contributory, Macklin was never fully reaccepted by the theatres. In the fall of 1744 Mills complains that "he has been excluded from both theatres." The managers were aware of the change. "Is there not now subsisting a Cartel between the Patentees of Covent Garden and Drury Lane very prejudicial to every performer?" asks Theophilus Cibber, a man who was again the cause of his own misfortunes.[210] The subtitle of one pamphlet of 1743 is "Historical, Critical and Prophetical Remarks on the Famous Cartel lately agreed on by the Masters of the Two Theatres."[211] Its author recounts the way in which the appearance of a theatre in Goodman's Fields gave the actors freedom, only to have them lose this liberty by the Licensing Act. A very good witness is Kitty Clive, who had been so loyal to Drury Lane in 1733. Eleven years later she writes, "As only two Theatres were authorized, the Managers thought it was in their Power to reduce the Incomes of those Performers who could not live independent of their Profession."[212] Interesting support comes in her explanation that when she was offered a smaller salary by Fleetwood she quit and went to John Rich, who offered her the exact sum that she had just refused from Fleetwood. Mrs Clive had influential and talkative friends, so that her trouble could be rectified, but a lesser player could not defy the cartel.

In sharp contrast to the repertory of the new theatres, where the emphasis was on new kinds of drama and on recent plays for stock, is the pattern at the major houses in the season after the passing of the Licensing Act. The acting period was shortened by the closing of the theatres upon the death of Queen Caroline, so that Rich's company played on only 136 nights. One new play was damned by the audience. Eighteen plays composed before 1642 were played on 48 nights; 20 Restoration plays on 42 nights. Thus on 90 out of 136 performances the audience saw plays that antedated 1700. At Drury Lane, an excellent company put on 58 different plays on 159 nights. They offered 3 new plays on 21 nights, one of which was *Comus*. Ten plays of Shakespeare were played on 26 nights, and 4 other Elizabethan plays on nine nights. A total of 22 Restoration plays were offered on 51 nights, with the remaining 52 nights devoted to 19 eighteenth-century plays. Here 86 of the acting nights were given to plays of the seventeenth century or earlier. As at Covent Garden, a large

210 In *A Letter from Theophilus Cibber . . . to John Highmore.*
211 *Tyranny Triumphant! and Liberty Lost* (1743).
212 *The Case of Mrs. Clive* (London, 1744), pp. 16-17.

number of nights were devoted to the comedy of manners and the heroic play.

The frequency of the offerings of the comedy of manners was to decline, however. The fortunes of the plays of Congreve will provide the most dependable example, for the moralists were condemning the older comedies of Etherege and Wycherley. In the second quarter of the century, Congreve's plays "gained steadily in popularity until in the four years before Garrick they comprised 6.2 per cent of the total offerings of the theatres, a quite remarkable achievement." After Garrick appeared on the scene, the number of performances of the comedies began to gradually diminish; when he became manager of Drury Lane, the totals fell off sharply. Though the comedies remained in stock at Covent Garden, the number of performances no longer constituted a noticeable part of the total productions at the two patent houses in the third quarter of the century. "Had Garrick been willing or able to undertake roles in more of Congreve's plays, they might not have declined so much or perhaps not at all."[213]

THE SHAKESPEAREAN REVIVAL

> Shakespeare (whom you and every Playhouse bill
> Style the divine, the matchless, what you will).
> —*Epistle to Augustus*, *ll.* 69–70

A factor which affected repertory greatly was an ascending series of revivals of the plays of Shakespeare, a concise account of which might be given. After a brief revival around 1700, the details of which are not fully known, Shakespeare's plays accounted for about 11 per cent of the total performances from 1703 to 1710 and about 14 per cent in the next seven years.[214] In the next few years a considerable increase occurred, chiefly at Rich's theatre in Lincoln's Inn Fields. Here 16 different Shakespearean dramas were presented on 66 nights in a season of 164 performances, truly an amazing record, and reference to it is important in order to demonstrate how early the Shakespearean revivals were under way. Nevertheless, it is perhaps

213 Emmett L. Avery, *Congreve's Plays on the Eighteenth-Century Stage* (New York, 1951), pp. 82, 106–7, 121. For Wycherley, see Emmett L. Avery, "The Reputation of Wycherley's Comedies as Stage Plays in the Eighteenth Century," *Research Studies of the State College of Washington*, XII (Sept. 1944), 131–54.

214 This and much of the material which follows come from my article, "The Increase in Popularity of Shakespeare's Plays in the Eighteenth Century," *Shakespeare Quarterly*, VII (Spring 1956), 189–202.

equally important to add that the movement may have been ahead of its time, for the treasurer's account books indicate that not many spectators came to these performances. In 1720–21 *The Merry Wives of Windsor* made money for the house, but 22 of the 66 total performances lost money, drawing under the amount needed for the fixed daily expenses. Hence, the representation of Shakespeare's plays accounting for 17 per cent of the performances from 1717 to 1723 may be a statistical fact, but should not be overestimated and does not have as much significance as the next cycle of expanding popularity.

During the next eleven years the proportion dropped considerably to a ratio of one Shakespearean performance out of eight. The reason for this has already been given and is quite instructive. When there were new plays on the boards like *The Beggar's Opera*, *The Provoked Husband*, *Pasquin*, and *The London Merchant*, and nineteen to twenty-six new plays a season, not much room was left for the Shakespearean drama. Of the five hundred performances at the New Haymarket from 1728 to the spring of 1737 only six were of Shakespearean plays.

However, a new cycle of Shakespearean popularity was under way by the 1734–35 season, aided and abetted by the Shakespear's Ladies Club.[215] Audience resentment against any new plays immediately after the Licensing Act also caused the managers to turn to Shakespearean revivals. The dearth of new comedies led to the selection of Shakespeare's comedies, five of which were brought out in 1740–41. During that season the ratio increased to one play of Shakespeare to every four performances, 25 per cent of the total repertory. To understand this unheard of increase, we must turn to theatre history.

First of all, Giffard had re-opened the Goodman's Fields theatre in an evasion of the Licensing Act, establishing a third company in competition for the play-going public. At Covent Garden, John Rich had engaged the beautiful actress, Margaret Woffington. To exploit this new actress, Rich's manager, Lacy Ryan, aided and abetted by the Prince of Wales, selected plays containing "breeches" parts, i.e., roles where women dressed in fashionable male attire. Accordingly, the shapely limbs of Mistress Woffington were displayed in the roles of Sylvia in *The Recruiting Officer* and Sir Harry Wildair in *The Constant Couple*. The latter part was indeed an innovation, never having been attempted by a woman before, and was an immediate success. From Rich's cash book, now at the Folger Library,

[215] Emmett L. Avery, "The Shakespeare Ladies Club," *Shakespeare Quarterly*, VII (Spring 1956), 153–58.

and from Rylands MS III, it can be seen that the play ran ten nights con-
secutively, to large houses. Davies and other contemporaries testify to the
sensation created in the theatre world by this program.

Drury Lane actresses had legs too; and there were other dramatists
besides Farquhar who had written plays in which a woman took a male
disguise. Accordingly, Fleetwood and Macklin, at Drury Lane, put *As
You Like It* into rehearsal, and on 20 December the company revived this
play for the first time since the Restoration. It was well received, achieving
a run of twelve nights, and, surprisingly enough, was not supported by any
kind of afterpiece, though the double bill had now become standard practice.
Encouraged by this reception, the company brought out *Twelfth Night*,
"never acted there," on 15 January 1741. On the same night, Giffard, at
Goodman's Fields, revived *The Winter's Tale*, "not acted 100 Years," and
both plays ran for nine nights. Covent Garden thereupon began to offer
some Shakespearean plays, and on twelve nights this month at least two
of the three theatres had a Shakespearean drama on the boards. In fact,
from mid-December to the end of March there were only six acting nights
without a Shakespearean production at one of the three houses.[216]

The climax was reached on 14 February, when Macklin interpreted
the role of Shylock in the new "natural" school of acting. The play was
acted twenty times, with great applause and considerable notice in the
press. The last revival was staged at Goodman's Fields, where *All's Well
that Ends Well* was offered to a London audience for the first time since the
closing of the theatres in 1642. The season continued with *Hamlet*, *1 Henry IV*,
and *The Merry Wives of Windsor* being played at all three theatres. By the
season's end, the Drury Lane company had produced 14 plays of Shakespeare
for a total of 85 performances in a season of 192 acting nights. The Shakespearean vogue was dominant.

By this time there remained only six plays which had not been revived.[217] Two of these—*Cymbeline* and *Romeo and Juliet*—were introduced at
the New Haymarket by Theophilus Cibber in the fall of 1744. The latter
was played to crowded houses in the early fall, and from the newspapers
we learn that an unusually high proportion of the audience were women.
Cibber followed this success by restoring the original *Cymbeline*. The crowds
proved his undoing. Very shortly, the managers of Covent Garden and

---

[216] See my article "Shakespeare's Plays in the Theatrical Repertory When Garrick Came
to London," *University of Texas Studies in English* (Austin, 1945), pp. 257–68.

[217] *Antony and Cleopatra, Cymbeline, Love's Labour's Lost, Romeo and Juliet, Midsummer Nights
Dream, Two Gentlemen of Verona.*

Drury Lane called upon the magistrate to enforce the Licensing Act and close the theatre.[218] In due time, when they acquired the kind of actors and actresses needed, Rich and Garrick produced *Romeo and Juliet* at their own theatres, often on the same night, and so frequently that it ranks as the most popular Shakespearean play in the third quarter of the century. But Theophilus Cibber had been quite right. Years before, the audiences had clamored for Booth: Booth as Brutus, Booth as Cato, and (our witness is Alexander Pope) applauded his entry before he spoke a word. It was all different now. Audiences were anxious to see Susannah Cibber or George Ann Bellamy lean from a balcony to a Garrick or a Barry.

REPERTORY IN THE 1740's

The theatres were now capitalizing on their excellent actors and actresses, reviving plays in which they could appear to advantage; they were producing expensive pantomimes; and they were importing excellent dance teams for the entr'actes. One theatre yet remained that was not following this program. William Hallam had gathered a troupe of players and acted regularly during the winter season for three years from 1744 until the spring of 1747, at the New Wells in Goodman's Fields, an unlicensed house. His last season may be examined to show the patterns of repertory at the New Wells. The house was lighted only 103 nights. One new piece was produced. Nine plays of Shakespeare were given on 33 nights, or almost one night in three. Eleven Restoration plays were shown, for a total of 19 performances. The remaining nights were devoted to eighteenth-century plays, for a total of 51 performances. Most of the Restoration plays were pathetic tragedies; in fact, 40 nights this season were given to tragedy. The next point of interest is the use of farces and ballad operas instead of pantomime as the afterpiece.

Much different was the situation at Drury Lane and Covent Garden. In the years 1741–47, Drury Lane brought out eighteen new plays (seven main plays and eleven afterpieces) during these seven years, but the main dependence was upon stock. The company presented from fifty to as many as seventy different plays during the season. At Covent Garden, John Rich offered only three new plays in these seven years: Cibber's *Papal Tyranny* (an adaptation from *King John*), Hoadly's *The Suspicious Husband*, and Garrick's

---

[218] See T. Cibber, *A Serio-Comic Apology*, and Genest, *Some Account of the English Stage*, IV, 171.

Miss in Her Teens; here too the company regularly presented as many as seventy different plays throughout the year.

Although the spring of 1737 provided the most excitement, the best acting in the period from 1729 to 1747 was seen in the last season, when there were again three companies competing for public favor. The center of attention was the Theatre Royal in Covent Garden, where John Rich, by engaging David Garrick, was able to announce him with Quin, Ryan, Mrs Pritchard, and Mrs Cibber in a series of the favorite pathetic tragedies such as *Jane Shore* and *The Fair Penitent.* The opportunity of seeing Quin and Garrick act leading roles in the same play drew thousands of spectators and elicited enthusiastic comment. Veteran playgoers tried to recall Booth and Mrs Oldfield, but the Covent Garden audiences felt that a better acting company had never been assembled than they were presently watching.[219] Drury Lane attempted to meet the competition by advertising its new leading man, the Irish actor Spranger Barry, and by featuring the dancing of Salomon and Mlle Violette. Meanwhile, Lewis and William Hallam, Mrs Lewis Hallam, Miss Maddocks, and Miss Budgell led a Goodman's Fields troupe through a winter season of a hundred performances of legitimate drama without offering a single pantomime. In fact, pantomime almost disappeared for the time, amazing as this fact may seem. The production of the best drama in the repertory by excellent actors and actresses nearly upset the dominance of the double-feature program. At Covent Garden, on 60 of the 170 acting nights no afterpiece was announced in the bills. The house opened to offer a five-act play; that constituted the evening's entertainment, with entr'acte dancing mentioned only four of these nights. Pantomimes were announced as afterpieces on but 23 occasions. These came at Christmas or at the interruption of the run of *The Suspicious Husband* caused by Garrick's illness. Even at Drury Lane, the management announced no afterpieces on 39 of the 158 nights the house was open.

Popular commendations of the splendid performances overlooked the final termination of legitimate drama at Goodman's Fields by the end of the season. Henceforth, three acting companies would no longer be in competition. Forgotten too was the dearth of new plays. The brilliance of the past season obscured the fact that the ensuing situation was unhealthy for creative drama.

The danger was not seen, and for very good reasons. The emergence of a new style of acting led by David Garrick, the presence of great actors

<hr>

[219] See Horace Walpole's letter of 5 Dec. 1746 to Horace Mann, *Yale Edition of Horace Walpole's Correspondence,* XIX, 342.

and actresses at both Drury Lane and Covent Garden, the excitement and variety provided by the skillfully designed programs—all these factors concealed what had happened; theatre-goers constituted only a tiny fraction of the London population of some 700,000, and the novel was replacing the drama as the dominant form of literary entertainment.

Dancing, Music, Singing, and Specialty Acts

Call for the Farce, the Bear, or the Black Joke.
—*Epistle to Augustus, l.* 309

ANY SURVEY of the Calendar of performances will show the great amount of singing, dancing, and music used in a night's production at a London theatre. Of this entertainment, dancing occupied the largest share. Formal ballet occurred in the pantomimes, and separate ballets were offered as entr'actes. In addition a profusion of individual named dances and hornpipes spiced every evening's program. Every theatre employed a considerable number of dancers. Of the seventy performers at Drury Lane in the season of 1730–31, the names of thirty-six were listed in the advertisements for dances, though many were primarily actors with the necessary versatility for dancing. Rich had eighty-eight members on his Covent Garden company in 1741–42, twenty-eight of whom were engaged only for dancing. As the lists of the different companies are examined, the reader will find that sometimes one in three was a dancer. In addition to these regular stock companies, separate houses offered nothing but dancing and miscellaneous entertainments, such as the New Wells, Clerkenwell, or the New Wells, Goodman's Fields, during the summer, or, best known of all, Sadler's Wells, a house that had plenty of money for dancers and scenery. It was at Sadler's Wells where innovations in the ballet could be found, such as on 22 August 1741, when "The Amorous Mandarins, a new picturesque Ballet, with a new Decoration in the Chinese Taste," was produced.

The relative popularity of dancing and singing fluctuated, of course. In the years immediately after the production of *The Beggar's Opera*, singing flourished. Yet dancing continued popular, with a constant stream of foreign dancers being introduced to the London theatres. In some seasons, as in 1742–43, the theatrical dance was the craze, and the names of the pieces and the dancers filled the notices. At Covent Garden, thirty-two named dances were performed; at Drury Lane, the two new dance teams, Checo and Chiaretta and Boromeo and Costanza produced twenty-one new dances.

Dances were the vogue at the King's Opera House, though the newspaper bills in the second quarter of the century did not include them.

During the 1742–43 season at the Opera, no dancers' names appear in the advertisements. We learn their names only from the libretto and from occasional news items to the effect that such and such a danseuse is ill and unable to perform in the opera and are thus assured of the place of dancing in the program. During the 1734–35 season, Marie Salle was working out the choreography for the intermezzi at the operas, and several new ballets were introduced during the season; yet the newspaper advertisements fail to name her or the other dancers.

The chief advance in ballet came from the work of this famous danseuse who had made several trips to England earlier in the century, and now returned to Rich's company on 8 November 1733. After performing in a number of dances during the late fall, she composed a new ballet, *Pigmalion*, produced on 14 January 1734. "This was a genuine, if miniature, *ballet d'action*," states Stanley Vince; "with simple but expressive choreography a team of eight dancers unfolded the familiar classical story."[220] A description of this ballet was published in the *Mercure de France*: "The statute, little by little, becomes conscious, showing wonder at her changed existence and all around her. Amazed and entranced, Pigmalion takes her hand, leading her down from the pedestal. Step by step she feels her way, gradually assuming the most graceful poses a sculptor could possibly desire, with steps ranging from the simplest to the most complex."[221] Throughout the period, Roger, Thurmond, Denoyer, Leviez, and various other ballet-masters worked out intricate ballets for the appreciative audiences. The spectators took the dances seriously and watched them, fervently intent, as can be seen from the following news item: "One William Wright, a young Man, who was in the Shilling Gallery, disapproving of Signora Domitilla's Dancing between the second and Third Acts, was without any provocation, kick'd, beat, and abused."[222]

The lesser theatres that offered legitimate drama often lacked choreographers and consequently tended to present dances that had already been created and produced at Drury Lane or Covent Garden. In fact, they would announce a dance, for example, as "after the Manner of the Fausans." Even so, some would try to develop new dances. On 15 October 1733, "A Dance of Court Cards, with King of Spades, Queen of Spades, Knave of Spades, King of Hearts, Queen of Diamonds, and Knave of Clubs" was inserted into *The Emperor of the Moon* at Goodman's Fields. A full ballet was

220 "Marie Salle," pp. 12–13.
221 *Ibid.*
222 *Daily Advertiser*, 23 Dec. 1742, for a performance of 18 Dec. It is noteworthy that Domitilla was by no means the leading dancer that season.

produced at the same theatre on 14 January 1742 entitled "The Welch-man's Triumph, or the Death of the Wild Goat."

As Foote was a noted egotist, and since it was the fashion in some years for London society to attend his matinees to witness his clever and ruthless mimicry, one might get the impression that he depended upon himself and his supporting players to draw spectators. A study of the daily announcements, however, will reveal that Foote employed a considerable group of dancers, carefully arranged for a variety of numbers. He rarely offered a program without presenting some named dances.

Popular as the dancers and dancing were, music remained an integral part of the evening's performance. From the specific naming of the compositions in the advertisements, it may be assumed that the audiences were attracted by the music. At Covent Garden on 8 May 1735, the day's advertisement included, "For the First Musick, a Concert for Hautboys; for the Second Musick, A Concerto of Geminiani; And for the Third, The Overture of Ariadne. The Act Tunes for French Horns, and Trumpets." The seceding players from Dury Lane, in possession of the New Haymarket in 1733–34, greatly increased the offering of music. On 6 October, 1733, they list "the first Concerto from Corelli" for the second Music, together with three musical pieces as entr'actes. Again, on 20 October, "For the 2nd Musick, the first Concerto of the 1st opera of Geminiani. For the 3rd Musick, an Overture composed by Mr Handel, for the Opera of Alexander," as well as two pieces and two songs for the entr'actes. Giffard's notices are also quite specific concerning the music, as can be seen from his advertisement for 8 May 1734: "For the 2nd Musick, a Concerto of the late Mr Wood-cook's on the little Flute. For the Third, the 8th Concerto of Corelli." At the prompter Chetwood's benefit at Goodman's Fields on 13 April 1733, four pieces of music were used as entr'actes.

The most popular composition of all was Handel's *Water Music*. It had been sporadically announced up until the 1732–33 season. Then it became the vogue; every theatre presented it frequently, and it shows up on the benefit nights. From this season on, it never disappears, and is listed throughout the season by every company, large or small. Individual favorites were the performers Burk Thumoth on the trumpet, and Job Baker "and his Kettle-Drums."

The enormous popularity of *The Beggar's Opera* increased what had already been a lively interest in singing. E. M. Gagey has carefully dealt with the large number of imitations in his study, *Ballad Opera*, so that no account of these new pieces will be given here beyond calling attention to their extraordinary number and popularity. As the vogue fell away, the practice of inserting songs into plays developed. Of course, such a practice was known in both the Restoration and the Elizabethan stage, but a marked expansion can be seen in the theatrical advertisements beginning with the 1744-45 season and continuing on past mid-century. Most revivals of older plays carried new songs which had been inserted. Drury Lane and Covent Garden both employed resident singers and hired additional ones when they were needed.

A great deal of singing was provided in the entr'actes. Many different lyrics were used, but the most popular at the established theatres were Kitty Clive's rendition of "The Life of a Beau," "The Flocks shall leave the Mountains," from Handel, Barrington's singing of "Arra[h] my Judy," "Was ever Nymph like Rosamund?" which Miss Arne sang frequently in 1733-34, and Waller's text of "Go, lovely Rose," set by T. A. Arne. At the little theatres, booths, and great rooms, far and away the most repeated piece was "Ellen a Roon."

The songs at the fairs were chiefly topical. Thus on 23 August 1743, with news of Dettingen announced, three booths at Bartholomew Fair announced a new song or ballad on "the retaking the English standard belonging to Sir Robert Rich's Regiment of Horse by George Darraugh."

Presentation of many of the announced songs modulated into what might be classified as specialty acts. For his benefit at Goodman's Fields, on 2 February 1742, Aspe chanted "L'Allegro and Il Pensoroso." On 26 October 1732 Goodman's Fields announced a "mimick Song by Stoppelaer [from Ireland] in the Character of a Ballad Singer." Tony Aston advertised from December 1743 to February 1744 "his learned comic demonstrative Oratory on the Face, with English, Irish, Scotch, and Negroe Songs . . . in proper Habits."[223] Unfortunately, no current journalist saw fit to provide us with more information about Aston's minstrel show, but the performance was not unique. Two years later, on 10 March 1746, was announced "the surprising Voice of a famous African who sings several Songs, with Mock Voices, particularly in Imitation of a young Child" (*Daily Advertiser*). Dialect pieces had been popular for some time, and "A Dialogue in the Scotish Stile" offered at Covent Garden on 24 May 1733 is but one of many such presentations.

---

[223] From unidentified newspaper clippings in Folger Library. For additional illustrations, see Emmett L. Avery, "Vaudeville on the London Stage, 1700-1737," *Research Studies of the State College of Washington*, V (June 1937), 66-77.

Some of the specialty acts were contrived entertainments, such as "A Burlesque Tragic Scene, call'd Sextus Quintilius, by Mr Penkethman and Mr Lyon," offered at Goodman's Fields on 15 May 1734. A new kind of entertainment was Barrington's rendition of Dublin street cries of hucksters and peddlers, later to become one of Shuter's most popular features.

An old custom of an actor's "riding an Ass to speak the Epilogue" survived throughout the period, in fact, was expanded in the 1732–33 season, when two players appeared mounted on donkeys to give the epilogue. The climax came on 29 May 1733, when a bill announced, "A New Epilogue to be spoken by Mr Wetherilt, Mr Morgan, and Mr Penkethman, riding on three Asses." Fortunately, the season was near its close. They were to be outdone in another way in the due course of time, when J. Petty, manager of the old playhouse in Tottenham Court, promised for 4 August 1735, "Entertainments, including 3 Wild Cats."

The Audience

The many-headed Monster of the Pit.
—*Epistle to Augustus, l.* 305

THE VEXING but fascinating problem of determining who constituted the theatre-going public must now be examined. It was not the heterogeneous audience that flocked to the Bankside theatres in Shakespeare's day, nor was it the relatively homogeneous elite who generally composed the audiences of the Restoration. To generalize further, we may say that the spectators at the London theatres in the second quarter of the century were not all members of fashionable society but included a much larger proportion from the middle class than did the audiences at the Comédie Française despite assertions to the contrary by H. Carrington Lancaster. To refute the notion that Parisian theatre audiences were restricted to the upper classes of a severely hierarchal society, Lancaster argues that if the total attendance in a given year were 150,000, "there must have been well over 100,000 different individuals who attended."[224] Stage history is a discipline that requires the utmost vigilance, and even the formidable researcher Lancaster fell into a statistical trap here. A hundred thousand different persons are not needed to achieve a season total of 150,000; in fact, as John Lough points out in his valuable study, *Paris Theatre Audiences in the Seventeenth and Eighteenth Centuries*, that total could be achieved by only 426 persons attending each of the 352 performances given during the season.[225] This is preposterous (as Lough admits), but not so preposterous as supposing 100,000 different persons in attendance. Actually, if 3,000 Parisians went to the theatre one evening each week, an entirely reasonable supposition, they would account for the total 150,000.

To obtain a more reliable estimate of the range of the spectators, Lough employs the excellent method of ascertaining the total number who attended during the run of a moderately successful new play. By applying this method to the London audiences, we can exclude the extremely high attendance figures for the first run of *The Beggar's Opera* on the grounds that Gay's ballad opera attracted a number of visitors who did not generally

[224] *A History of French Dramatic Literature in the Seventeenth Century*, as quoted by John Lough, *Paris Theatre Audiences in the Seventeenth and Eighteenth Centuries* (London, 1957), p. 49.
[225] *Ibid.*, p. 51.

frequent the theatre, and we can disregard the box-receipts for a new play that attained only three or six nights, since the full audience potential was not exhausted by so short a run. A later play of Gay's, *Achilles*, had an excellent run of seventeen nights in February and March of 1733, during the first season of the new theatre in Covent Garden, and we may assume that most patrons of the theatre went to see this new play, though we must remember that some may have witnessed more than one performance. Exact attendance records are not known, but the box-receipts exist. Just under £2,100 was taken in during the initial run. This sum would represent about 13,500 paying spectators, with no allowance for those who might have attended on more than one night. Toward the end of our period, Hoadly's comedy *The Suspicious Husband* was acted on twelve consecutive nights in February 1747 until it was taken off the boards because of the sudden illness of the leading performer, Garrick. During the run the receipts were about £2,300, representing at least 14,500 persons in attendance. Receipts of £186 on the night before Garrick's illness would suggest that the full audience potential had not yet been reached.

Another approach would be to determine the total seating capacities of the combined theatres. Unfortunately, we cannot obtain this information accurately. Drury Lane could accommodate about 1,000; Covent Garden and Lincoln's Inn Fields each held 1,400, and the normal capacity of the King's Opera House was also around 1,400. Goodman's Fields held about 700; the little theatre in the Haymarket may have held slightly more, say 800. If we add these totals together and apply them to a week's performances during the middle of the winter, assuming Drury Lane, Covent Garden, and Goodman's Fields open on six nights, with opera on two nights, and the little Haymarket theatre open on the other four nights, the total capacity would be 24,600; in other words, in the years before the Licensing Act, all the theatres together could not accommodate much more than 25,000 spectators for a week's performances. Restricting our calculations to the patent houses and the opera house (but considering the latter for only its regular Tuesday and Saturday performances), the total capacity available for a week's performances would decrease to about 17,200.

By using extant records of box-receipts, we can turn to specific performances and attempt to learn how many spectators attended on a single night or an individual week. On 26 December 1732, the two patent houses were open; there was an opera at King's, with the King and Queen and three princesses present; Goodman's Fields and Lincoln's Inn Fields were also lighted, and a play was announced in Southwark. The treasurer's receipts show £93 7s. 6d. at Covent Garden, or about 700 paid admissions, and £65 12s. at Lincoln's Inn Fields, or about 450 spectators. Credit Drury Lane with the same attendance as at Covent Garden, and estimate that Goodman's Fields was half full, or 350. With royalty present, assume that the boxes were three-fourths full at the opera and half of these spectators had a servant in the gallery, together with 100 persons in the pit, a total of 550. About 100 persons might have gone to the theatre in Southwark. The total of these estimates would be 2,850, not unlikely during Christmas week but somewhat above the normal attendance on other nights during the season. Counting a second performance of the opera and disregarding the Southwark theatre entirely, the entire week's attendance, on the basis of the figures for 26 December, would be 14,300.

One additional week may be scrutinized, March 26–31 in 1733. Drury Lane again acted each of the six nights; two were command performances, and on Saturday a new pantomime was brought out. Hence one might conjecture that the house might have been three-fourths full on each night. The receipts for Covent Garden, acting six nights, represent an estimated attendance of 4,800. Goodman's Fields was also open each night, with two performances being benefits, and we may suppose it was drawing about two-thirds capacity during the week. The New Haymarket was open only twice, and a conservative estimate would be around 800 for the two performances. Lincoln's Inn Fields was open on Monday night, with receipts of £131 10s. 6d., or about 800 people. On Tuesday, 27 March, the opera house had one of the largest audiences ever seen there, according to a notice to be quoted later in this section, and we may suppose a full house; for the other opera night, we can return to the previous estimate of 550. The totals would be as follows:

Drury Lane	4,500
Covent Garden	4,800
Goodman's Fields	2,832
New Haymarket	800
Lincoln's Inn Fields	800
King's	1,950
	15,682

These figures throughout are based on estimates and should not be accepted as the presentation of fact. If we were to place any dependence upon them, one could conclude that during the 1732–33 season there was a core of about 13,000 or 14,000 regular theatre-goers and that in a holiday period the total attendance during a week might be around 15,000. Even so, the latter total might include many spectators who went to a play on one night and to the opera on another night in the same week, a standard pattern for Horace Walpole, Lord Hervey, and the Earl of Egmont. The totals are considerably below those for spectators at the Comédie Française during the same years, where a moderately successful new play drew about 18,000 in attendance.[226] Voltaire calls attention to this difference in alluding to Parisian theatre audiences for the years 1735–50: "Dans notre nation on n'aime pas véritablement la littérature. Une pièce réussit pleinement, 5 à 6,000 personnes la voient dans Paris, 1,200 la lisent, non sic à Londres."[227]

Determining the extent of the representation from the different classes in London is also a complex matter. Starting at the top, we can find an immediate increase of royal support over that of the previous era. Further-more, the Hanoverian tribe was more numerous than that of the later Stuarts. Additional princesses meant a higher total of command perform-ances. Under the second George, more Britons took pleasure at seeing royalty present at public entertainments, and royal attendance at the theatres increased the popularity of both royalty and the theatres.[228]

"Last Saturday night," reports the London Daily Post and General Advertiser on 22 January 1739, "his Majesty, his Royal Highness the Duke, the Princesses, with several Foreign Ministers and their Ladies, were at the Theatre-Royal in Covent Garden, to see the Tragedy of Macbeth, with the Entertainment of Perseus and Andromeda. So great a Concourse of People came in order to see his Majesty there, as has scarcely been seen; many Persons who came to the Play-House at Four o'Clock offering any Price, if they could possibly be admitted." His Majesty played his role as well as any of the performers on the stage, for the newspaper account continues, "In the Fury Dance of Macbeth, Mr Haughton had the Misfortune to dislocate his Ankle-Bone, and fell down upon the Stage, and was obliged to be carried off; upon which his Majesty was graciously pleased to send him Ten Guineas instantly, and to order him to be taken care of."

The King and Queen Caroline preferred opera, and the newspapers record the presence of some member of the Royal family at the King's Opera House for about half of the fifty nights that constituted the operatic

226 Ibid., pp. 178–80.
227 As quoted by Lough, Ibid., p. 179.
228 See the following advertisement by the French company for a performance on 27 Feb. 1735: "Places may be taken next the Boxes built on the Stage for their Royal Highnesses, Princess Amelia, and Princess Caroline." (In both the Daily Advertiser and the London Daily Post and General Advertiser.)

season. Attendance at the new oratorios was most fashionable, as may be seen by the following report in the *Daily Advertiser* of 28 March 1733: "Their Majesties, together with his Royal Highness the Prince of Wales and the Princesses, were again at the King's Theatre in the Haymarket, to see Deborah, the New Oratorio in English, at which was likewise present one of the most numerous Audiences of Nobility and Persons of Distinction that has been ever seen in any Theatre." The King and Queen would take pains to appear at the two patent theatres on benefit nights for famous players, such as the tragediennes Mrs Porter and Mrs Horton, but it was the Prince and the Princesses who saw legitimate drama regularly. In the early years they generally went to the Drury Lane theatre, in 1731–32 attending the house twenty-three times to eight appearances at Lincoln's Inn Fields, but as the years passed they divided their attendance about equally between the two companies. They appeared very rarely at the theatres from 1743 to 1746, but the combination of the suppression of the rebellion, when it was good for royalty to be seen publicly, and the excitement of the great season in which Quin and Garrick played together in Rich's company during 1746–47 drew more royal attendance than in any previous season of this period.

The most striking example of the way in which the theatres catered to public interest in their rulers occurred in the season of 1733–34, when the impending marriage of the Princess Royal to the Prince of Orange inspired every manager to prepare a number of ballets, dances, oratorios, and festivals, each with new costumes, scenes, and choreography, in celebration of the royal nuptials.[229] The Prince of Orange arrived in London on 7 November 1733, and by that time, each theatre was ready with an afterpiece designed to draw spectators who were interested in either the social events of royalty or the new entertainments, or both. Each of the pieces was successful, and they were witnessed by enormous numbers in the theatres.

On occasion, some of the Brunswicks attended performances at other places besides the patent houses. Drawn by the novelty of Fieldings' new pieces, the Duke of Cumberland and the Princess Amelia went to see a musical version of *Tom Thumb* at the New Haymarket on Monday 4 June 1733 (*Daily Advertiser*, 5 June). Their report must have been favorable, for the *Daily Advertiser* reported on Thursday 7 June, "Last Night his Royal Highness the Prince of Wales, with a vast Concourse of the Nobility and Gentry, was at the New Theatre in the Haymarket, and saw the Opera of Operas, or Tom Thumb the Great." We know the identity of at least one

[229] See Avery, "A Royal Wedding Royally Confounded," pp. 153–64.

member of the "vast Concourse," as the Earl of Egmont recorded his presence on this night.[230] The crowds kept coming, for on Friday night the "two youngest Princesses" appeared, this time with only a "great Concourse of Nobility and Gentry" (*Daily Advertiser*, 9 June). On the following Monday, "the vast Concourse" returned, this time under the leadership of the "Conde de Montijo, the Spanish Ambassador" (*Daily Advertiser*, 12 June).

It must be pointed out that people did not go to see Fielding's productions at the New Haymarket because they were consumed with indignation against Sir Robert Walpole; they went because they found pleasure in the lively entertainment provided by "the Grand Mogul's Company of Comedians." On Monday, 23 May 1737, the *Daily Advertiser* announced that the "Dutchess Dowager of Marlborough will be at the Theatre in the Hay-Market this Night, to see the *Historical Register*." The Earl of Egmont repeatedly notes his attendance at Fielding's new pieces. In fact, *Applebee's* noted the presence of Sir Robert Walpole himself at the New Haymarket on 22 March 1733, during Passion Week, when all theatres were supposed to be closed.

Royalty even appeared to watch the performances at booths in the fairs. On the afternoon of Thursday, 17 August 1732, Prince William, the Princesses Mary and Louisa, accompanied by "his Excellency Ach Mohamet Ambassador from the Bey of Algiers" attended the Tottenham Court Fair to see the pantomime "the Life and Death of Dr. Faustus" (*Daily Advertiser*, 19 August). In August 1741, when plays at four booths at Bartholomew Fair were being presented by players from the regular London companies, the Duke of Cumberland chose to go to the fifth booth, where the program consisted of tumbling and rope dancing (*London Daily Post and General Advertiser*, 24 August).

But while royalty, aristocracy, and the top men of quality could set fashions and bring social sanction to the theatre, their influence could not fill the four theatres running during the 1730's. Such influence in the Restoration had not been able to maintain two theatres for more than a short time. The genuinely "vast Concourses" filling the theatres were drawn from other social classes. From the petitions filed with Parliament in connection with a proposed act to reform the theatres in 1735, we know that merchants, large and small, were becoming theatre-goers. The request performances at all theatres "by several Merchants" shows this group taking an interest not only in attendance but also in the repertory. The

[230] *Diary*, I, 384.

Freemasons bespoke at least two plays every season in the 1730's and 1740's. For a small theatre like Hallam's New Wells in Goodman's Fields, ten rows of the pit had to be roped in to reserve places for them. These occasions were in no way surreptitious. The Masons would repair usually to the Fleece Tavern in full regalia, and under the leadership of the Grand Master, proceed to the theatre. We can assume that two hundred or more persons were in the procession.

The young law students, the Templars, comprised a very influential group. They often requested particular plays, and were regular in attendance at first nights. As *Common Sense* for 27 May 1738 observed, "They are a set of Gentlemen who never fail to assist the first Night at everything new which is exhibited on the Stage." From a speech in parliament in 1733, we learn that "the Theatre in Goodman's Fields is chiefly supported by Captains of Ships, and seafaring Men." From another petition to Parliament in 1735, it appears that large numbers of apprentices were also attending the Goodman's Fields theatre.[231]

TASTE AND CHANGING TASTE

> . . . the People's Voice is odd,
> It is, and it is not, the voice of God.
>   —*Epistle to Augustus, l.* 89

A close relationship existed between actor and audience throughout the century. If a spectator in the pit wished a tune played, a song sung, or an epilogue restored, he loudly called for it to be done.[232] A large number of the spectators were habitués, experienced theatre-goers, and they felt a proprietary interest in the proceedings. Let an actor offend them, and he would have to come forward and apologize. If some unexpected contretemps threatened to affect the regular procedures, the problem was often laid before the audience. The *Daily Advertiser* of 14 January 1736 describes such a crux on the preceding night: "The Gentleman who perform'd the Character of Osman in The Tragedy of Zara the first night having declin'd it, that Part was read last Night; and it being submitted to the Determination of the Audience, whether the Play should be continu'd, or the Repetition of it deferr'd till somebody was studied in the Part, they unanimously declared for the Continuation of the Play."

[231] Pedicord, *The Theatrical Public in the Time of Garrick*, p. 35. See also Emmett L. Avery, "Cibber, *King John*, and the Students of the Law," *Modern Language Notes*, LIII (1938), 272–75.
[232] See the *Universal Spectator* of 11 June 1743, where a person boasts of calling for "the Black Joke."

At James Quin's intended benefit on 9 April 1747, when Garrick was still too ill to act as advertised, the notice stated, "If any Gentlemen or Ladies shall be displeas'd with the alteration in the performance of the play, the money shall be returned."[233] The *Daily Post* of 17 October 1733 reported that "some passages in the Farce call'd The Livery Rake, or the Country Lass, not being approved by the Audience, the Company of the Revels will not perform it again till proper alterations are made by the Author." The control exerted by the audience was not a matter of opinion, as can be seen from a comment made by the *Grub St. Journal* on the two following newspaper notices which it had reprinted:

Last night the new Comedy call'd, *The Old Debauchees*, and *The Covent Garden Tragedy*, were acted for the first time, at the Theatre Royal in Drury Lane, with universal Applause (*Daily Post*, 3 June). We were partly misinform'd as to the reception of the two Pieces play'd on Thursday Night last . . . we are assur'd the Comedy call'd *The Old Debauchees* did meet with universal Applause; but the *Covent Garden Tragedy* will be acted no more, both the Author and the Actors, being unwilling to continue any Piece contrary to the opinion of the Town (*Daily Post*, 5 June).

At this point the editor of the *Grub St. Journal* added the comment, "*For* unwilling *Read* unable." Lest anyone think the *Grub St. Journal* was indulging in cynicism, let him look at the news article in *Applebee's* on a performance at the New Haymarket on 22 March 1733: "At the performance of Love Runs all Dangers . . . one of the Commedians took the Liberty to throw out some Reflections upon the Prime Minister and the Excise, which were not designed by the Author; Lord Walpole, being in the House, went behind the Scenes, and demanded of the Prompter, whether such Words were in the Play, and he answering they were not, his Lordship immediately corrected the Comedian with his own Hands very severly" (31 March).

The best thing to do was to take the audience into confidence and lay all the cards on the table, as did the employees of the New Haymarket in an advertisement of 12 August 1734, saying "As the Summer Season has prov'd very unsuccessful, the Servants humbly hope that in Consideration of it the Town will favour them this Night" (*Daily Advertiser*).

The close attention paid by the audience to acting techniques can be found throughout the period. Two particularly informative selections should illustrate this feature of the audiences: in the late spring of 1746, when James (Love) Dance left Hallam for an engagement at Covent Garden and was advertised to play Bayes in *The Rehearsal* on 2 May, a role he played

[233] From an unidentified newspaper clipping in the Folger Library.

frequently at the New Wells, the following letter appeared in that day's *General Advertiser*.

> *Tom's Coffee House, Cornhill*
> *Wednesday four o'Clock*
>
> Mr. Bayes,
>
> By the unanimous Desire of a Number of your Friends here assembled, who intend to sit in judgment upon you on Friday, I take upon me to advise you in some particulars, as to your present Undertaking. Let not any Success you might meet with at an End of Town where the Audience must be compos'd of a different Class of People from what you might expect at Covent Garden, tempt you to think of Mimicking an Actress whom the Town doats upon; and particularly avoid Puffing; a Scheme long ago worn threadbare, but not even an Epilogue from the Gods would be of any Service now; and therefore if you have anything that's new, and fiery Flights of Fancy, and all that, let them lie dormant till the Time of Action, and then endeavour to elevate and surprize. Value these Hints.

Other similar comments or notices appear, showing that the acting of a new leading man is being watched by experienced audiences, close followers of acting and the drama.

On the other hand, we have the poet Gray's letter to John Chute (24 May 1742), in which Gray complains humorously that in two nights spent attending Pergolesi's *Olimpiade* (advertised as *Meraspe*) from the vantage point of the gallery, he observed that no one else recognized the music. On 15 November 1743 the bills for the opening night at the King's Opera House announc'd, "will be reviv'd an Opera *Roxane*, or *Alexander in India*. The Musick compos'd by Mr Handel." But what the singers offered that night was Lampugnani's *Rossane*, the composer's first contribution to the house for which he had just been hired as the resident composer. Yet all through the sixteen-night run, the bills continue to say, "The Musick compos'd by Mr Handel." Students of the opera will concur in saying that this situation simply could not have taken place with the audience at Italian opera houses.

Changing taste is reflected by comments from the audience. The Reverend T. Newton, eagerly watching Garrick during his spectacular first season, at the Goodman's Fields house, wrote bitterly reproaching him for playing one of the recruits in *The Recruiting Officer*. "You should not," writes Newton, "demean yourself by acting anything that is low or little. . . . If I was an actor, surely I would rather wish to be a Raphael than a Hogarth; if I was a poet, I would choose infinitely rather to be a Milton than Hudibras."[234]

[234] 14 Jan. 1742. Quoted in *Private Correspondence of David Garrick*, I, 46.

Remarks like these, many more of which could be quoted, show that the reading public for whom Swift and Pope wrote and the theatre-goers who applauded the plays of Congreve and Gay were yielding to a new audience affected by a recrudescence of English Puritanism. Outside the theatre, Richardson's *Pamela* and Young's *Night Thoughts* were being provided for this new middle class audience: within, the "weeping comedies" and the *drame* from France were supplanting the comedy of manners. "It is not surprising," writes Winton Dean, "that Handel, who saw no necessary opposition between religion and laughter, was sometimes incomprehensible to his age, and that works like *Susanna* were dismal failures."[235] Dean has provided an excellent, heavily documented account of the intrusion of the didactic and anti-aesthetic views of the new middle class made prosperous by the world of commerce, and the reader is referred to it rather than having it repeated here.[236]

To this audience Handel addressed all the later oratorios; for their benefit he abandoned the system of seasonal subscriptions in favour of single tickets for each performance; for their benefit, it is to be feared, he lowered his standards in the spirit of his remark to Gluck in 1746 that the English liked something they could beat time to—the spirit in which he wrote *Judas Maccabaeus*.[237]

Handel had brought out his magnificent oratorio *Hercules* (hardly a sacred oratorio) in 1745 to the accompaniment of complete indifference on the part of the London public, who failed to appear for the performances. In desperation, Handel published his famous letter on the English language (*Daily Advertiser*, 17 January). When Handel started his Lenten oratorio season in 1747, he discontinued the established method of the subscription, as Dean states above, and offered tickets at the door instead (*General Advertiser*, 6 March). The year 1747 provides a convenient dividing point in the study of the eighteenth-century theatre, because of the many changes, of which this is but one.

[235] Dean, *Handel's Dramatic Oratorios*, p. 135.
[236] *Ibid.*, "The Oratorio and English Taste," pp. 128–49. See also F. W. Bateson, *English Comic Drama, 1700–1750* (Oxford, 1929), pp. 145–48. On the catering to this changed audience by offering pantomimes, see Emmett L. Avery, "The Defense and Criticism of Pantomimic Entertainments in the Early Eighteenth Century," *Journal of English Literary History*, V (1938), 127–45.
[237] Dean, *Handel's Dramatic Oratorios*, p. 136.

COMMAND AND REQUEST PERFORMANCES

The repeated use of the statement "By Desire" or "By Desire of several Persons of Quality" in theatrical notices can lead the reader today into considering these phrases as pure clichés of advertising, lacking any referential meaning. Nevertheless, sufficient information exists to indicate that the procedure whereby a theatre-goer chose a particular piece to be staged, or "bespeaking," as the arrangement was termed, was widely practiced and has significance in that it demonstrated audience participation in the selection of the repertory. A selected number of examples will be given to indicate the nature of the evidence existing to document the authenticity and prevalence of "bespeaking." The most definitive assurance comes from a command performance by royalty.

At the end of the notice for Drury Lane in the *Daily Advertiser* of 28 September 1734, the statement follows: "By Command of his Royal Highness, on Monday next will be presented a Play, call'd *Amphitryon*." On 5 November 1729 the Drury Lane notice in the *Daily Post* announced *The Conscious Lovers* for the next night; on 6 November the play was changed to *The Way of the World*, "By Command" of the Prince of Wales.

Yet bespeaking was not limited to royalty. The note added to the Drury Lane advertisement of 21 September 1734 in the *Daily Advertiser* is quite explicit: "The Letter from some Gentlemen of the Inner-Temple (desiring the first Part of King Henry the Fourth to be play'd soon) was receiv'd, and, in Compliment to their Request, that Play will be Acted on Tuesday next." Equally clear is the language of a note added to an advertisement for Rich's Covent Garden company, "The Play of Love for Love, which was bespoke for this Day, is deferr'd on account of a principal Comedian" (*Daily Advertiser*, 15 November 1733). Factual indication of a change in the program appears in a note added to an advertisement for the New Haymarket during the run of the *Historical Register* in Fielding's last season: "N.B. Mr Lacy being oblig'd, at the particular Desire of several Ladies of Quality, to perform Pasquin instead of the Historical Register, etc. the Tickets deliver'd out for the Latter will be taken this Night, which will be the last Time of performing Pasquin this Season (*Daily Advertiser*, 4 May 1737). Not all requests were for the selection of the pieces to be performed; on 19 January 1743 Giffard was requested to play the farce *Bickerstaff's Unburied Dead* as a curtain raiser before the main play of the evening, instead of using it in the customary position of afterpiece (*London Daily Post and General Advertiser*).

One further example comes from the end of the period under consideration in this Introduction. John DeVoto, the scene designer for most of the London theatres in the 1730's, had now transferred to the New Wells in Goodman's Fields. In January 1746 he had been preparing assiduously for his benefit night, scheduled for 29 January 1745. His advance notices stated that the main play would be *The Orphan*, with the part of Monimia to be attempted by his daughter, "her first time on any Stage." However, on the day of performance, the play was changed to Cibber's *Love Makes a Man*, and the notice reads, "At the particular desire of several Gentlemen and Ladies we were obliged to change the Play" (*Daily Advertiser*). We can assume that DeVoto would not have laid aside his plans for his little girl's debut on the stage unless there had been considerable pressure. That the change was financially profitable is attested by the bills of 3 February announcing that since the theatre had been filled on the night of 29 January tickets delivered out for DeVoto's benefit would be taken at the later date.

That the custom of bespeaking was known and alluded to can be demonstrated from a letter of Aaron Hill's to Alexander Pope on 17 December 1731. Commenting on the failure of *Athelwold*, Hill writes, "It is possible, after all, that some persons of *rank*, and distinction to *bespeak* Plays, and compel audiences, may be kind enough to *Athelwold*, to introduce him, now and then, into civiler company, for the sake of the *Players*."[238]

In addition to individual requests of a manager to produce a certain play, a concerted arrangement appeared in the 1730's on the part of some women, unidentified, but of social standing, not only to restore the plays of Shakespeare to the stage but to have them acted from authentic texts. This group of "Shakespeare's Ladies," as they were sometimes called, has had its promotional activities on behalf of a Shakespearean revival described at length by Emmett L. Avery, but a brief account will be given here.[239] They began, writes Professor Avery, with bespeaking plays by Shakespeare at Drury Lane in January 1737. Then they went farther than requesting the manager for plays; they apparently raised money by subscription for the production of the Shakespearean drama at Covent Garden. To a prologue spoken by Havard on 12 February 1737, an explanation is appended in the printed copy, "alluding to the Ladies Subscription this Winter for the Revival of Shakespear's Plays."[240] Fielding paid tribute to the work of

238 *The Correspondence of Alexander Pope*, ed. George Sherburn, III (Oxford, 1956), 258.
239 "The Shakespeare Ladies Club," pp. 153–58.
240 All quotations are taken from Avery's article, "The Shakespeare Ladies Club."

these women by advertising an "Address to the Ladies of the Shakespeare Club." Other acknowledgments and praises appeared elsewhere, and an excellent appraisal came from James Ralph in 1743, five years later, in which he speaks of the advantage of reviving old plays, "and the Ladies of the *Shakespear* Club, gave a very noble Instance of it being their Inclination. Indeed, if ever the Theatre receives new Life, it must come from this Quarter." Now after these encomiums, let us see what the ladies achieved. From the contemporary accounts, they were most active in the two seasons 1735–36, 1736–37. In those two and the following season eight plays from good texts and five adaptations of Shakespeare were produced. More impressive possibly are the statistics of totals; of the 650 performances offered by London theatres in 1735–36, 91, or 14 per cent, were of plays by Shakespeare; of the 539 in 1736–37, 92 were Shakespearean; of the 306 in 1737–38, 68 were Shakespearean, or 22 per cent. Apparently the concerted audience requests changed the repertory considerably.

AUDIENCE BEHAVIOR

As opposed to the well behaved and long-suffering theatre audiences of the mid-twentieth century, the spectators at a play in the eighteenth century were very much alive. The auditory had strong emotions and did not hesitate to express them. When the actors were struggling with their presentation of the tragedy *Medea* at its premiere on 11 December 1730 at Drury Lane, Lord Hervey observed that "the house was in one continued roar of laughter from the beginning of the 3d act to the end of the 5th."[241] At another night at Drury Lane, Lord Hervey was sceptical about the sincerity of the emotions, but he records their expression for us:

In the evening I attending His Majesty to the Theatre in Drury Lane, where Mrs Porter play'd Queen Elizabeth most excellently (with a cane) for her own Benefit, and to the fullest audience that ever was seen. The Dowager D[uche]ss of Malborough was there with the D[uche]ss of Bedford and the D[uche]ss of Manchester. The Alpha and Omega of these three wept at the moving scenes. Tender creatures! And in one part of the play where Essex says,

"Abhor all Courts, if thou art brave and wise, For there thou never shall be sure to rise. Think not by doing well, a fame to get, But be a villain, and thou shalt be great,"

[241] *Lord Hervey and His Friends*, p. 61.

her Grace of Malborough cried charmingly, and clapt her hands so loud that we heard her [a]cross the theatre into the King's Box.[242]

Bored with the opera another night, Lord Hervey records that he "thought the Opera would never be finished, they encored so many songs."[243] On 17 March 1730 Leveridge received "a universal Encore" for his performance that night at the theatre in Lincoln's Inn Fields (*Daily Journal*, 18 March). Of the Prince of Wales' attendance at the New Haymarket on 18 April 1737, the *Daily Post* stated that "he seem'd so pleas'd" that it was expected that he would return to see Fielding's play the *Historical Register* again; but the quickening details come from the *Diary* of the Earl of Egmont, who "went to the Haymarket Playhouse, where a farce was acted called Eurydice Hiss'd an allegory on the loss of the Excise Bill. The whole was a satire on Sir Robert Walpole, and I observed that when any strong passages fell, the Prince, who was there, clapped, especially when in favour of liberty."[244] Not all the actors were on stage. The Earl of Egmont records another charming episode, the nuances of which did not escape the rest of the audience: "The Prince and Princess of Wales, the Duke, the Princesses were all at the Play. When the Prince came into the box he made a bow to the Duke and Princesses; the Duke returned it, but the Princesses did not, upon which the house hissed them. Very soon after Princess Carolina sounded away, upon which the Princesses left the Play, the Duke leading them out. When he returned, he made another respectful bow to the Prince."[245] At the premiere of *The Double Deceit* at Covent Garden on 26 February 1736 there was a disturbance in the audience even though four members of the Royal family were present. The actors continued with the performance, but the author was so upset by this rudeness that he withdrew the play.

Exuberant as the spectators were, serious disturbances were infrequent and destructive riots occurred only two or three times. Much has been made of the few genuine riots in the eighteenth-century London theatres; yet, while there was often a good deal of impromptu noise, the audiences were generally orderly and resented disturbances. Of the many thousand performances from 1729 to 1747, a remarkably small number were marked by disturbances. What may mislead the modern reader is that the spectators frequently engaged in conversation while the play was going on, they brought their dogs with them on occasion, and there would be sporadic outbursts of noise to which little attention was paid. Since customs have

[242] *Ibid.*   [243] *Ibid.*, p. 115.   [244] *Diary*, II, 390.   [245] *Ibid.*, p. 511.

changed, and a modern audience remains as quiet as if at a concert, mention by stage historians of any kind of noise gives the impression that the theatres were always in a tumult. An exchange of points of view over an incident in the theatre where the audience broke into an uproar while a play was being acted may provide us not only with a reason for the modern belief that early eighteenth-century audiences were rowdy but also with a realization of a major difference between those audiences and ours. The incident is the reception of Henry Fielding's *Universal Gallant* on 10 February 1735 at Drury Lane. In his preface to the play, dated 12 February, Fielding complains bitterly that the audience were prejudiced in that they would not allow the play to be heard. To this charge, Aaron Hill makes a statement in the *Prompter* of 18 February:

> Here I had the Opportunity of making an Observation very much in Favour of the Town, *Viz* that the accusation of BAD TASTE is very *falsely* and *maliciously* brought against them, since if the Town had really the bad Taste, they are represented to have, the Play would have run the remaining Part of the Season, in an *uninterrupted* Course of *Applause*. I had likewise an Opportunity of observing much more *Impartiality* than I expected, in the Behaviour of the Audience, for till almost the third Act was over, they sat very quiet, in hopes it would mend, till finding it grew *worse* and *worse*, they at length lost all Patience, and not an *Expression* or *Sentiment* afterwards passed without its *deserved Censure*.

Here the aged critic touches upon an essential characteristic of the sophisticated Augustan theatre-goers. They did not have the slightest intention of putting up with a play that bored them, that they disliked, or that they thought failed to make good sense. But the more sophisticated the modern spectator, the more he shrinks from any exhibition of feelings— even applauding too vigorously is a sign of bad taste. Furthermore, and here we reach one of the contributions we hope our history of the London stage will make, there is such a change in theatrical procedure. In the twentieth-century theatres, at least two intermissions are generally scheduled in the program the usher hands the entering patron. If his taste is outraged by such a poor exhibition that he does not want to sit through it, he can walk out and smoke a cigarette at intermission time or else slip out quietly and go home. Not so, in a London theatre in the years of *The Dunciad*. Between each of the five acts of the main piece, at the end of the play, and between the two acts of the afterpiece, the theatre-goers had their opportunity to see Checo and Chiaretta the latest imported dance team, or Mlle Salle dance in a translucent robe, or hear Susanna Arne Cibber sing "Was ever Nymph like Rosamund?"

The chief kind of disturbance arose from concerted attempts to ruin a play on its opening night, an unpleasant practice to which Allardyce Nicoll has very properly called attention in his account of eighteenth-century audiences.[246] Some of these organized attempts to hinder a performance were unmotivated, apparently emanating from coarse malice; other claques proceeded from political faction. No statement of cause is given for a group who tried to make trouble on both 28 and 30 October 1736, when they tried to stampede the audience by shouting "Fire!" After this effort failed, they repaired to the upper gallery at the Lincoln's Inn Fields theatre to hiss the actors (*Daily Advertiser*). A year earlier, the *Daily Advertiser* records the efforts of "young Clerks to raise a riot, who were for that purpose marshall'd by the Cunning Lawyer their Master," at an isolated production in the York Buildings (*Daily Advertiser*, 24 September 1733).

The Templars, or law students, had long since passed condemnation on the entire Cibber tribe, and people in the Town knew in advance of their plans to spoil the reception of Colley Cibber's *Papal Tyranny in the Reign of King John*, so much so that Cibber withdrew the play, even though rehearsals had been completed and new scenes painted. Theophilus Cibber felt the lash in January 1739. "I hear their will be a vast riot to night at the Play," wrote the nearly illiterate but noble Lady Stafford on 4 January, "for young Cibber is to act and the Templars are resolved to hiss him off the stage."[247]

After the passage of the Licensing Act, motivation was clear: any new play would encounter systematic opposition. William Shirley gives a detailed account of the troubles on the first night of his tragedy *The Parracide* at Covent Garden in 1739, and reports his distress that, "twenty or thirty Persons should enter into an Association against a Person or his Productions, without having the least knowledge of either, but that it was a New Play, and had been Licens'd. That my Enemies came resolv'd to execute, before Trial, may be gather'd from their Behaviour ere the Play began, for at Five o'Clock they engag'd, and overthrew the Candles in the Musick-Room, . . . expelling the Ladies from the Pit, and sending for Wine to drink."[248]

Unruly footmen occasionally gave trouble. Some of them annoyed the ladies by coming into the Opera House with "lighted Flambeaux"; the footmen resisted the guard sent to quiet them, whereupon soldiers were

---

[246] *A History of English Drama*, II, 13–24.
[247] *The Wentworth Papers, 1705–1739*, ed. James J. Cartwright (London, 1883), p. 541.
[248] From the dedication in *The Parracide* (1739).

brought in. They killed one footman and drove the rest out. An actual riot was caused by the footmen at Drury Lane on 21 February 1737, when they demanded entrance into "their Gallery." The footmen were present in great numbers, so that Thomas de Veil was forced to read the Riot Proclamation, just as the servants began to "hew down the passage door" to the gallery. They quieted down, but some damage had been done to the theatre (*Grub St. Journal*).

The best known and the most completely organized riot took place at the New Haymarket theatre on Monday night, 9 October 1738, when a company of French comedians attempted to open for the winter season. The Lord Chamberlain had made a tremendous blunder in giving them a license at all; practically any Londoner could have predicted a serious explosion if foreigners were authorized to play when English companies had been restricted. Accounts of the riot appear in at least four newspapers on the following day, and further accounts soon appeared in the biweekly and monthly periodicals. All are highly partisan, and undoubtedly exaggerate. Benjamin Victor was in the audience, and from his own account, together with the reports in the press, the main details can be traced. The theatre was packed, "not a hundredth Part being able to get into the House"; those on the outside contented themselves with breaking windows in the theatre.[249] The audience was unanimous, reported the *Daily Post*, "every Body having the greatest abhorrence of Papists coming over to a Protestant Country to Pick Protestant Pockets . . . Potatoes and Pippings sold for 1s. and 18d. a Dozen at the Door of the Theatre" (*Daily Post*, 11 October). When the disturbance started, the French ambassador and some other people in the boxes left, only to have their seats immediately filled by members of the crowd outside.[250] What especially infuriated the mob was the appearance of two files of British grenadiers, when the curtain went up.[251] The magistrate de Veil ordered these soldiers off the stage, and the French actors tried to start their play. When they found that they couldn't be heard above the din of the assembly, they withdrew and sent out twelve men and ten women for a "Grande Dance,"[252] in which, "to please the Audience, one of the Mademoiselles fairly shew'd her A——, but it being *Foreign Goods*, gave no Content."[253] Members of the audience began a systematic shouting of "Remember the poor English

[249] *Daily Post*, 11 Oct., and Victor, *A History of the Theatres*, I, 54.
[250] *London Evening Post*, 10–12 Oct.
[251] Victor, *A History of the Theatres*, I, 54–55; *Daily Advertiser*, 10 Oct.
[252] Victor, *A History of the Theatres*, I, 54.
[253] *London Evening Post*, 10–12 Oct.

Players in Gaol" and "No French Strollers;" the pelting of missiles increased; de Veil was persuaded not to read the Riot Act; the French company were driven off the stage, "out of the back Windows" and into Suffolk Street.[254] No further damage was done to the theatre itself beyond the window breakage, yet the events certainly constituted a grand riot.

---

[254] *Ibid.* See also Victor, *A History of the Theatres,* I, 55; Sybil Rosenfeld, *Foreign Theatrical Companies in Great Britain in the 17th and 18th Centuries* (London, 1955), pp. 22–24.

Production

"A NEW Play requires the greatest Exactitude in its first representation," writes Aaron Hill, "as the Impression given an Audience is generally conveyed to the whole Town, and the Success of the Play depends, in great measure, upon it" (*The Prompter*, 6 May 1735). Here the veteran critic utters a universal truth concerning the production of a new play in the Augustan Age. Few plays could shake off the results of an unfavorable response to accidental or negligent flaws in the first night's staging. Not only the new plays but also the revivals of older drama and the stock plays required great care and intelligent planning for presentation. Since a full and detailed account of the total aspects of production is given in the Introduction to Part 2, no attempt to duplicate it will be made here. Corroborative testimony or examples of changing practices will demonstrate the main features of production during the years 1729–47. Procedures tend to become static in a tradition-minded society like that of the theatre, and changes seem to come about almost by accident. The acquisition of a resident house dramatist had not yet developed, as it was to do after mid-century. All companies had a resident librettist or artificer for pantomimes. Thurmond performed this service for Drury Lane until he left during the squabbles of 1733 and moved over to join Giffard at Goodman's Fields. The eminent Shakespearean editor Lewis Theobald was the improviser for some of the most profitable pantomimes Rich ever offered, such as *The Rape of Proserpine*, *Orpheus and Eurydice*, and *Perseus and Andromeda*. Theobald doctored the last named of these on several occasions. After Thurmond's departure, Theophilus Cibber got up the pantomimes at Drury Lane more successfully than anything else he ever attempted in the theatre. Thurmond's most popular achievements were *Harlequin Doctor Faustus* and *Harlequin Sheppard* (the latter named after the juvenile delinquent Jack Sheppard whom Defoe made famous).

Though the processes of staging remained similar, the important companies began to add composers of music, song writers, musicians, and choreographers as resident members of their company, as opposed to the older practice of simply paying such specialists for particular works.

Most of the prominent composers in the early part of the period composed or arranged music for John Rich, particularly J. C. Pepusch, John F. Lampe, John E. Galliard. In the 1730's Prelleur and Eversman seemed to compose and arrange only for Giffard's company. Later, Thomas A. Arne became what might be called resident composer at Drury Lane, where his music for *Comus* had become very popular.

Resident choreographers at Drury Lane were Roger during 1729–30, John Thurmond, until 1733, M. G. Desnoyer, 1735–40, and then Leviez for the rest of the period. Glover and Lalauze were the chief ballet-masters at Covent Garden. After 1733 Thurmond joined Holt at Goodman's Fields.

After a new play had been accepted by management, the author chose the cast and read the play to the assembled players in the greenroom. Revivals of older plays were cast by the manager, of course, and the awarding of parts was closely watched by "the Town."[255] The next step was to have the prompter copy out the parts for each player so that memorization could begin.

REHEARSALS

Some time after the players cast for a new work had been given their separate parts or "sides," the rehearsals started. They were held in the late morning; Giffard conducted his rehearsals at Goodman's Fields in 1735 from 10 A.M. to 1 P.M. (*London Daily Post and General Advertiser*, 31 March). They were held at the theatre, though the player Fielding announced on 17 August 1734 in preparation for Bartholomew Fair that he would "Rehearse his Play, and Practise his Musick, at his own House . . . at Ten this Morning." Members of the cast were required to attend,[256] on pain of a forfeit, though C. B. Hogan points out that not all of them had to be there at once; when a player had finished his lines he might leave.[257] Rehearsals usually were carried on for two weeks. If a play were put on in shorter time, it was usually a matter for unfavourable comment. Hewitt, complaining about the misfortunes of his own play *Tutor for the Beaus*, wrote in his Preface, "The Comedy made it's Appearance under many Disadvantages . . . It was read for the first Time to the Performers,

255 See the complaints about managerial miscasting in the *Daily Gazetteer*, 31 Oct. 1744.
256 "The Rehearsals of The Ephesian Matron having oblig'd Mr. Bridgwater to a close attendance."—*Daily Advertiser*, 17 April 1732.
257 "An Eighteenth-Century Prompter's Notes," *Theatre Notebook*, X (Jan. 1956), 37–44.

Tuesday the 15th, and acted Monday the 21st." There was general derogatory gossip about Macklin's *Henry VII*, a play got up in a hurry because of the topical connection in 1746. Macklin himself admitted in his Preface that the drama was put in rehearsal act by act; the only revisions were at the rehearsals. When Giffard wanted to produce *King Arthur* in the season of 1735–36, he started rehearsals on 1 December for a scheduled opening on 15 December; the production could not be got ready, and the actual performance was postponed until 17 December. The summer company at Covent Garden in 1733 announced on 10 August that "The Fancy'd Queen, advertised to be play'd Tomorrow, is deferred till Thursday next, the same not being yet perfect." Close to the first night, managers of the opera would hold public rehearsals known to twentieth-century audiences as previews. These were at the Haymarket Opera House, although the opera *Sabrina* was rehearsed in the morning of 25 April 1737 in Heidegger's own lodgings. Traditionally they were held at noon, and the Earl of Egmont speaks of the public rehearsal of *Flavius* on 17 April 1732 as being at noon.[258] Such public rehearsals were rare occasions at the theatres, although the *Daily Advertiser* of 11 May 1737 reports a public rehearsal the previous day of *The Dragon of Wantley*; its premiere was to be on 16 May. Rehearsals for *Pamela*, which appeared on 9 November 1741, began on 22 September at Goodman's Fields. T. Cibber had *Romeo and Juliet* so far along in rehearsals that he was inviting guests to them a week before the play opened on 4 September 1744.

Mishaps could threaten the production schedule. The printed text of *Tutor for the Beaus* lists a Miss Hughes as playing the leading feminine role; however, this attribution was not the original arrangement. Mrs Giffard had taken the role first, but on Thursday night, 17 February 1737, she was suffering from an illness that had incapacitated her during most of the season and she returned her "lengths." This setback came at a bad time, as the play had been announced for Monday 21 February. The part was then assigned to another member of the company, a Mrs Hamilton. Unfortunately, she reported on early Saturday afternoon at rehearsal to say that she could not memorize the part unless there was drastic cutting of the lines. Her proposed remedy could not be followed, "the Nature of the Part not admitting." Now Giffard turned to Miss Hughes, who accepted the role in a very cheerful way, memorized the lines, and played the part without a blunder two nights later.[259]

---

258 *Diary*, I, 257. See also Deutsch, *Handel*, p. 288.
259 See J. Hewitt's Preface to *A Tutor for the Beaus* (1737).

Difficulties might arise even closer to curtain time. A temperamental actress might not come down to the theatre on the night of performance, or an actor might be "indisposed," a term which generally meant over-consumption of liquor. Two solutions were possible: the scheduled play might be given, but the prompter or stage manager would read the part, or a stock play could be substituted. If the latter decision were made, and if the manager had been notified in the morning, he had to change the announcements in the papers. Sometimes the stage hands reported that the machinery used for the elaborate pantomimes had broken down and could not be repaired in time for the performance. On 8 October 1737, a member of the Drury Lane company noted, "Phaeton posted but the Devil to Pay done" (Egerton 2320). Since the notice in the *London Daily Post and General Advertiser* for that day lists *The Devil to Pay* as the afterpiece, we know that *The Fall of Phaeton* was in the large posters. From this knowledge, we can infer that the posters were put up at an earlier hour than copy was sent to the newspaper office.

While some members of the audience might complain over the length of the complete program, the managers had to plan a full evening's entertainment for such nights when the main piece was only a three-act play. Consequently, notices in the 1730's begin to announce a triple feature, as on 23 January 1734, when Drury Lane revived Vanbrugh's *Cornish Squire*, with new music by J. F. Lampe and a new dance inserted. This farce remained a two-act piece, and another farce of two acts, *The Intriguing Chambermaid* was added, with the pantomime *The Harlot's Progress* afterwards. In the 1740's when there was a mild revival of the masques, three pieces often had to be scheduled to make up the program.

TIME OF PERFORMANCE

Throughout the greater part of the eighteenth century a London play-goer knew that the major theatres began at six o'clock; without a theatrical bill he would not know the starting time at one of the minor theatres. With the rise of new theatres in the 1730's, the managers began to experiment in the hope of finding a starting time that would draw more people. The newly-opened Goodman's Fields house moved the starting time back in its first season, but it reverted on 21 September 1730 "to begin positively at Six o'Clock, the Beginning later the last Season being found very

Inconvenient."260 The other alternative was an earlier hour. However, if a manager moved the hour up to five o'clock he found his house in direct competition with the pleasure gardens and wells that produced pantomimes in the late afternoon. Furthermore, the working public who attended the theatre were barely able to make a six o'clock curtain,261 and various managers experimented with a later hour. Traditions were strong; the audience was satisfied with seven o'clock performances because of the heat in the early summer, but otherwise the time was six o'clock.

When legitimate drama was first offered at the James Street theatre, the actors began in the spring of 1734 to play at seven o'clock, and for the next five years that was the usual starting time at that place. Productions at York Buildings in 1734 followed no pattern, some starting at seven and some at six. In the following season the performances started at six-thirty or seven. Henry Fielding, responsible for so many other changes in dramatic tradition, changed from six to seven very early in the spring of 1736. On 30 April 1737, his famous satire, *The Historical Register*, was advertised to begin at seven.

This trend was altered by 1740, when the promoters at the smaller house began experimenting with an earlier hour. The actors at James Street reverted to a six o'clock hour during 1740 and 1741, and for a scheduled performance on 28 December 1741 moved up the hour to five. Early in 1741 plays were starting at seven at the New Haymarket, but in the following season the starting hour varied from six to six-thirty, although continuing with a summer schedule of seven. The manager of the New Wells, in the London Spa, Clerkenwell, began at five o'clock in the summer of 1742. During his difficulties with the law in his short but exciting season at the New Haymarket in the fall of 1744, T. Cibber also tried the five o'clock starting time. He may have felt that the managers of the patent houses would let him alone if his productions were scheduled at a different hour. On Easter Monday 1745 Hallam changed from six to seven at the New Wells, Lemon Street, Goodman's Fields.

The various players in the booths on the Bowling Green during the time of Southwark Fair in September showed no consistency at all. One troupe, playing in the New Theatre on the Bowling Green in October

---

260 But on 21 Jan. 1731 the Goodman's Fields advertisement states that "complaint being made of beginning too late, it is resolv'd for the future to begin every Night at exactly six o'Clock."

261 "Compare this to your mechanick of pleasure who is to frequent the theatre. . . . He must be a fine gentleman, leave his work at five at the farthest . . . that he may be drest and at the playhouse at six.—*A Letter to the Right Hon. Sir Richard Brocas* (London, 1730).

1746, started by beginning their play at seven, moved back to six for their next performance, to six-thirty for the next one, and concluded by beginning the rest at seven. At the new theatre erected by Shepherd over in Mayfair, the promoter moved up to four o'clock, but soon changed back to six and then to six-thirty.

In 1729 the King's Opera House opened at the same time as the regular theatres; however, by the 1740's the opera began at six-thirty.

The most notable innovation, however, was to be tried by Samuel Foote at the little theatre in the Haymarket, where in 1747 he presented the first matinee in English dramatic history.[262] Actually this noonday performance was not so surprising an innovation as it is generally supposed to be. There were at least three kinds of entertainment drawing noonday crowds in the time of George II: prizefighting, public breakfasts, and auctions of paintings. In the 1740's prizefights were held at a booth in Tottenham Court, at the little theatre in the Haymarket, and at Broughton's Amphitheatre. The formula for the time of performance was, "The Doors open at Ten, and the Masters mount at Twelve Noon." This was the starting hour for many years, especially for prizefights at the New Haymarket. From the middle of the winter until the end of spring, there was a prizefight in London every week or ten days. Fairly large crowds attended, since Broughton, the chief promoter, gave the winner "the first Ten Guineas out of the Box," (i.e., the day's receipts). Public breakfastings were increasing, with notices appearing regularly in papers. Singers were employed at these affairs and sometimes punch and judy shows; otherwise they could hardly be called entertainments.

Meanwhile, the auctions of allegedly imported paintings had been enjoying a vogue that was almost to become a mania by the middle of the century. In the spring of 1747 the newspapers list from two to as many as six auctions on the same day. In the winter of 1746–47 the notices of the spurious "imported originals" were augmented by those listing collections of pictures from great private estates. On 3 January 1747 the famous auctioneer Cock announced the sale at auction of the effects and property of the late James Brydges, Duke of Chandos. Such interest was displayed and such great crowds desired admittance to see the objects which they believed Pope to have described in "Timon's Villa,"[263] that Cock announced he was going to charge 2s. 6d. admission. "Curiosity will excite Numbers

[262] This section is condensed from my article, "On the Origin of Foote's Matinees," *Theatre Notebook*, VII (Jan. 1953), 28–32.
[263] Alexander Pope, *An Epistle to Burlington*, II (1731), 79–152.

of Persons to crowd there as Spectators ONLY," Cock pleaded in his advertisements of the auction. Of the prominent auctioneers at this time, Cock, Ford, Geare, and Lamb began at 11:30 A.M., Prestage and Howard at noon, hours which would not have been maintained in the absence of popular attendance. Consequently, it is not surprising that such a close student of the London public as Samuel Foote should elect on 25 April 1747 to begin his productions at the New Haymarket at noon and to announce them in advertisements that are combinations of the usual newspaper notices of prizefights, auctions, and public breakfastings. By summer time, Foote shifted back to a conventional hour, but in the years to come he produced his pieces at twelve or one as long as he acted in the regular season.

Dependable evidence about the length of the entire performance is exceedingly rare. Such information became a desideratum to contemporary theatre-goers, and eventually became available in 1767 when Brownsmith issued a timetable. The occasional notices of "all will be over at Nine" appended to theatrical advertisements may justly be classified as promises rather than reliable testimony. The manager Hallam's statement in the advertisement for the opening night of the winter season of 1745–46 at Goodman's Fields, that the main piece and the farce would extend from 6 P.M. to 9:30 P.M., indicates the policy of the house; and we may accept it as fairly accurate since Hallam was not producing the extravagant pantomimes that occupied so much time at the patent houses. On 25 January 1733, when Lord Hervey had gone to see Mrs Porter play Queen Elizabeth in *The Unhappy Favorite*, the play was "done by nine a clock."[264] Banks's tragedy is a full-length, five-act drama, and other plays may not have lasted so long as it. On the other hand, an additional hour would be needed for a pantomime used as afterpiece. A communication in the *Daily Journal* of 23 December 1736 tells of the writer's attendance at Drury Lane on a night when *Macbeth* and *Harlequin Restor'd* constituted the double feature. Exasperated, he left at ten-thirty, at which time the pantomime had not yet ended. He complains that *Macbeth* ran to nine-thirty with the entr'actes. The letter may reflect only the author's dislike of overly long spectacles, but his reference to specific hours indicates that many a night's production ran over four hours.

[264] *Lord Hervey and His Friends*, p. 157.

THE PROMPTER'S DUTIES

When the evening's entertainment started, the prompter assumed authority and took charge of the proceedings. His station in the theatres was at the first entrance on the actor's left side (the right-hand side of the stage, to a person in front of the footlights). The location of all exits and entrances marked in working copies of a play is designated with reference to his position. At the Opera House in the Haymarket, the prompter was located in a hooded box at the front of the stage, in full view of the audience, after the Continental manner.[265]

Supplying the occasional line (needed by the player's loss of memory or else the proverbial intoxication) was only a part of the prompter's responsibilities. Armed with a whistle to be blown for a change in scenery and a bell to call for music, the prompter ruled the activities (*The Prompter*, 12 November 1734). Actors had to be called for entrances, offstage noises were signalled, and entr'acte dancers summoned. Above all, the timing of the various segments of the evening's program had to be maintained. If a player were taken ill during the performance, the prompter must place the under-prompter in the wings and step into the role of the stricken actor. If the audience wanted extra renditions of "The Roast Beef of England" and were upsetting the time schedule, the prompter had to summon the manager and try to keep the program moving.

PROLOGUES AND EPILOGUES

Adapters of Shakespeare's plays may have deleted comic episodes from a tragedy in preparing a text for the eighteenth-century stage, but the ending of any tragedy, old or new, was followed immediately by a flippant, even ribald epilogue. Some objections were raised against this antiphony, the question being raised very sharply by the poet of the age, Alexander Pope, in a letter of 12 September 1738 to Aaron Hill: "I have often wished to live to see the Day when Prologues and Epilogues should be no more. I wish a Great Genius would break thro' the silly, useless formality. But at least I would have one good try, to leave the Audience *full* of the *Effects* of a good tragedy, without an Epilogue" (*Correspondence*, IV, 127). To this uttered wish, the respondent made an immediate and practical reply:

---

265 Lawrence, *Old Theatre Days and Ways*, pp. 35–36. I have not found a primary source earlier than Lawrence's citation of a periodical reference in 1761.

What you say, against Prologues and Epilogues, is a truth, which I heartily feel. . . . But he ought to be very well *mounted* who is for leaping in hedges of custom. As my affairs stand, at present, I should find it imprudent to give away the third nights (which till now I have always left to the House). And I doubt [i.e., doubt not] those disorderly hearts, which must throw the *first* night into uproar, upon retrenching a popular folly, might have effects for the above reason alone to be apprehended.—23 September, *Correspondence*, IV, 129

Hill's answer is supported by the record; prologues and epilogues continued to form a part of the evening's entertainment throughout the rest of the century. The custom was so thoroughly entrenched that mention of them is only occasionally included in the playbills or newspaper advertisements. For most of this period and for the Calendar of performances in Part 4 of the present Work, the principal source for identifying the speakers of prologues and epilogues is the printed edition of the play, where both the authors and the speakers are given. Thus while the speaking of a prologue and an epilogue was a universal practice at a premiere, it is difficult to determine whether the practice extended to subsequent performances of the play in its initial run. Thus for the first night of *The Lady's Revenge* at Covent Garden on 9 January 1734 nothing appears in the advertisements to indicate a prologue or epilogue, nor is any such mention in the notices for the next three performances of the play. However, in the author's Preface is the news that Ryan spoke the prologue every night, but that Mrs. Younger spoke the epilogue on the third and fourth nights. Who spoke the epilogue on the first night? Was any epilogue given on the second night? Had one actress spoken an epilogue on the first two nights and Mrs Younger presented a different epilogue on the remaining nights? (Printed editions of Restoration and early eighteenth-century plays occasionally include more than one prologue or epilogue.)

Henry Fielding seems to have announced his prologues and epilogues more than any one else. Of course, if a particular prologue or epilogue happened to become fashionable, its inclusion in the program was mentioned in the advertisements. Thus the "Prologue and Epilogue proper to the Tragedy" was promised for *Chrononhotonthologos* on each performance from 22 February to 5 March 1734. After a play went into repertory the prologue and epilogue were usually dropped, but on a revival of an old play that had dropped out of stock a new prologue and epilogue were composed and spoken for the occasion. New ones were also given for a production bespoken by a large group such as the Masonic brethren, or in connection with some current event, such as the rebellion of 1745 in Scotland, at which time all

of the theatres had prologues and epilogues spoken by woman "in the charac-
ter of a (Female) Volunteer." For a performance on 4 November 1746 at
Covent Garden, Horace Walpole provided a new epilogue on the suppression
of the rebellion to be spoken by Mrs Pritchard in the character of the Comic
Muse.[266] A gag by Theophilus Cibber soon became popular at the smaller
theatres, with various plays ending with epilogues "spoken by Nobody."
Some verged on the specialty acts, such as Cushing's "Prologue on Modern
Tragedy spoken in the Character of a Jew,"[267] or a "New Singing Prologue"
given on 29 November 1729.

In the Introduction to Fielding's *Don Quixote in England*, the Manager
asks for the prologue, whereupon the Author raises a number of objections.
The Manager echoes Aaron Hill's reply to Pope, saying the audience would
insist upon having one. The Author then makes an amusing generalization
about the monotonous similarity of the prologues, where the first twelve
lines inveigh against indecency, "and the last twenty show you what it is."

The prologues and epilogues were rehearsed and the speakers drilled
in gestures as carefully as in the preparation of the plays and afterpieces.
Amusing testimony appears in a couplet from a prologue spoken at Drury
Lane under the triumvirate.

> *Then if I should mistake a Word, you know,*
> *There's Mr Wilks within would Snub one so—*[268]

At six o'clock the prompter had signalled for the curtain to be pulled
up, where it would stay for the duration of the program at most theatres.
Fielding, however, began the practice of lowering the curtain at the end of
a scene and raising it to begin the next scene, but there is no evidence
that other managers continued this innovation.

When the afterpiece ended, a leading actor or the stage manager
stepped forward and announced the main play and afterpiece for the next
performance, just as in the Restoration (Egerton 2320). However, toward
the end of the period under discussion a new feature was added at closing
time. It was the singing of "God Save the King." Authorities differ on
setting the date when this custom originated. From our records the earliest
example takes place on 10 March 1738, when a concert at the Swan Tavern
concluded with the rendition of this song. On 1 March, 1739, the *Daily*

---

266 *General Advertiser*, 4 Nov. 1746.
267 At the theatre in Lemon St., Goodman's Fields.—*Daily Advertiser*, 10 March 1746.
268 In *The Country Lasses* (1715).

Advertiser bill announcing a benefit production at the little theatre in the Haymarket for John Biggs states specifically that the program would conclude with "God Save the King." The enterprising Giffard had also announced that the program at Goodman's Fields of 29 April 1742 would "conclude with the Coronation Anthem." By the time of the Rebellion of 1745 all the theatres used it as the 1745–46 season got under way; at Drury Lane on 28 September 1745, "the Gentlemen belonging to that House performing the Anthem of 'God Save our Noble King'"; at the Lemon Street theatre in Goodman's Fields on 28 October, "to conclude with the Chorus of "Long Live the King"; and at Covent Garden on 26 December at the end of the play, "God Save the King."

INDEX